W   I   L   D

B   L   U   E

M   E   D   I   A

ELEMENTS *A series edited by Stacy Alaimo and Nicole Starosielski*

WILD

THINKING THROUGH SEAWATER

BLUE

Melody Jue

MEDIA

DUKE UNIVERSITY PRESS / *Durham and London* / 2020

Cover designed by Courtney Leigh Baker
Text designed by Matthew Tauch
Typeset in Portrait and Cronos Pro by Copperline Books

Library of Congress Cataloging-in-Publication Data
Names: Jue, Melody, [date].
Title: Wild blue media : thinking through seawater /
Melody Jue.
Description: Durham : Duke University Press, 2020. | Series:
Elements | Includes bibliographical references and index.
Identifiers: LCCN 2019024145 (print) |
LCCN 2019024146 (ebook)
ISBN 9781478006121 (hardcover)
ISBN 9781478006978 (paperback)
ISBN 9781478007548 (ebook)
Subjects: LCSH: Seawater. | Technological innovations. |
Ocean engineering.
Classification: LCC GC116 .J84 2020 (print) |
LCC GC116 (ebook) | DDC 304.209162—dc23
LC record available at https://lccn.loc.gov/2019024145
LC ebook record available at https://lccn.loc.gov/2019024146

Cover art: Giant kelp forest off the coast of Gull Island
marine protected area (Santa Cruz Island), November 2018.
Courtesy of the author.

For my dad, Rodney Jue, with love

CONTENTS

Photo gallery appears after page 80

PREFACE / Into the Blue

If it is true that we often remember the photograph rather than the actual event, then my memory of diving in Mexico is blurred. Gliding behind my dive partner in pleasantly clear water, I recall entering a shipwreck through a dark window and encountering a bloom of orange and pink tunicates and anemones encrusted inside. As we drifted toward a window, I raised my small GoPro camera toward the other diver's fins, clicked, and then sailed through the opening behind him (plate 1). Yet when I uploaded the pictures to my laptop much later, I was surprised to find that the bright undersea bouquet of orange and pink had registered as blue-green smears of light in the digital image. I struggled to reconcile my memory of the shipwreck with its muted signature, recognizing the scene only by the faint outline of two crossed flippers and window openings, surreally distorted. The photograph paled in comparison to my memory of warm life inside, brightly ensconced in every crevice available. Yet something about the photograph drew me—perhaps the contrast of right angles against the soft, bumpy texture of life growing on the ship below, or the way the flippers gently signify human presence within the soft, greenish room.

Is there any stability of color underwater? I have looked at the wreck photo so many times now that I feel the blur of amphibious memory, shifting between the vibrant scene as my eye remembered it and the view of the GoPro camera saturated by blues and greens. Clearly the camera's eye registered light differently from mine. In fact, what the photograph preserves is the difference between my human eyes and the camera's sensor, and our varying sensitivities to ambient light at forty feet underwater. Yet light changes the deeper one goes. Explorer William Beebe famously wrote about the gradual erasure of warm colors as he descended down the water column in his Bathysphere in 1928, describing the transition from "a golden yellow world to a green one" upon plunging into the ocean.[1] At six hundred feet down, the water became a "dark, luminous blue." After seven hundred feet, "blue tapers into a nameless gray, and this finally into black," and "the sun is defeated and color has gone forever, until a human at last penetrates and flashes a yellow electric ray into what has been jet black for two billion years."[2] Here Beebe depicts the ocean as an optical medium for the experience of color, dependent on whose eyes are looking and at what depth. Perhaps blueness is not an abstract feature of the ocean, but an experience that comes into being through the particularities of embodiment and positionality.

Yet from a historical perspective, the ocean has not always been blue. The Old English word for "white"—*hwit*—was used to describe the ocean and suggests brightness or radiance. In this sense, the reflective surface of the ocean could be hwit, or the gleaming of stars. Homer's *Odyssey* repeatedly refers to the ocean as "the wine-dark sea," in part because ancient Greek—like many older languages—did not have a word for what we would today call "blue."[3] Although scientific convention stabilizes blueness to a particular wavelength (450–95 nanometers), other cultural uses of words for color are not always anchored to a specific range in the light spectrum. During a recent trip to Taiwan, I was reminded that the color *qing se* (青色) can mean blue as in blue sky (*qing tian*, 青天), green as in green pepper (*qing jiao*, 青椒), blue-green as in lichen (*qing tai*, 青苔), green as in fresh vegetables (*qing cai*, 青菜), or black as in a young person's hair; it even appears in the word for teenager (*nian qing ren*, 年青人). In these examples, *qing se* describes things exhibiting "nature's color" and the vitality of youthfulness. Seeing blue depends, then, not only on physiology but on cultural standardizations of vision.

Wild Blue Media takes its name from the common association of blueness with the ocean, even though the experience of blueness above water or below is not a stable thing. Blueness has been useful in branding the emergent field of ocean humanities, or "blue humanities," which turns to the world's oceans as environments for scholarly inquiry, challenging the assumption that saving the environment means being concerned with forests.[4] Indeed, viewed from outer space, it would seem that the Earth is more blue than green. The "Blue Marble" and "Pale Blue Dot" photographs take their names from this orbital point of view, as do documentaries about the world's oceans like BBC's *The Blue Planet* and *Blue Planet II*. Oceanographer Sylvia Earle also considers blueness as a figure for the planetary in her book *The World Is Blue: How Our Fate and the Ocean's Are One*, while the name of her foundation, Mission Blue—dedicated to creating marine protected areas ("hope spots")—suggests more of a utopian pursuit of earthly care. In these examples, blue stands in metonymically for our oceanic planet seen from outer space.

Wild Blue Media intentionally signals these cultural associations while also aiming to evoke a more unsettled understanding of blue through its echo of the phrase "wild blue yonder." Although "wild blue yonder" originates in a U.S. Army Air Force song as a reference for the sky, it figuratively describes any kind of journey into the unknown or toward a limitless expanse. "Yonder" suggests that ocean media can be thought of as a horizon of possibility, just beyond our immediate experience but nonetheless part of the fabric and flesh of the world. This book shows that what we thought were the limits of media—computers, telephones, satellites, cables, movies, newspapers, radios—shift when we venture into the ocean. Further, *Wild Blue Media* explores how oceanic environments challenge some of the most ingrained and sedimented concepts in media theory: interface, inscription, and database storage. More than an account of media objects or even media processes, *Wild Blue Media* is about thinking through the ocean as an environment for thought, and accounting for the positionality of the critic along the way. Going "into the blue" means becoming aware of habits of perception that reflect the fact that we are acculturated to certain conditions of gravity rather than the buoyant and vital fluidity of the ocean, among other environmental and cultural factors.

The "wildness" of *Wild Blue Media* signals that the conditions of mediation we find in the ocean may be unruly, testing the limitations of a human point of view. Whereas wilderness was traditionally conceived as that space outside human habitation and culture, wildness can be much closer to home. As William Cronon helpfully distinguishes, "*wildness* (as opposed to wilderness) can be found anywhere: in the seemingly tame fields and woodlots of Massachusetts, in the cracks of a Manhattan sidewalk, even in the cells of our own bodies."[5] Wildness can crop up far away or closer to home, such as in Werner Herzog's science fantasy film *The Wild Blue Yonder*, which pretends that footage of jellyfish in the Antarctic Ocean is from an alien planet. This ironic move folds the desire for venturing into the blue unknown back into reenchantment with the Earth. Yet wildness also deals with the untamed, the out of control, the unmarked. For Jack Halberstam, wildness "skews toward collapse and works always on behalf of failure."[6] I think of the ocean as a wild milieu for testing our most habitual concepts and categories, an environment within which they might fail or break. Wildness might point to the limits of the human sensorium, or the thresholds of perceptibility. This is not to reify the ocean as an absolute other, like the sentient planetary ocean of Stanisław Lem's novel *Solaris* that repeatedly deters scientific study. It is, however, to say that we might have something to learn by testing our ways of speaking about media in the ocean.

So while the ocean has not always been blue—also hwit, also wine-dark—perhaps blue is as good as any place to start. Perhaps blue marks our initial position at the surface, oriented by the scientific metrics of the light spectrum. Perhaps blue signals a promise to engage with the oceans as distinct from terrestrial and aerial environments while recognizing their interconnection through the material flows of the weather and global capitalism. Perhaps blue illuminates an awareness of human endangerment from sea level rise alongside the ways that anthropogenic pollution, ocean acidification, and overfishing are wrecking global ocean ecosystems. Perhaps blue invites a certain humility, recognizing that culturally specific ways of speaking about the world may undergo further changes in the cold buoyancy of the water column.

Perhaps blue is just the beginning.

ACKNOWLEDGMENTS

Wild Blue Media emerged with the help of many enlivening forces. I would like to thank Kate Hayles for guiding this project from its early stages, and for her continued mentorship from North Carolina to California. Stefan Helmreich generously read every inch of my writings about the ocean, and his influential book *Alien Ocean* helped me see how interdisciplinary writing about the ocean was possible. Thank you to Zach Blas and Lauren Pawlak for their steadfast friendship and generosity of spirit. I am grateful to Stacy Alaimo and Nicole Starosielski for their enthusiasm for this project and all things ocean, and to my supportive editor at Duke University Press, Courtney Berger.

I'd like to thank all my colleagues at UC Santa Barbara in the Departments of English and Film and Media Studies, especially Bishnupriya Ghosh and Rita Raley for reading through early drafts of the introduction. I would also like to thank Alenda Chang, Jeremy Douglass, Ken Hiltner, Alan Liu, David Novak, Bhaskar Sarkar, Janet Walker, and Tess Shewry for helpful conversations about this book in its final stages. Thank you also to the graduate students of "STS Perspectives on Ecology" and "Feminist and Queer Science Studies" for their curiosity and original thoughts.

At Duke University, I was supported by a James B. Duke Fellowship and a Katherine Goodman Stern Fellowship, which generously granted me time to finish writing an early version of the manuscript. I'd like to thank Mark Hansen, Rey Chow, Priscilla Wald, and Kate Hayles (again) for making sure that the project emerged organically, without falling into too prescriptive a form. Special thanks to Mark for his encouragement to see scuba diving as a form of phenomenological research during a formative stage of the project. Thank you to those who read portions of my ocean writing and influenced the trajectory of the project: Kaila Brown, Gerry Canavan, Jui-an Chao, Kita Douglas, David Dulceany, Ainehi Edoro, Anne Garréta, Michael Hardt, Jessica Hines, Jonathan Howard, Calvin Hui, Jess Issacharoff, Fredric Jameson, Deanna Koretsky, Carolyn Laubender, Mary Caton Lingold, Marina Magloire, Negar Mottahedeh, Meghan O'Neil, Renee Ragin, Christopher Bautista Ramos, Jennifer Rhee, Dan Richter, Abby Seeskin, Barbara Herrnstein Smith, Cheryl Spinner, Whitney Trettien, Jasmina Tumbas, Susan Willis, and Pinar Yoldas. Thank you to Tiwonda Johnson-Blount for her seamless administrative support. At the Duke University Marine Lab, thank you to Cindy Van Dover, Dan Rittschof, Bill Kirby-Smith, Xavier Basurto, Janil Miller, and many others for welcoming me to teach at the lab for a few summers, and generously including my classes on field trips. At UC Davis, I am grateful to Colin Milburn for his unconditional encouragement and guidance at a time when I did not know what I was doing! I would also like to thank Fran Dolan and Evan Fletcher for their early support and wonderful presence as teachers.

Some parts of this book were previously published, and benefited from the rigorous editorial feedback of Lucia Allais, Sylvie Bissonette, and Matthew C. Hunter. I would also like to thank Jamie Skye Bianco, Jeremie Brugidou, Heather Davis, Jody Deming, Andy Hageman, Jenni Halpin, Eva Hayward, Tung-hui Hu, Samantha Joye, Rahul Mukherjee, Astrida Neimanis, Rafico Ruiz, Chris Russill, Paul Saint-Amour, Alyson Santoro, John Shiga, Christopher Walker, and Chi-Ming Yang for helpful conversations along the way. I'm inspired by the Ocean Memory Working Group and look forward to future collaborations.

I was lucky to have several fantastic dive instructors, Larry at Island Divers Hawaii and Rigo at Scuba Libre in Playa Del Carmen; thank you for teaching me to be a more coordinated fish, keeping me safe in the process, and helping me manage my seasickness. A big thank you to my

Auntie Cherie and Uncle Mike for hosting me in Honolulu while I took advanced diving training for two weeks and to both them and my Uncle Roger and Auntie Wendy for being extra supportive of my dad.

Even though this book was finished under the shadow of my dad's cancer diagnosis and passing in 2019, I am grateful for the love, support, and humor of my mom, my sister Lori, and my partner Ben. Thank you for looking after my well-being. Dad, you gave me a good start with your video recordings of fish at the aquarium, trips to the beach, and many viewings of the original *Star Wars*. I think you can see where your influence as a scientist mattered, and this book is dedicated to you.

INTRODUCTION / Thinking through Seawater

One summer a few years ago, I stood on the sandy edge of a rock jetty in North Carolina's Outer Banks. After trudging along a quarter mile of beach with scuba gear in tow, it was a relief to enter the cool water, weightless and buoyed by the prostheses of a wet suit, tanks, and air-filled vest (BCD).[1] As I swam out to deeper water with my classmates, our instructor reminded us of strategies for descending: let all the air out of your vest, breathe normally, and pinch your nose every time you exhale to equalize your ears with the ambient water pressure. Failing to do so, he reminded us, would result in sinus pain—so we would be wise to equalize (pinch) early and often. Our lungs would form an interface with the life-sustaining technology of regulators from which to breathe, connected by hoses to the air tanks strapped to our backs. Through another pocket of mediating air (in our goggles), focused vision would be possible, though slightly magnified.[2] As we descended into the smooth liquid depths, brushed by streams of bubble exhalations, I was reminded that "breathing underwater is an unnatural act."[3]

Despite being a swimmer, I found it difficult at first to maintain a controlled, level posture while moving through the water. Seasoned divers are distinguished by their calm, horizontal glide, with arms lightly folded across the chest to prevent any equipment from brushing the seafloor.[4] This posture comes from the familiarity of spending hours underwater and achieving neutral buoyancy (to neither rise nor sink), adjusting the air volume in one's vest as needed. Yet as a new student of the sea, I was not yet comfortable. Whenever I felt myself sinking out of control, or dangerously close to a patch of sea urchins on the rock jetty, I would immediately try to stand upright and put my flipper feet below me, braced to stop my "fall." Standing upright was clearly a habit formed from my anthropoid experience of gravity. It was as if my body still thought it was on land, falling through air rather than water, attempting to ensure a safe landing and overriding what I knew I was supposed to do. I quickly realized that becoming a good diver was going to require extensive rehabituation: I needed to rewire the reflex to stand up and get used to how the act of breathing affected my motion, slightly sinking with each exhalation and rising with each inhalation.[5] It would be some time before, as Jacques Cousteau once put it, I would experience my "flesh feeling what the fish scales know."[6]

The practice of learning to dive has directed my attention to how our instinctive postures, embodied habits, and muscle memory are all adapted to the gravitational conditions of walking on land and breathing air (amid a range of abilities). Indeed, these terrestrial habits of movement and orientation are so ingrained as to be virtually invisible, unless one experiences their interruption through a change in body state (a growth spurt, dizziness, injury) or a change in milieu (parachuting, swimming, diving).[7] Although many people around the world grow up intimately with the oceans—through swimming, freediving, sailing, fishing, surfing—there are, as of yet, no biologically amphibious humans; the demand to "surface" is an orientational constraint for all human beings that, as I show in this book, has specific impacts on language and figurative speech.[8] If one agrees with Ludwig Wittgenstein's observation that to imagine a language is to imagine a form of life, then it is clear that human languages have taken form within a range of terrestrial and coastal environments that, at minimum, all share the experience of gravity and horizontal (rather than volumetric) movement.[9]

By sinking deeply into the ocean in *Wild Blue Media*, I aim to show how the ocean is just the beginning of developing a broader sensitivity to the role of milieu in the fields of media studies, literary studies, science and technology studies, and the environmental humanities. I see the ocean as a vital starting place to develop what I call *milieu-specific analysis*, calling attention to the differences between perceptual environments and how we think within and through them as embodied observers. By offering entirely different conditions than land—increased pressure, three-dimensional movement, light refraction and magnification, and the inability to tell the direction of sounds, to name a few—the ocean is a material and imaginative space for the conditions of perception that we have taken for granted. Milieu-specific analysis acknowledges that specific thought forms emerge in relation to different environments, and that these environments are significant for how we form questions about the world, and how we imagine communication within it. However, the challenge with milieu-specific analysis is not to reify the ocean as a stable object, since what the ocean "is" is also a matter of "for whom." There should also be a historical consideration, since the way we come to know the ocean is through many accumulated moments of contact through our bodies, cultural practices, and technological instruments. Thus, instead of seeing the ocean as a decodable structure that determines thought, we can think of it as a dynamic milieu whose characteristics manifest by actively moving within it (as a human, octopus, plankton, or other) and through mediated forms of contact.[10]

The importance of mediation here is key: in order to study the ocean—especially the deep ocean—scientists need a variety of instrumentation, satellites, remotely operated vehicles (ROVs), submersibles, sonar, and other technical prostheses for sampling and sensing.[11] Early oceanographers like Marie Tharp built up entire maps of the seafloor from the data of sonar pings, revealing a textured landscape of the deep that no one had quite anticipated.[12] Today, computer technologies perform the work of signal transduction, converting acoustic measurements into visual renderings.[13] Rather than being immediately present to us, the (deep) ocean emerges as an object of knowledge only through chains of mediation and remote sensing—measurements that allow us to build up imaginative pictures of what life in the ocean is like, often from points of view that would be physically impossible to inhabit without the protection of a submersible.[14] As Rachel Carson wrote, "To sense this world of waters known to the creatures of the sea we must shed our human perceptions of length and breadth and time and place," either imaginatively or with the help of remote-sensing visual technologies.[15] Her "underwater traveler" pictures conditions in the depths of the ocean that include "enormous pressures" and "glacial cold," nonvisual sensory elements learned about from the mediation of remote technological devices.[16]

Attending carefully to the conditions of mediation—or how we come to know about distant and expansive ocean ecologies—is not only a speculative act but also of vital significance for environmental activism and environmental justice today. Consider the Deepwater Horizon "spillcam" feed: when the oil rig blew up in 2010, the public demanded that camera footage at the base of the oil well be made public.[17] For weeks on end, one could tune into a 24/7 live feed of oil gushing forth from the broken well, lending an eerie immediacy to an event that everyone could only experience at a distance. Yet as Susan Schuppli writes, the footage was political not only as a form of virtually witnessing the disaster but because scientists with an understanding of fluid mechanics used the footage to calculate the actual number of gallons per day leaking forth—a number much higher than BP's own estimate.[18] Such calculations were key in the lawsuits that followed, providing a baseline for estimating ecological injury. However, the importance of spillcam as a witness should not overshadow the fact that media themselves have considerable energy demands, depending on the very infrastructure of extraction that they sought to document in its spectacular failure; media contribute to petroculture even as they document it. The field of environmental media studies tackles such contradictions, balancing a consideration of media representations, media infrastructures, and media materiality.[19]

While other threads in environmental media studies also seek to articulate the ocean *as* a medium (a point I address later in this introduction), *Wild Blue Media* argues that our preexisting conceptions of media and mediation need to undergo recalibration in the milieu of the ocean. Media theory has been using a conceptual vocabulary that derives its sensibility from terrestrial and anthropocentric contexts, and then deploys this same vocabulary to describe mediation in the ocean. If we have grown used to talking about networks, information, data storage, recording, transmission, inscription, and interfaces in relation to computer technologies, to what extent do these terms adequately address processes of mediation in the ocean? In order to gain perspective on the terrestrial biases of concepts in media theory, *Wild Blue Media* develops a methodology of *conceptual displacement*. This science fictional strategy involves imaginatively submerging media terms into the ocean to see how they hold up in a liquid milieu of pressure, salinity, and coldness (among other qualities). Methodologically, each of the first three chapters of this book submerges a different term—interface, inscription, and database—in order to see how our understanding of them necessarily shifts under the ocean. Such a task requires a form of amphibious scholarship that remains attentive to the milieu specificities of ocean environments (be they shallow, pelagic, or deep) and the critic's own norms—keeping track of surprising contexts for the use of concepts, or where they acquire new valences. Chapter 4 brings these new oceanic valences of interface, inscription, and database to bear on the complex dynamics of mediation in underwater museums, developing an amphibious perspective through my own practice of scuba diving.

However, the process of developing an amphibious perspective through oceanic immersion has its constraints. After all, preparing to dive involves an exchange of terrestrial immobility for aquatic mobility. Imagine struggling into a thick wet suit on the surface of a rocking boat, strapping on a heavy weight belt and tank, a set of awkward fins, and, finally, a large mask. Sweating all the way, often steadied by a crewmember, you rejoice when you finally plunge into the cool relief of the water, your weight buoyed by the ocean. Finally, you are in the element in which your prosthetically augmented body moves best, and you may even forget that you are wearing equipment at all. The diving equipment "comes into being with the seascape," as Stephanie Merchant writes, and what was once heavy and uncomfortable goes unnoticed in its functionality—that is, unless your mask fogs, or your skin chills too much, or your ears hurt from the pressure.[20] You are suspended between remembering and forgetting the equipment that enables aquatic immersion in the first place. At the threshold between ocean and air, there is no universal condition of perfect adaptation. However, we can investigate "the physical and the conceptual in/accessibility of [specific] environments," as Stacy Alaimo names one possible intersection between disability studies, crip theory, and environmental humanities.[21] This accessibility is always a question of technical mediation, facilitated through simple and complex technologies—from wearing goggles with their vision-enabling pocket of air, to sonar systems of mapping.[22] Recognizing how difficult it is to escape the gravitational pull of the Earth, the utopian and science fictional impulse of this book is to explore the ocean as a force for conceptual reorientations that sometimes estranges what we thought was familiar. By bringing you, reader, into the oceanic depths, I aim to take you out of immersion from the habits of thought cultivated at your desk.

Conceptual Displacement as Science Fictional Strategy

In "Orientations Matter," Sara Ahmed writes that philosophy is full of tables—the object most at hand for sedentary philosophers, contemplating indoors. Tables function as "orientation devices": the repeated act of working at a table, as anyone reading this is well aware, often leads to slumped shoulders, achy backs, neck problems, and joint pain: "Our body takes the shape of this repetition; *we get stuck in certain alignments as an effect of this work.*"[23] For Ahmed, bodies "acquire orientation" through the repetition of certain actions, actions that coalesce around objects like tables and other sites of labor (or the ground we walk or roll on).[24] In his writings about the weather, Tim Ingold also questions how the physical location of the office has impacted scholarship: "Perhaps it is because we generally think and write indoors that we have such difficulty in imagining how any world we inhabit could be other than a furnished room, or how, cast out from this interior space, we could be anything other than exhabitants."[25] If writers, artists, and theorists have traditionally been situated at a table in front of a computer to reflect on representations of the ocean from a distance, what form of thought might take place from within the water column, pressed on all sides by the fluid salinity of seawater? To what extent might the ocean operate as a necessary "disorientation device" for theory and philosophy, a milieu that denatures our normative habits of orienting to the (terrestrial) world through language?

Drawing on the experience of sensory estrangement when I first learned how to dive, *Wild Blue Media* develops conceptual displacement as a method of defamiliarization to make our terrestrial orientations visible. This science fictional method of thinking with the ocean productively estranges the terrestrially inflected ways of theorizing and thinking to which we have become habituated. Thinking with the ocean involves asking *How would ways of speaking about (x) change if you were to displace or transport it to a different environmental context, like the ocean?* Even in this, one must be specific about which part of the ocean—littoral, pelagic, benthic—is involved in the displacement and its cultural histories, but the important thing is to think through the affordances of whichever oceanic environment one specifies.[26] Like divers who want to "stand up" when they feel out of control underwater, conceptual displacement is about recognizing what terrestrial habits we carry with us through the act of imagining familiar concepts underwater, displaced from the normal scene of humanities writing. The ocean is a kind of anti-environment to the desk, repositioning critics in the ocean in order to prompt them to rethink the efficacy of their most habitual concepts and vocabularies (plate 2).[27]

As I explain in this book, the displacement of concepts in the ocean can show how our uses of metaphor and figurative language—the ways we habitually speak—fall within a milieu-specific, or surface-specific, way of talking about the world. Even when we believe we are speaking literally, the way that we ordinarily speak draws on subconscious uses of metaphor.[28] Conceptual displacement works by amphibiously holding the tension between the milieu specificity of the ocean with the milieu specificity of the observer's normative environment, to the best of one's estimation. In this way, conceptual displacement is rigorously self-reflexive, attending to the ways that theorists and writers draw on their normative habits of orientation within a particular environment. This relationship between habit and habitat is key, as both share an etymological root word (Latin: *habitāre*) that has to do with dwelling. I see conceptual displacement as a method of dislocating terrestrially nurtured thought into the ocean, a process that may involve physical immersion, technically mediated immersion, and speculative immersion through fiction, film, digital media, and the arts.

Conceptual displacement as methodology has strong ties with the genre of science fiction. Writer Philip K. Dick once defined science fiction as a genre predicated on a certain "conceptual *dislocation*," or estrangement from one's familiar experience. In good science fiction, "the conceptual dislocation—the new idea, in other words—must be truly new (or a new variation on an old one) and it must be intellectually stimulating to the reader; it must invade his mind and wake it up to the possibility of something he had not up to then thought of."[29] This resonates with Darko Suvin's classic definition of science fiction as the genre of cognitive estrangement, imagining a world that is logically continuous with what we know about reality while introducing something new that defamiliarizes the present. For Suvin, good science fiction necessarily exhibits a "cognitive" function (plausibility within scientific knowledge of the universe) and "estrangement" provided by the strange newness of a "novum," a new thing, invention, or set of circumstances.[30] In *Wild Blue Media*, the ocean provides an estrangement effect on terrestrial conceptions of media and mediation, providing a new set of environmental circumstances under which to consider their efficacy.

Of course, many science fictions have imagined the ocean—or extra-terrestrial oceans—as dramatic spaces harboring unforeseen forms of alien life and ecologies. Jules Verne's classic novel *20,000 Leagues under the Sea* is perhaps the most famous nineteenth-century text to take readers imaginatively into the ocean in *The Nautilus* submersible, describing marine life and a monstrous kraken. Stanisław Lem's *Solaris* imagines a sentient ocean planet that frustrates human efforts to understand it, while feminist science fictions like Joan Slonzcewski's *A Door into Ocean* and Nnedi Okorafor's *Lagoon* focus more on alien biological diversity in the ocean (and in Okorafor's case, an Afrofuturist vision for breaking dependency on petroleum).[31] However, *Wild Blue Media* is not only about the genre of published ocean science fiction as such. By seeing the ocean as a milieu capable of providing estrangement effects, this book employs an expansive notion of science fiction as a genre that includes cultural discourse in nonbook and nonfilmic forms.

Stefan Helmreich's pathbreaking study *Alien Ocean: Anthropological Voyages in Microbial Seas* offers one way of seeing science fictionality beyond published novels and films, through its identification of the "alien ocean" as a common trope that emerges across a variety of cultural contexts, including microbiology, documentary film, and aquarium exhibits. For example, David Attenborough's narration of the deep sea in *Blue Planet* documentaries becomes science fictional when he notes that "more people have been to outer space than to the bottom of the deep ocean," an environment that is home to "alien" life forms that live there in a milieu of pressure and darkness.[32] Aquarium exhibits also evoke the strangeness of "alien" sea creatures, drawing parallels between science fictional imaginations of the cosmos and the deep ocean. For Helmreich, the alien ocean is not a reification of the ocean as always alien and science fictional; rather, the alien ocean is a specific cultural construction that one can identify in many places that include, but are not limited to, ocean science fiction. What this implies is an understanding of genre as a mobile lens of interpretation that can describe phenomena not normally under the purview of literary study. I see similarities between Helmreich and scholars such as Lisa Yaszek and Lindsey Thomas, who show how public policy writing and emergency preparedness plans—documents that require writers to speculate ten, fifty, or one hundred years or more in advance—can also act as science fictions.[33] For me, what makes the ocean science fictional is not an ontological connection between space aliens and sea creatures but rather the effect of cognitive estrangement underwater, of shocking the reader out of their normative habits of thinking and speaking about the world that belie our terrestrial acculturation. It is from this expansive understanding of genre that I think of the ocean as a natural environment for science fiction, estranging our terrestrial perspectives on space, life, and normativity in relation to the specificity of seawater—a locus for situated knowledge.

Situated Knowledge and Objectivity

In *Wild Blue Media* I approach terrestrial bias not as a flaw but as a form of what Donna Haraway calls "situated knowledge." In the mythology of objectivity, objectivity aspires to a form of disembodied, disinterested, critical distance—a point of view Haraway calls the "God trick," or view from nowhere. Rather than throwing out objectivity all together, Haraway instead advocates for a new understanding of what it means to be objective, marked by the "engaged, accountable positioning" that takes into consideration who wants to ask particular questions in science, and why we decide they are worth funding.[34] From this framework, scientific facts about the world do not simply exist in some universal repository—scientific facts about the world are established *for* particular human communities through particular measuring instruments, sensing technologies, and cooperation. Indeed, scientific questions and their funding—especially gender, race, and genetics—may reflect the assumptions and values of one community but not others. To situate knowledge is to address the "radical historical specificity, and thus contestability, of every layer of the onion of scientific and technical constructions."[35] In a move toward epistemic humility, Haraway finds value in the "partial perspective," an acknowledgment of the conditions of possibility from which a point of view emerges.

Haraway's call for situated knowledge participates in a broader critique of the myth of objectivity by scholars in feminist science studies. The term *feminist* in feminist science studies includes more than advocating for more women in STEM fields, formulating research questions pertinent to women's lives, and critiquing normative gender roles. *Feminist* also means directing and challenging the idea that there is one universal perspective shared by all. In this way, situated knowledge draws on earlier articulations of "standpoint theory" by Dorothy Smith, Sandra Harding, and Patricia Hill Collins, which consider how differences in power, interest, and situation relate to the questions one might ask, or features of the world that may be most relevant to those asking.[36] In Smith's words, "From the point of view of 'women's place' the values assigned to different aspects of the world are changed," a point that Collins complicates by adding the dimensions of race and class.[37] However, qualifying one's standpoint is not always an easy matter of laying out intersectional filiations—sometimes elements of one's standpoint are more subtle, invisible, or taken for granted. As Haraway cautions, "Location is the always partial, always finite, always fraught play of foreground and background, text and context, that constitutes critical inquiry. Above all, location is not self-evident or transparent."[38]

If one unacknowledged standard of objectivity has been a human being standing on the ground, then oceanic organisms offer quite different perspectives, having adapted to the physical conditions of the ocean in ways that differ profoundly from those on land. For example, mantis shrimp have sixteen types of light-sensing cones in their eyes (rather than the three that human beings possess), attuning them to a much broader range of the electromagnetic spectrum. Many other sea creatures rely on hearing (like whales) and/or sense of smell (like sharks). Furthermore, to us, other sea creatures would seem to possess modes of synesthesia that combine at least two of "our" senses. Octopuses can taste with their tentacles, as Sy Montgomery beautifully relates in *The Soul of an Octopus*, and so can some crustaceans. The range of perceptual capacities of ocean organisms—that we learn about through scientific instrumentation and sensing devices—should humble us into considering how our own sensory attunements are a very narrow band through which parts of the world might be perceived.

I imagine "terrestrial bias" as a necessary partial perspective—one that, once recognized, erodes the dream of a master language that would be totally objective, distant, and adequate to articulating and describing the world in its entirety. The milieu of the ocean offers an epistemological check on human knowledge formation, presenting entirely different conditions for perception, sensation, and life than terrestrial environments.

My theorization of milieu-specific analysis asks that we consider the observer's milieu in addition to the role of culture, class, gender, race, ability, and other identitarian categories and how the observer's orientations within a particular (terrestrial) milieu relate to the ways that they speak about the world and orient to the world through language. Knowledge developed in terrestrial environs—of which there is, of course, much cultural and historical variation—is situated knowledge, as is knowledge situated in the depths of the ocean. Thus, rather than thinking of the terrestrial bias in media theory as synonymous to something false or incorrect, I would like to think of it as a situated perspective that responds to the fact that we live on land, are bound by gravity when we walk, and experience daily life as immersion in invisible air rather than water.

Terrestrial Bias and Milieu-Specific Analysis

To get a sense of the extent to which living on the Earth orients our thought, think of all the ordinary ways of speaking about the "ground": they are a well-grounded individual, they have no grounds to make that claim, their expertise is grounded by many years of fieldwork. In each of these formulations, "ground" appears as the equivalent of stability or evidence. As a result, "ground" creeps into our metaphorical ways of talking about validating points of view or arguments. Take, for example, the way David Abram describes the importance of the environment for cognition in *The Spell of the Sensuous*:

> Thus, the living world—this ambiguous realm that we experience in anger and joy, in grief and in love—is both the soil in which all our sciences are rooted and the rich humus into which their results ultimately return, whether as nutrients or as poisons. Our spontaneous experience of the world, charged with subjective, emotional, and intuitive content, remains the vital and dark ground of all our objectivity. And yet this ground goes largely unnoticed or unacknowledged in scientific culture.[39]

Here, Abram's metaphors for being in touch with the living world all relate to the contact zone of "soil" that our sciences are "rooted" in, the "rich humus" and "dark ground" as the condition for "all our objectivity." Abram goes on to discuss the work of phenomenologist Edmund Husserl and his argument that the Earth "provides the most immediate, bodily awareness of space, from which all later *conceptions* of space are derived."[40] Thus, "*all* bodies (including our own) are first located relative to the ground of the earth, whereas the earth itself is not 'in' space, since it is the earth that, from the first, *provides* space."[41] In philosophy and beyond, it is the Earth's surface under an atmosphere that has been taken as the default environment for human thought, and the foundation of intuition about spatiality.

I see these figurations of "ground" not as wrong or falsifiable, but as a common way of developing a picture of reality through an environmental imagination situated terrestrially. I agree with Abram (and Husserl) that in Western culture, the phenomenological experience of space was learned on the still Earth. However, I disagree that this is the whole picture; we should not mistake the grounding of human thought, reason, and intuition on the Earth as objectivity itself, or as the most neutral way of cognizing the world. Terrestrial contexts are but one milieu for cognition to press up against; thought might develop entirely differently in an aquatic environment like the ocean. As a Californian used to earthquakes, I am, of course, aware that the ground is a dynamic and fluid medium across geologic time scales, but I maintain that the ground commonly figures as a foundation for knowledge, or as a locus of stability in the duration of a human life.

As another example of terrestrial bias, consider how Pierre Bourdieu's concept of the habitus uses the reference point of the ground. In Bourdieu's original formulation, the habitus is "embodied history, internalized as a second nature and so forgotten as history."[42] It is both the product and producer of a set of individual and collective practices that shape particular "schemes of perception, thought and action," as well as what is taken for granted, "procedures to follow, paths to take."[43] The habitus, a product of history, "ensures the active presence of past experiences, which, deposited in each organism in the form of schemes of perception, thought and action, tend to guarantee the 'correctness' of practices and their constancy over time."[44] Like silt that gathers at the bottom of a river, or a kind of sediment, the habitus—which suggests both habit and habitat—is figured as a kind of accumulation of earthy history. If our experience dwelling on the surface of the Earth (or at least the surface of a boat) contributes to this past, sedimented in our very schemes of perception, then habitus brings us to a greater consideration of the ways that a terrestrial bias informs conceptual formation in philosophy and theory.

I bring up the terrestrial bias in Abram's and Bourdieu's work as two examples that stand for a broader trend in critical theory and academic writing that takes, as its normative starting point, an observer at the surface of the Earth that is its own form of situated knowledge. This book could have been written as a survey of works in Western philosophy and criticism that most exemplify a terrestrial bias (and such a project has still to be written).[45] However, I feel that it is more constructive and more expansive to develop a theory of milieu specificity that addresses the situated nature of all knowledge production for specific observers. Objectivity is to be found not in a universal perspective (what Haraway calls the "view from nowhere") but in the particularities of embodied knowledge in milieu-specific conditions that stretch us to think through the ocean—or the sky, high-altitude mountains, or low-gravity environments such as the moon and Mars.

Milieu-specific analysis figures as a general conscientiousness of the environmental conditions in which scholars produce theories. As I develop it here, milieu is not simply the climate of a critical text, or a general influence, but constitutes something that the theorist actively orients within, through language. Attending to milieu—a word with a rich history ranging from mechanics to biology that, in Georges Canguilhem's usage, alternates between being "a centered space" or "mi-*lieu* [mid-*place*]," and a "decentered space" (intermediary field) or "*mi*-lieu [*mid*-place]"—stresses the tension between the observer and the environs they think from.[46] Thus, one of the requirements for the study of the ocean as an epistemic environment for thought is to attend not only to the material specificities of the ocean but also to the particular observer/perceiver who is interacting with the ocean.

Milieu-specific analysis differs from earlier writings on "medium specificity" in the fields of art history and media theory through its particular invocation of the environment, although both attend to materiality. Marshall McLuhan's famous statement "the medium is the message" in *Understanding Media* looked to the importance of physical form in relation to symbolic content. "The electric light is pure information," he wrote. "It is a medium without a message, as it were, unless it is used to spell out some verbal ad or name. This fact, characteristic of all media, is that the 'con-

tent' of any medium is always another medium."[47] Thus, the "message" of
a medium is the "change of scale or pace or pattern that it introduces into
human affairs."[48] John Guillory traces a longer history of the concept of
medium going back to Aristotle, while noting, "The emergence of the media concept in the later nineteenth century was a response to the proliferation of new technical media—such as the telegraph and phonograph—
that could not be assimilated to the older system of the arts."[49] In the
1950s, art historian Clement Greenberg defined "medium specificity" as
the critical attention to the substance or material of an artwork, particularly in Modernist painting.[50] Whereas Greenberg's medium specificity
focused on the object itself, Katherine Hayles's "medium-specific analysis" in the early twenty-first century emerged from her call to develop
vocabulary specific to the materiality of media technologies while not
isolating them as objects.[51] Critical of the poststructuralist tendency of
the late twentieth century to use the vocabulary of text to describe anything and everything, Hayles argues that the vocabulary of "text" based
on the printed page is inadequate to address the materiality of media. As
an alternative, her medium-specific analysis attends to the specificities of
form while also being aware of how different media may cite or imitate
one another. The implications for the study of oceanic milieu specificity
should be clear: just as it was a problem for the vocabulary of textual analysis alone to describe and analyze media, it is also a problem for terrestrial
analytics to describe mediation in all its forms. Through the act of imagining media studies underwater, we can become more aware of the calcified habits of our (theoretical) storytelling, and their predilections for the
solid, the fixed, the reliable, the static.[52] Milieu-specific analysis poses the
following question: *In what environmental milieu do scholars write their theory,
and to what extent does it inform their thinking and writing?*

Although *Wild Blue Media* focuses on the ocean, milieu-specific analysis is a form of attention that is equally at home considering the particularities of swamps, glaciers, atolls, grassy plains, cityscapes, and more, extending the purview of the environmental humanities to more than just
green or forested environments. Essay collections like *Prismatic Ecology:
Ecotheory beyond Green* offer a way to begin thinking milieu specifically,
resisting the "green branding" of environmentalisms in favor of a broader
spectrum (pink, gold, violet-black, and more) of color-based iconography.[53]
One might also find a hint of milieu specificity in ethnomusicologist Steven Feld's theorization of rainforest "acoustemologies" specific to lush

canopy environments, Barry Lopez's observation that the extreme alternation of seasons characterizes the Arctic environment, or David Valentine's discussion of gravitational differences on future Martian colonies or space stations.[54] Because milieu specificity opens to the particularities of any milieu, it need not rest on the dialectic tension between ocean and land alone but in the saturated push and pull of what Kamau Brathwaite calls "tidalectic" relation.[55] Concerning the messiness of environmental boundaries, Tim Ingold observes, "Rainfall can turn a ploughed field into a sea of mud, frost can shatter solid rocks, lightning can ignite forest fires on land parched by summer heat, and the wind can whip sand into dunes, snow into drifts, and the water of lakes and oceans into waves."[56] In what Ingold calls the "weather-world," elements co-saturate each other, making clear distinctions between environs but a dream of purification.[57] Perhaps in another way, the Earth and more specifically its oceans are saturated by human agency. Oil extraction directly contributes to global climate change, ocean acidification, sea level rise, and coral bleaching, while new industrial-scale fishing methods have led to the collapse of many fisheries stocks.

Indeed, it is impossible to do responsible work about the ocean today without addressing anthropogenic effects—a tension exhibited by BBC's *Blue Planet II* documentary series, which concludes nearly every episode with a self-awareness of anthropogenic changes in the ocean. Considering BBC's long history of making nature films absent of humans, its shift to include human influence is both heartening and a grim sign of the state of the ocean today, relative to historic baselines. Yet such sea changes affect not only marine life but human communities as well. Sea level rise and regional collapses of fishing stocks have been affecting vulnerable coastal and island communities on an incremental scale, enacting a form of what Rob Nixon calls "slow violence" rather than the more spectacular violence of something like an oil rig explosion.[58] As an instance of slow violence, the encroachment of sea level rise leads to "displacement in place" of climate refugees, Nixon's formulation for the way that people may face dislocation without having moved at all.[59]

The imaginative strategy of conceptual displacement that I articulate in *Wild Blue Media* is shadowed by these literal oceanic displacements of people and living beings, displacements that are projected to accelerate dramatically in the next century. Chapter 1 concludes with a discussion of submergence as a strategy of climate change protest, focusing on the example of the Maldives' underwater cabinet meeting in 2009. Chapter 2 demonstrates this tension between human displacement and speculative displacement, engaging Vilém Flusser's writings on migrancy alongside his media fable about the vampire squid. Chapter 4 offers another view, considering what it means to think about submerged history through the example of Jason deCaires Taylor's underwater museum and its visual relation to Middle Passage history. By demonstrating how to *think through* seawater rather than take the ocean as a discrete object of analysis, this book hopes to inspire new tactics of artistic and political resistance against climate change in both its global and local effects.

The Ocean Humanities

The method of "milieu-specific analysis" not only calls attention to the terrestrial bias of critical theory but also changes the practice of scholarship in the emerging field of ocean humanities. The ocean humanities—also sometimes called the "blue humanities" or "thalassography"—distinguishes interdisciplinary work on the ocean from the broader umbrella of environmental humanities.[60] Distinct from green forest spaces, the ocean figures as a vital confluence of overlapping theoretical approaches that deal with global climate change, indigenous cultural histories of seafaring and navigation, shipping routes and global capitalism, the alterity of marine organisms, the Middle Passage, technologies of ocean mapping and remote sensing, marine resource extraction, maritime literatures, and more.[61] Such topics usually require expertise from more than one field—for example, geography and history, literature and media—giving rise to a number of interstitial scholars who loosely identify under the umbrella of the ocean humanities.

However, milieu-specific analysis differs from previous work in the ocean humanities by engaging with the ocean as an environment for thought rather than as an object of analysis or region for the study of cultural representations. By dwelling with the epistemological implications of thinking through the ocean, this book calls on critics to track their own areas of terrestrial bias, even within their studies and theorizations of the ocean. One of the closest articulations of thinking "through" the ocean comes from Stefan Helmreich in his generative conclusion to *Sounding the Limits of Life*, where he discusses the ocean as "a medium through which living and knowing happens." What Helmreich calls "theory underwater" implies "not merely theorizing underwater things, but subjecting theory to unfamiliar conditions as well—of pressure, saturation, waterlogging—seeing how it deforms as it merges with what it seeks to describe."[62] What is key about this formulation is the feedback loop between knower and known, human and ocean. "Subjecting" (or better, submerging) theory underwater, or what I call "conceptual displacement," is precisely about tracking the deformations of what we thought we knew through the unique materiality and physical conditions of the ocean. For example, in chapter 1 I take a special interest in the role of "pressure" as an environmental factor that literary readings and media analyses have often ignored, in part because pressure is not easily represented in visual terms. Pressure is what helps me read "interface" as a distributed and volumetric phenomenon rather than solely a matter of surface.

Indeed, one of the key areas where *Wild Blue Media* differs from existing studies of oceanic literature is through its focus on interpretation within the depths rather than at the surface, which is most common in studies of seafaring literature.[63] Although the surface of the sea can also produce sensory estrangement—which I know all too well from my own experiences of seasickness—this book privileges vantage points from within the water column, and texts that dwell with the challenges of narration from this point of view. By focusing on interpretation from within the water column, I provide an alternative to the unacknowledged spatial configuration that has informed literary interpretation for quite some time: the idea that the interpreter is located on the surface of things. From the surface, the interpreter either plumbs the hidden depths of the text (as in the hermeneutics of suspicion) or considers other "surface" or topographic features of a text (as in the varieties of "surface" reading outlined in Stephen Best and Sharon Marcus's issue of *Representations* in 2009).[64] In chapter 1, I discuss the implications of moving the critic into the water column through my own immersed readings of oceanic science fiction and ocean memoir that engage with this positionality. *Wild Blue Media* calls on the ocean humanities not only to consider representations of ocean environments in literature and media but also to attend to the ocean as an *environment of interpretation*.

Another challenge in the ocean humanities has been to develop a critical vocabulary specific to the ocean, in spite of a tendency toward terrestrial mimesis.[65] For example, literary scholar Ian Baucom writes that a hydrographic imaginary in literary studies serves not only to "trouble or reorganize" but also to "multiply our maps of the 'real,' to render visible some additional fraction of all those worlds virtually present within the world. . . . What we know of the world depends not simply on what 'exists' but on where we stand."[66] By directing our attention to "the place where we stand," Baucom acknowledges the terrestrial position of most literary critics. Yet even the term *hydrographic* emulates the geographic; "thalassography" (sea writing) parallels geography (Earth writing); Gary Kroll's "ocean ethic" echoes Aldo Leopold's land ethic; "seascape" derives from landscape.[67] Many of the neologisms developed to address the ocean environment—like hydrography, or seascape—are modified versions of terms that we use to talk about the land. There is truth to Dan Brayton's claim that the "deep encoding [of the land] in the terminology and conceptual categories that define ecocritical inquiry profoundly limits our object of study and keeps us from reaching beneath the surface of what Mary Oliver calls the 'green and black cobbled coat' of the sea," but even this poetic image relies on an anthropomorphic reference (the cobbled coat) to describe the ocean in human terms.[68]

Wild Blue Media does not simply create a new critical vocabulary specific to oceanic conditions, mapping out a new terrain for neologisms or "wet theory."[69] Instead, it foregrounds the methodology of conceptual displacement as a means for gaining perspective on habits of description, interpretation, theoretical orientations, and assumptions about environmental context. I aim to leave the critic somewhat at sea, unsettled from their habituated ways of speaking about the world. *Wild Blue Media* not only shifts critical inquiry to the site of oceans but more importantly asks scholars to reflect on the invisibilized environment or milieu that they think within as well as on how this grounding has informed the way that they have (up till now) deployed concepts and categories and even used prepositions (as I discuss in chapter 2).

My focus on the ocean as a science fictional medium of estrangement may seem to be at odds with the focus on kinship and connectivity in postcolonial studies of ocean literature, but I actually see them as complementary projects with the common goal of rethinking norms in Western thought. Many indigenous-focused spatial studies theorize the active formation of feelings of kinship with oceanic regions and cultural heritages, which, to a certain extent, functions as a reenchantment process. This tactic of reenchantment with more-than-human ecologies has the effect of making apparent the habits of thought that inhere in Western philosophy in contrast to alter/native epistemologies. As a polysemic milieu, the ocean can of course support both indigenous characterizations of the ocean as a familiar home and science fictional characterizations of the ocean as a space of alterity. This book is in companionable conversation with indigenous perspectives on the ocean like Karin Ingersoll's *Waves of Knowing*, with the mutual goal of denaturalizing Western habits of thought and perception.[70]

In thinking through the element of seawater, *Wild Blue Media* draws on a genealogy of elemental philosophy. Gaston Bachelard's *Water and Dreams: An Essay on the Material Imagination of Matter* carefully delineates how water offers "its own rules and poetics" that often evoke the womb, the unconscious, drowning and death. Bachelard writes of how "a being dedicated to water is a being in flux. He dies every minute; something of his substance is constantly falling away," a figure that recurs throughout literary imaginations of undersea bodies.[71] Feminist theorists have also taken an interest in the element of water in relation to feminine alterity, or in water's "gestational" properties that do not fall under the frame of a sexual binary.[72] This vital materiality of water as a medium of becoming changes how we might think about conditions of storage. Chapter 3 takes this up specifically to consider the difference between representations and renderings of seawater in digital media, and the materiality of seawater itself. By tracking what aspects of seawater's materiality are foregrounded or elided, I show how the ocean makes possible a different notion of storage than do digital technologies.

Seawater also changes how we think about the porosity of embodiment, a question I address in chapter 1, on theories of the interface in relation to the human lung. By focusing on the physiology of breathing underwater, I show how the interface is not only a boundary or surface but can also extend through membranes to have volumetric effects. This transcorporeal understanding draws on feminist theories of posthumanism by Stacy Alaimo and Astrida Neimanis that consider bodies not as isolated containers but as porous to distributed material flows that connect to global elements. Alaimo's theory of "transcorporeality" describes the human as "substantially and perpetually interconnected with the flows of substances and the agencies of environments."[73] Such a perspective sees embodiment in terms of buoyancy, "a sense that the human is held, but not held up, by invisible genealogies and a maelstrom of often imperceptible substances that disclose connections between humans and the sea."[74] For Alaimo, these substances may include vital elements like water as well as poisons like mercury, where transcorporeal interconnection might indicate sustenance or vulnerability. Building on Alaimo's work and theories of phenomenology in *Bodies of Water: Posthuman Feminist Phenomenology*, Neimanis argues that Enlightenment conceptions of human beings that have become intuitive—as bounded, autonomous, individual, discrete— have done the particular damage of obscuring a different material reality that has been with us all along: our existence as bodies of water. By rewriting water back into the picture, Neimanis aims to present a more faithful account of subjectivity that—because of its distributed nature—should more appropriately be called "posthuman." The posthuman subject that emerges from these watery feminist materialisms should change our self-conception, encouraging us to see our own distributed embodiment as a condition that is attached to the ecological welfare of a sphere larger than our own body. Channeling this work, *Wild Blue Media* also keys in to the ways that images of bodies underwater resonate differently depending on specific geographies, cultural histories, and race.[75] Chapter 4 on "Underwater Museums" shows how images of bodies underwater should not evoke pure wonderment alone but also the hauntings of the Middle Passage, the refugee crisis in the Mediterranean, and other traumatic geopolitical events.[76]

Where *Wild Blue Media* differs from new materialist methodologies is through its comparative focus. Rather than tracking the flows of materials, it focuses on the relationship (and tension) between the interpreter's normative environment of interpretation and the ocean as an environment of interpretation. Perhaps the best demonstration of this occurs in chapter 2, on vampire squid media, where I show how Vilém Flusser's *Vampyroteuthis Infernalis* operates as both a speculative fiction about media in the ocean and as a fable about photography. Here, Flusser realistically images how the vampire squid would use ink clouds and skin paintings as its own liquid communication media in the deep sea. However, he allows moments to break through where he wonders how vampyroteuthic our own society might become through new imaging techniques, never losing track of the fact that it is a human observer framing all observations about the vampire squid. The comparison of vampire squid epistemology in the abyss and human epistemology on land functions as a mode of self-critique, qualifying the very text that we read with the knowledge that it could have been written under different environmental conditions. The methods of milieu-specific analysis and conceptual displacement that I outline in this book concern such epistemological questions that are essentially comparative in nature, studying the contrast between the observer's own norms and those in the ocean.

A Sea Change in Media Studies

Milieu-specific analysis is a mode of media studies and literary criticism that involves close attention to the conditions of perception in a given environment, and to the techniques of mediation possible within that environment. What are the affordances of mediation in the ocean, for which particular observer, and through what narrative techniques is this communicated? To make this speculation, however, requires prior scientific knowledge about the ocean through techniques of remote sensing. Rachel Carson wrote that although we can no longer live in the ocean like our aquatic ancestors, we can still "re-enter it mentally and imaginatively," inventing "mechanical eyes and ears that could re-create for his senses a world long lost, but a world that, in the deepest part of his subconscious mind, he had never wholly forgotten."[77] For Carson—who never learned to dive—narrative was her prosthetic technology, her way of imagining deep ocean processes and their role in the history of the Earth and the origins of life. However, the "mechanical eyes and ears" that Carson wrote of prefigure the many ways in which we scientifically sense the ocean, augmenting the human sensorium through technical prostheses like hydrophones, sonar technologies, lasers, CTD (conductivity, temperature, depth) sensors, and more.[78] The very design of ocean-sensing technologies anticipates the gap between what is perceivable for humans and what is perceivable in the ocean. Indeed, faithful speculations about the milieu-specific conditions of the ocean depend on a prior body of knowledge developed by oceanographers and marine biologists. Yet because the technique of conceptual displacement complements milieu-specific analysis, it is not enough merely to describe the conditions of mediation in the ocean, as distant observers. We have to take a hard look at how the conceptual vocabularies and grammars familiar to media studies hold up under conditions of oceanic submergence, subjected to changes in pressure, temperature, salinity, movement, and the presence of microscopic life. Conceptual displacement is what brings the observers into the scene of mediation, testing out their readiness to orient within the affordances of a particular ocean environment.

Wild Blue Media expands on key studies of media in the ocean, including works by Nicole Starosielski, John Shiga, Helen Rozwadowski, Stefan Helmreich, and John Durham Peters, to consider how media and mediation occur *through the ocean*.[79] The preposition matters: media "in" the ocean make the ocean seem like a mere container or external environs to be bracketed out from the corrosiveness of saltwater, whereas media "through" the ocean positions the ocean as an optical and sensory medium that the observer actively orients within. A study that focused only on nouns (concepts) would miss this important grammatical detail concerning the role of the chosen preposition, a topic I discuss more extensively in chapter 2. If we have grown used to deploying these concepts only in terms of computational technologies, what necessarily shifts when we relocate their use to oceanic conditions? This epistemic shift is about cultivating a certain humility, aware of how mediation might seem otherwise from another embodied point of view in the milieu of the ocean. Through the speculative method of submerging familiar concepts in new media studies—interface, inscription, and database—*Wild Blue Media* tests how we think about environmental media and mediation underwater.

Although cameras, scuba gear, film, underwater habitats, and digital ocean simulations do make their appearances in this book, my focus is not primarily on media objects but rather on the tension between concepts in media studies and oceanic contexts. Because of its epistemological focus on the environmental conditions of scholarly writing, *Wild Blue Media* differs from existing work in the field of media studies that has primarily dealt with human communication and technical objects that store, record, or transmit information.[80] This includes the history of printing, the advent of sound recording technologies like the gramophone, the history of photographic experimentation and cinema, as well as infrastructural feats like the laying of telephone wires and fiber-optic cables. "Mass media" named an older practice of studying newspapers and television, while "new media" studies has tended to focus on computational technologies, networks, and algorithms. Erkki Huhtamo's and Jussi Parikka's articulation of "media archaeology" takes a longer historical look at media objects beyond the "new," rummaging through "textual, visual, and auditory archives as well as collections of artifacts, emphasizing both the discursive and the material manifestations of culture."[81] In a systemic sense, scholars like Matthew Fuller propose studying "media ecologies" and their capacities, examining their "interrelationship with knowledge and time management processes, intellectual property regimes, database and software design" and more.[82] By contrast, Neil Postman uses the environmental metaphor of "media ecology" to think about the affordances of media as environments but in doing so risks separating nature and culture in simplistic ways that neglect the way that media technologies themselves depend on natural resources and energy for their condition of possibility.[83]

Such a question is, however, very important in the field of "environmental media studies," which considers a variety of entanglements between media technologies and natural resources. These include the carbon footprint of cinema and digital technologies, the role of media in climate change activism, the way that elements of the environment might facilitate or disrupt communication, the role of the environment as a recording medium or transmission medium, and the role that elements of the natural environment play in media infrastructures.[84] In *Sustainable Media*, Nicole Starosielski and Janet Walker explore "connections that inhere between media *about* the environment and media *in* the environment"—a perspective that outlines something of a feedback loop between environmental activism through media, and the resource dependency of media.[85] Environmental media studies weighs the cost of "the massive amount of energy drawn and expended to power media systems, the extraction of materials to construct media technologies, and the toxicities of use and disposal" against the ways that media "provide a means to come to terms with and help ameliorate the ecological harms produced by industrial processes."[86] The conclusions to chapter 1 and chapter 3 specifically consider the implications of milieu-specific analysis for environmental activism, including how an expanded notion of the interface and a scale-specific consideration of seawater could lead to different forms of environmental awareness and artwork.

Indeed, one of the key aims of *Wild Blue Media* is to expand where we would traditionally look for media, or instances of mediation. Toward this, I draw from recent work in both media theory and environmental media studies by scholars such as John Durham Peters. Peters's approach has been to see the environment *as a medium*, stretching the definition of media to include not only technical objects but also tree rings, ice cores, geologic strata, and other elements of the natural environment. In this view, the environment is a medium when it demonstrates a functional similarity to anthropogenic technologies of storage and transmission. Peters makes precisely this claim in *The Marvelous Clouds: Toward a Philosophy of Elemental Media* through an analogy between what communication technologies do and what elements of the environment do: "If we mean mental content intentionally designed to say something to someone, of course clouds or fire don't communicate. But if we mean repositories of readable data and processes that sustain and enable existence, then of course clouds and fire have meaning."[87] Such a claim operates through the logic of the retrospective view, where both old and contemporary media technologies allow us to look back at the environment and see the technical work that it has been performing all along: the sky for orientation, geologic strata for storage, ocean for acoustic transmission.[88] In this view, the environment functions analogically as a kind of media infrastructure, or at least presents the conditions of possibility through which transmission, storage, and recording might occur.

Another point of view contends that, rather than trying to define or even expand the definition of what media are, critics should focus on processes and events that encompass biotechnical life. In *Life after New Media: Mediation as Vital Process*, Sarah Kember and Joanna Zylinska call for a shift from studying media objects to studying processes of mediation. Drawing on the philosophy of Henri Bergson and Jacques Derrida, they see objects as only temporary stabilizations within the ongoing becoming of the world. Instead of media, "mediation" becomes a "key trope for understanding and articulating our being in, and becoming with, the technological world, our emergence and ways of intra-acting with it, as well as the acts and processes of temporarily stabilizing the world into media, agents, relations, and networks."[89] Attending to mediation across such varied practices as photography, face transplant surgery, home security surveillance, the Large Hadron Collider, and credit crunch, Kember and Zylinska show how "life itself under certain circumstances becomes articulated as a medium that is subject to the same mechanisms of reproduction, transformation, flattening, and patenting that other media forms . . . underwent previously."[90] The key word here is "articulation"—to be articulated as a medium is not about a stable ontological identity (this is a medium, that is not) but about being enfolded into an assemblage such that something performs the function of a medium. In a similar vein, Eva Horn advocates engaging with media in terms of processes, transformations, and events. In "There Are No Media," Horn writes, "Media are not only the conditions of possibility for events—be they the transfer of a message, the emergence of a visual object, or the re-presentation of things past—but are in themselves events: assemblages or constellations of certain technologies, fields of knowledge, and social institutions."[91] Horn's more explicitly anti-ontological approach to media avoids answering the knotty question of "what media 'are'" and instead, like Kember and Zylinska, attends to processes of mediation that gradually unfold.[92]

The implication of these anti-ontological theories is that "mediation" would cease to focus on anthropogenic technologies and instead address more distributed phenomena in the world, like the BP oil spill, the Fukushima Daiichi nuclear meltdown, and other protracted events. Indeed, perhaps the key factor that Kember, Zylinska, and Horn introduce is time, along with a broader appreciation of duration as part of media processes. By thinking through temporary stabilizations rather than the persistence of objects, all three scholars take a more processual view that complements environmental justice frameworks like Nixon's "slow violence," attentive to forms of violence that normally extend past human scales of time.[93] *Wild Blue Media* shares an interest in temporal processes of mediation particularly in chapter 1, where I develop a reading of the human lungs as an interface and show how starting from this biological tissue actually involves gas saturation of the entire body. What this allows me to identify are larger-scale instances of interface—for instance, the way our carbon economy saturates the ocean (an important absorber of heat and excess carbon), resulting in increased acidification to the detriment of shelled creatures and coral reefs around the world.

However, this book is not only about making media theory more aware of its conditions of theorization. The reason why it is important for environmental scholars to think about mediation now has to do with a latent media imaginary in discourses about the Anthropocene and climate change. We can see this imaginary at work in descriptions of the sediment or ice cores as "books" of the past, or the idea that in the Anthropocene humans are writing the geologic record. At the same time, other conversations about anthropogenic climate change lament the erasure of different records through sea level rise (submerging human communities), ocean acidification (dissolving the shells of crustaceans and corals), global warming (causing coral to bleach and die), and more. As I have written about elsewhere, scholarship has tended to superimpose understandings of human media onto environmental processes.[94] Because these conversations about climate change and the Anthropocene both consciously and subconsciously draw on the language of media, it is time to think more critically about the media terminology we are using and the milieu in which it emerged. Answering this question, however, involves not only considering environments of thought, or environments of mediation, but the nature of the embodied observer to whom they are meaningful.

Zoological Comparative Media Studies

In addition to considering environments of mediation, *Wild Blue Media* asks that we also consider the perceptual capacities of the observer to whom these descriptions are meaningful. The importance of the observer takes us to a question that Peters raises in *The Marvelous Clouds* about the species specificity of media. By asking if the ocean is "the greatest medium or the limit point of any possible media," Peters challenges readers to consider how noise for one observer might be information for another.[95] His comparison of whale communication with human communication leads him to argue, "Media are species- and habitat-specific and are defined by the beings they are *for*," as it makes no sense to study whale communication outside the enabling medium of seawater.[96] This focus on the body is key, and addresses the role that animal studies might play in environmental media studies by not assuming a normative sensory apparatus. Peters provocatively suggests that zoology might become "the open book of comparative media studies."[97] This offers a powerful complement to Hayles's formulation of "comparative media studies" in *How We Think*—also the name of an interdisciplinary master's program at MIT.[98] Like comparative literature, comparative media studies emphasizes juxtaposition, attentive to the materiality of media across a variety of instantiations. A zoological comparative media studies addresses not only differences in media materiality and form but also the species specificity of media under particular environmental conditions.

Wild Blue Media depends on the balanced accounting of both species specificity and milieu specificity, attending to the roles of environment and observer in their embodied, cultural, and historical context. This comes through most visibly in chapter 2, on "vampire squid media," which considers inscription from the perspective of the vampire squid living in the deep abyss in Vilém Flusser's speculative media fable *Vampyroteuthis Infernalis*. In this chapter, I pay close attention to the differences in embodied perception for the vampire squid compared with a human observer, attending to the situated and partial perspectives of each. I also attend to the way that Flusser thinks about the conditions of recording information underwater, and how his speculation folds back (as a fable) into his thinking about the significance of photography. This work finds an echo in Flusser's observation that "one can do gymnastic exercises with perspective," its own form of zoological comparative media studies.[99]

Through this attention to species specificity, *Wild Blue Media* shares kinship with Eduardo Kohn's *How Forests Think: Toward an Anthropology beyond the Human*. Drawing on Peircean semiotics, Kohn explores how something like a tree falling in the rainforest might signify quite differently to a human, compared with a monkey or other forest creature. A similar argument can be found in Jacob von Uexküll's writings on *Umwelt* from the 1930s.[100] Von Uexküll contrasts what he calls the Umwelt, or perceptual world of the tick, with its more general "surroundings," as noticed by human beings. Drawing on the biosemiotic imaginations of Peters, Kohn, and Uexküll, I argue that what count as media depend on whom we imagine they are useful to, with human beings as the normal reference point. However, just because a variety of perceptual worlds may exist specific to individual animals does not mean that there is not overlap and ecological vulnerability. I do not take Uexküll's theory of Umwelt as evidence that there is no common "world" to be shared by all species. While this may be true at the level of perception, this cannot be true at the level of materiality or transcorporeality. Nuclear radiation, for example, exerts its effects whether or not a living being is aware, an invisible threat whose effects often register many years after exposure.

Zoological comparative media studies raises a key question about perception and narrative: Through what means might one approximate the point of view of an animal? Toward this, Eva Hayward's oceanic work is a powerful example of thinking about mediation and phenomenology in species-specific ways while also accounting for transcorporeal interconnection. To us, other sea creatures would seem to possess modes of synesthesia that combine at least two of "our" senses. Octopuses can taste with their tentacles, while coral polyps are both light sensitive and touch sensitive. Hayward's work on the "fingery-eyes" of cup corals productively shifts the traditional focus of phenomenology on the human body to the perceptual attunements of marine invertebrates, who operate within perceptually different worlds.[101] From naturally occurring transsexual fish to asexual jellies and colonial organisms, sea creatures destabilize our expectations of heteronormativity, individuality, and perception across species. In *Wild Blue Media*, I consider these lessons about species-specific perception as a lesson about media anthropocentrism, or how media designs (necessarily) favor human perceptual capacities—a form of partial perception and situated knowledge. *Wild Blue Media* explores the milieu specificity of processes of mediation, while being aware that what is noise for a human might be information for a dolphin. Meaning emerges in species-specific and milieu-specific contexts and habituations of perception.

Chapter Descriptions

As a chimera in form, *Wild Blue Media* channels the literary and science fictional technique of conceptual displacement in order to denature what we have come to expect out of our media technologies. Following this introduction, each of the three core chapters of this book takes a concept in media theory—interface, inscription, and database—and submerges it underwater. These key terms roughly correspond to Friedrich Kittler's definition of media in terms of "recording, storage, and the processing of information."[102] While Kittler's terms operate fairly intuitively in terrestrial contexts—we might imagine recording as typing on a computer, storage as a hard drive, and information processing as the printing of a text file or rendering of an animation—the ocean environment presents other challenges. If seawater is a storage medium, then it is not the same kind of "storage" we imagine that happens with a digital database, where all the records stay put. The ocean also changes how we understand the possibilities of recording or inscription in the sense of making marks on a page or a stone tablet. Underwater, any in-*script*-ions would be eroded, washed away, or overgrown with marine plants and animals. Rather than Kittler's third term, "processing," I use "interface" as my third term to think within the ocean, considering how the conditions of pressure in the ocean necessitate a three-dimensional rather than flat understanding of the interface. In these ways, the alterity of the ocean environment challenges how we have traditionally thought of the conditions for media as dry processes. However, it is important to me that this book not be read as a "keywords" project, which has a kind of encyclopedic logic and no rationale for its delimitation. Instead, I intend interface, inscription, and database to serve as a kind of generative matrix for thinking through the conditions of possibility for media in the ocean environment, a matrix I bring together in a final chapter on underwater museums.

Chapter 1, "Interface: Breathing Underwater," plunges the reader into the ocean through its analysis of how narratives of scuba diving change the way we understand the concept of the interface in media theory. I trace the ways that the watery etymology of the term *interface* as the surface between two fluids has reified a particular way of understanding of it as a surface. While media theorists have described the interface as any surface across which human users can exercise control (screens, keyboards), diving suggests a relationship with technology that is less about control than about participation and vulnerability. By starting with the lungs rather than other forms of technical interfaces, I develop a theory of interface through the biological process of tissue saturation. Tissue saturation involves considering the role of time and pressure (measurable in atmospheres) on divers, where not just the lungs but the whole body figures as a distributed interface. I blend readings of diving memoirs by Jacques Cousteau and Sylvia Earle, two of the most visible figures in ocean environmentalism, with ocean science fictions by Greg Egan and James Blish that portray submerged humans. These literary texts demonstrate key media perspectives on thinking about interfaces, meditating on the process of breathing underwater, the significance of time and pressure, and on the surface as a kind of "chronotope."[103] They also lead me to identify the anthropocentrism embedded within one of the key debates in literary studies: "surface reading" versus a hermeneutics of suspicion, both of which assume the interpreter does their work from the plane of a surface, gazing down into the depths (psychological, textual, or other). By attending to the physiological conditions of diving underwater in these two narrative accounts, I show how oceanic immersion suggests a different interpretive vantage point, involving a distributed technical interface between air, body, regulator, and tanks that provides a temporary condition of amphibiousness. This new physiological and ecological way of looking for instances of saturated interface in the world—for example, in phenomena like ocean acidification—models a way of bringing together oceanic theories of mediation alongside matters of climate change and environmental justice.

The ocean not only changes the way we think about interfaces; it also changes how universally we should think about the concept of inscription in media theory. As a cold liquid environment swirling with dissolved chemicals and planktonic life, the ocean presents conditions of mediation that may have less to do with marks and the reading of signs than on residues and processes of camouflage. Chapter 2, "Inscription: Vampire Squid Media," follows Vilém Flusser's unusual text *Vampyroteuthis Infernalis*, which takes up the challenge of imagining what forms of media would exist for the vampire squid living in the deep abyss. In the abyssal environment of *Vampyroteuthis infernalis*, inscription on paper or even stone tablets is eventually eroded by seawater or encrusted with growth; Flusser's vampire squid communicates through the noninscriptive media of liquid ink clouds and skin paintings. Flusser considers how the unique physiology of the vampire squid gives rise to particular forms of spatial cognition, what kind of media would be available to the vampire squid living in the deep abyss, and what might constitute lasting forms of information storage underwater. If the squid were a theorist, how would it metaphorically speak about its world? Flusser models a science fictional perspective on media theory by assuming that the entity using media is a cephalopod rather than a human. In so doing, he also asks that we consider the role of both the environment and human desire in shaping what kinds of media we design—and value.

The two methods I develop in this book, milieu-specific analysis and conceptual displacement, are both explicitly Flusserian. Conceptual displacement, as I have already written, links Flusser with critical traditions in science fiction studies and the productive estrangement that emerges from such situations. In asking about the possibility of media in the abyss, Flusser's vampire squid fable also models a version of milieu-specific analysis as the attention to the significance of the environment of critical, theoretical, and philosophical writing. Indeed, it is the abyss that characterizes how Flusser imagines the vampire squid's media (ink clouds, skin paintings), ephemeral forms that make their impressions through memory rather than through marks on pages or stone. The abyss also contributes to the way that the vampire squid orients to its world through language. Through a discussion of Lakoff and Johnson's theories of orientational metaphor, I show how Flusser's vampire squid might bring us to a greater awareness of the terrestrial bias in the ways we figuratively speak about the world.

However, Flusser's vampire squid fiction also operates on an allegorical level, as a fable about photography. I argue that Flusser's fictional science fable imagines the abyssal world of the vampire squid as a pretext for considering photography as a medium that marks a transition in society from valuing objects, like individual photographs, to the information transmitted, such as a film negative. Unlike earlier theories of photography (Roland Barthes, Susan Sontag, Joel Snyder), *Vampyroteuthis infernalis* is different in form, taking the abyss as a literary environment for media theory. Evoking the methodological tradition of science fiction's "cognitive estrangement," *Vampyroteuthis Infernalis* invents a comparative epistemology between human and vampire squid in order to gain critical distance on photography. Yet Flusser also wonders whether society might be becoming more "vampyroteuthic," valuing the inscription of information directly on subjects rather than on objects. At this allegorical level of interpretation, the vampire squid fable works as a sort of alien mirror within which to recognize similarities with our technological present. In this way, Flusser's speculation never loses sight of the human observer as "mediating" what it is possible to know about the vampire squid, avoiding the pitfall of physiological determinism.[104] The chapter ends by imagining the role of liquids in photography and digital media, using Ted Chiang's "The Story of Your Life" and "Exhalation" to consider not only media materiality but the significance of interpretation in terms of what counts as a mark or inscription. I define "noninscriptive media" not in permanent ontological or material terms that are limited to substances like fluids and gases but in terms of recognition on behalf of the reader or interpreter, developing my own fable about the Hawaiian bobtail squid and symbiotic counterillumination.

Moving from inscription to questions of storage, chapter 3, "Database: Proteus and the Digital," analyzes the assumption that the ocean is a "natural database" by looking at how two different data visualizations, Google Ocean and the artwork ATLAS *in silico*, render seawater. Where chapter 2 concerns metaphorical estrangement, chapter 3 explores the stakes of naturalized metaphors—when flows of information and oceanic databases obscure the material differences between digital technologies and oceanic media. I show how a conception of information storage in computational contexts values the preservation of data intact, something that would be challenged by an environment of seawater. Indeed, the chemical and vital properties of seawater transform what is stored underwater through processes of erasure, encrustation, and saturation. Seawater asks us to rethink terrestrial notions of the archive or database as informed by the language of earth and sediment, and instead consider storage in terms of seawater's capacity for protean transformation. The scale at which we look at seawater matters; the protean properties of seawater are meaningful at a macroscale (as in Google Ocean), but on increasingly microscopic scales, processes of abstraction make seawater commensurate with digitality (as in ATLAS *in silico*). In this way, milieu-specific analysis constitutes a sensitivity to representations of the ocean in digital media, including the questions of how the ocean is visually rendered as an object for interaction and interpretation—and the descriptive language that obscures these mediations.

Wild Blue Media concludes with chapter 4, "Underwater Museums: Diving as Method," which brings together considerations of interface, inscription, and database to ask: what changes when we imagine the "museum" underwater, and how can scuba diving become a humanities practice? I discuss my exploration and documentation of Jason deCaires Taylor's underwater sculpture museums in Isla Mujeres, Mexico, and the nearby cenotes (underwater caverns) in Tulum, Mexico. The sculptures not only exist as tourist sites that scuba divers can visit but are more commonly encountered as a series of high-quality photographs circulated online (and even as a Google Street View destination). I approach the sculptures from the perspective of comparative media studies, looking at the way they exist across digital, oceanic, and terrestrial installations, drawing on my training as a scuba diver to study them in situ. As a point of contrast, I compare Taylor's underwater museum with naturally occurring cenotes or underwater limestone caverns, considering the role of optical phenomena, bubbles, the halocline, and other boundary matters. I make the case for scuba diving as a humanities methodology that not only figures as a form of witnessing but also constitutes a meaningful interpretive practice that trains the diver to read from below.

I write this book, in part, due to my lifelong obsession with the wonderfully enchanting alterity of marine creatures and as a response to the real anthropogenic threats that the ocean faces today. To channel Walter Benjamin's statement about historical memory, the ocean flashes up in the moment of danger that is climate change.[105] Yet the years that have gone into crafting this book have not focused on marine spatial planning, or fisheries regulation, or climate change policy. I think of this book as a "pre-activist" book, in the hopes that thinking through the ocean will alter and add to the storytelling and analytical techniques available to everyone.

INTERFACE / Breathing Underwater

As a first step into an oceanic theory of mediation, let us turn to Jacques Cousteau—perhaps the most famous marine storyteller—and dive with him into *World without Sun* (1964), a film that explored and celebrated the science fictional possibility of human habitation underwater. The film begins with a disc-shaped yellow submarine slowly cruising under the Red Sea, off the coast of Sudan. It wobbles slightly via jet propulsion and moves forward under dappled rays of light that filter down from the surface, as clouds of fish casually stream by. The view shifts and the submarine dips under the hood of a yellow structure. As the habitat looms above on the prongs of three supporting legs, the camera looks up to show the submarine fantastically reflected in the mirror of a silvery moon pool—an interface between ocean and air, opening to the habitat above. A diver swims freely overhead to assist the submarine, and we now realize what the submarine has been doing all along: it is docking.

If a media theorist were to enumerate the kinds of technical interfaces present in *World without Sun*, they might begin by naming the hard things: the body of the submarine, the control panel of the submarine that allows the steersman to control its propulsion jets, or perhaps the regulator through which the diver breathes compressed air. Technical interfaces, after all, are commonly understood as surfaces—like keyboards, screens, and dashboards—through which a user exerts control and interprets information. A more ecologically minded theorist might point to the contact between air and water, which relates to the definition of an interface in chemistry, as the boundary between two fluids.[1] Yet in order for humans to live underwater, there must be successful management of the life-sustaining element of air. The submarine, habitat, and scuba (self-contained underwater breathing apparatus) tanks are all carefully regulated pockets of air, sealed off from the surrounding milieu of the ocean in order to sustain human life.[2] Interfaces with the air, then, should include the silvery film of the moon pool as well as the human lungs themselves: one a flat surface between fluids, the other a three-dimensional and biological surface. It is this second interface—the lungs—that most interests me. Since human movement underwater turns out to be dependent on an ecology of air, what would change if we took the human lungs in scuba diving, rather than computer screens, as a site through which to theorize the interface? If, as Johanna Drucker writes, "we face the challenge of reading interface as an object and of understanding it as a space that constitutes reading as an activity," how might a focus on the lungs recalibrate our sense interpretation—a question central to debates in literary theory?[3]

In order to rethink the interface concept through the lungs—whose delicate alveoli are tucked into the very interior of human bodies—this chapter begins by offering a gloss on recent critical discussions of the interface in media theory, which center on computers and other digital technologies. Since the flurry of writings on new media from the 1990s, the concept of the "interface" has been predominantly tied to computers and screen culture, surfaces that display interactive visual iconography. Yet unlike discussions of screen technologies, the interface in diving involves not only a visual capacity to interpret signs (such as the readings of one's gauges measuring depth and remaining air) but also somatic feedback of how one's air cavities—ears, sinuses, head, lungs—feel. Bodily discomfort is an important nonvisual sign that indicates how the diver should proceed. Thus proprioception—knowledge of the body's orientation in space and inner feeling—is key to how interpretation takes place for human beings underwater.

Unlike screens and keyboards, the interface in diving extends from the lungs into body tissues as they absorb extra air (nitrogen and oxygen) breathed at a pressure equivalent to the diver's depth. In this picture, the interface between self and world materializes as tissue saturation, a thick extension of dissolved gasses in the blood stream. These physiological and environmental conditions of scuba require a new conception of interface in terms of both space and time: as a distributed volume rather than a surface, and as a duration effect of breathing air at higher pressures.[4] Rethinking the interface in the milieu specificity of the ocean, for a human being, requires a corollary concept of saturation.

As primary source material for this type of phenomenological reading of the interface, I turn to nonfiction narratives, or memoirs, of oceanic immersion in scuba diving that usefully document the sensory and cognitive estrangement of breathing underwater. I focus on Jacques Cousteau's autobiographical account of his early experiments with the aqualung in *The Silent World* and Sylvia Earle's *Sea Change: A Message from the Oceans* because of their clear descriptions of the physiology of breathing underwater and the technology that facilitates it. Drawing on my own experience as a scuba diver, I read Cousteau and Earle as unintentional "media theorists" who show how the interfacial conditions of diving begin with the surface of the lungs but also involve the complexity of air tanks, regulator, air, lungs, and bodily absorption of air into the tissues. This biochemical and distributed sense of interface shifts away from the flatness of surfaces by considering the liquid volume of the human body and oceanic milieu.

Cousteau and Earle emphasize not only the tactility and liquidity of the ocean but, most importantly, the function of *pressure*. For every thirty feet, the pressure around a diver increases by a factor of one atmosphere (atm). It is the factor of pressure that characterizes how long a scuba diver might safely spend underwater before surfacing, a matter of physiology that I will soon discuss. My consideration of the ocean as a milieu of varying pressures (depending on depth) shows how milieu-specific analysis needs to consider more than saltwatery materiality; it also needs to consider other physical conditions and their implications. Pressure is both a milieu-specific and an embodiment-specific effect of thinking through the interface in the ocean, an effect that does not come under consideration with screen technologies or terrestrial conditions of perception.[5] Pressure brings our attention to the physiology of human lungs, such that interface means thinking in terms of volumes, duration, and tissue saturation.

Through their detailed attention to the phenomenology of breathing

underwater, Earle's and Cousteau's ocean memoirs share a certain kinship with ocean science fiction, which also concerns itself with explaining
sensory estrangement and the speculative possibilities of human habitation under the ocean (either through prosthetics or bioengineering). For
example, Jules Verne's late nineteenth-century novel 20,000 *Leagues under
the Sea* famously imagined the adventures of Captain Nemo and his submarine *The Nautilus*, and the possibility of proto-scuba gear such that men
could walk in suits on the seafloor. More biologically centered fictions
like James Blish's "Surface Tension" and Greg Egan's "Oceanic" imagine
amphibiously modified human beings that can breathe underwater or on
land, which I discuss in this chapter.[6] Because of their shared investment
in describing the conditions of human submergence in the ocean, I blend
discussions of ocean science fiction with ocean memoir throughout this
chapter, juxtaposing their phenomenological narratives to draw out an
embodied and milieu-specific theorization of the interface in scuba diving. By using diving memoirs and science fiction texts as documentation
of the phenomenology of diving, I show how questions of mediation suffuse literary narratives about the ocean.

Although this chapter starts with human immersion underwater in a
way that perhaps looks like anthropocentrism, I see it as a way of cultivating an awareness of our necessarily anthropo*genic* perspectives. Human embodiment is a form of situated knowledge that accounts for the
epistemic conditions from which we—as scholars, artists, and passionate
observers—begin. While I begin with human divers, submergence underwater ultimately leads to broader multispecies connections. Once we learn
how to look for the particular kind of interface that emerges in scuba
diving that involves molecular exchange, distribution across a volume,
and duration, it becomes easier to recognize other examples of this type
of interface elsewhere in the world. When Earle says that the oceans are
the blue "lungs" of the planet, referencing the sheer volume of oxygen
that marine algae produce, it carries affective power: the analogy between
human body and ocean body figures as a narrative tactic that asks us to
care for the environment in the same way that we would care for our own
vulnerable bodies.[7] Attending to saturation may lead to larger-scale consciousness of other interfacial volumes, such as the sea as it absorbs CO_2
from the atmosphere. In this way, interface/saturation provides a way of
addressing messy biotechnical saturations across meaningful thresholds
of livability.

Surface Tension: Theories of the Human-Computer Interface (HCI)

Since the 1980s, the term *interface* has appeared in a variety of media theory contexts to describe technical forms of relation between human users and symbolic content. Sometimes the interface indicates a concrete physical thing: for example, a computer screen, a control panel, a video game controller, a computer (typically referred to as "human computer interface," or HCI). Other times the interface is imagined as a surface that allows a user to control, to communicate with, or to otherwise exert influence.[8] Either way, interface tends to be constellated within configurations of dry technologies, even for theorists trying to think about different senses of the interface beyond HCI. For example, Joanna Drucker lists "control panels, dashboards, toaster ovens, home entertainment units, plumbing fixtures, and card catalogs" as examples of typical interfaces, while Alexander Galloway writes that his concept "the Interface effect" is "about windows, screens, keyboards, kiosks, channels, sockets, and holes— or rather, about none of these things in particular and all of them simultaneously."[9] Both theorists agree that the interface is never a matter of a thing or one technology in isolation. However, their lists are indicative of our terrestrial bias toward thinking and theorizing technologies, which typically extend as far as computers and their prostheses—technologies that would be ruined by water should it wash over them. I rehearse some of the literature on human-computer interfaces below, from media theory and cognitive science, to draw out a few key commonalities that normally define interfaces: interpretation, reading, and visuality.

In some interpretations, the interface is potentially everything semiotically meaningful in one's environment. For example, in "The Interface Theory of Perception," Donald Hoffman argues that "our perceptions constitute a *species-specific user interface* that guides behavior in a niche."[10] Hoffman draws on the early twentieth-century Estonian biologist Jacob von Uexküll's influential writings on animal perception worlds, or *Umwelten*, to argue that human perception is not of "reality" directly but of cues in our perceived environment—a modernized version of Plato's cave allegory, in which we only ever see shadows of things themselves. He compares the interface of perception to the way the trash icon on a computer screen is not the computer code itself but a representation that allows us to interact with it. Although Hoffman does not account for how matters of culture, ideology, gender, race, or the unconscious figure into our nonconscious habits of perception, he sees perception as a useful fiction that "constructs the properties and categories of an organism's perceptual world," and thus "different species have different interfaces."[11] In this view, we do not experience reality directly but rather its icons—Platonic shadows on the wall of the cave.

Other scholars foreground the role of legibility and the visual hermeneutics of "reading" the interface. Like Hoffman, Joanna Drucker's writings on the ubiquity of interface begin from the premise that anything semiotically meaningful can function as an interface for human beings, yet she complicates Hoffman's argument by foregrounding practices of interpretation. Because anything that signifies can be an interface, "interface, increasingly, will be the experience of being in the world."[12] Drucker sees the interface not as a matter of representation but as a matter of performance: "We face the challenge of reading interface as an object and of understanding it as a space that constitutes reading as an activity."[13] In this picture, reading activates or actualizes interfaces as interpretive sites for specific readers; thus, reading is a fundamental way in which we encounter the world. Although we might question whether "reading" is an adequate verb for nonvisual forms of interpretation that take place across interfaces, like hearing or proprioception, the tactility of braille does suggest one possibility.

In another view, an interface is the cumulative effect of multiple channels of infrastructure and power, as articulated by media scholar Alexander Galloway in *The Interface Effect*. Like Drucker and Hoffman, Galloway retains a strong emphasis on the interface as a site of visual interpretation but moves away from focusing on interfaces as things and instead theorizes interfaces as effects. Here, Galloway understands the interface as "an 'agitation' or generative friction between different formats," exemplified by the home screen in World of Warcraft (WOW).[14] He reads this screen not as a door or window but as a "factory floor, an information-age sweatshop."[15] The politics of WOW's interface is not that it connects a virtual world with the player's world through a window but that it embeds forms of cooperative labor inside play. By highlighting cooperative labor as an effect of WOW's interface, Galloway shows how "power today resides in networks, computers, algorithms, information, and data," inhabiting the largely invisible or nonrepresentational conditions that underlie visual interfaces.[16] The lesson to be learned from Galloway's argument is that an interface can come into effect not only as a surface of interaction or interpretation but as a distributed material phenomenon conditioned by unrepresented processes and forms of power. Distribution is useful for thinking through technical interfaces and also—as we will see—environmental ones.

One text that begins to think through a more environmental sense of the interface is Branden Hookway's *Interface: A Genealogy of Mediation and Control*. Hookway uses the material and mathematical properties of fluids to theorize the interface as not a thing but as a modulated effect. Hookway begins with the definition of interface coined in 1869 by engineer James Thompson, who defines "interface" in relation to the contact between two fluids: "[It is] as if the fluid everywhere possesses an expansive tendency, so that pressure must everywhere be received by the fluid on one side of a dividing surface (or as I call it *interface*) from the fluid, or solid, on the one side, to prevent the fluid from expanding indefinitely, or to balance its expansive force."[17] This usage predates by thirteen years the definition cited by Matthew Fuller and Florian Cramer in their article "Interface" in *Software Studies*: the interface is "a surface forming a common boundary of two bodies, spaces, phases.[18] Based on the etymological history that links "interface" to chemistry and thermodynamics, Hookway argues that, "*interface* and *fluid* meet in mutual self-definition."[19] However, Hookway's engagement with fluidity is at an extremely abstract level, focusing on only one material quality of fluids: to produce separation and internal difference.[20] This generic notion of fluid/fluidity neglects the meaningful material differences between fluids like seawater, freshwater, air, specific gasses, and plasmas, in terms of both their chemical properties and the material imagination of these substances.[21] As I argue in chapter 3, theories about digital media often draw on an abstract sense of "fluidity" that does not have the properties of any particular fluid (freshwater, ocean, other). Even so, Hookway's sense that interface is always a matter of surface interaction is an enduring conception that persists in media theory, and even in fiction.

One classic science fiction story that dramatizes Hookway's sense of the interface as a surface between two fluids is James Blish's short story "Surface Tension." The story takes place on the swampy world of Hydrot, full of an ocean and primitive life in puddles. These conditions prove inhospitable to the human ship that crash landed with hopes of "seeding" the universe with human colonies, and in desperation, the scientists decide to engineer microscopic humans as their descendants, adapted to freshwater puddles. "Surface Tension" then follows the actions of a microscopic human named Lavon, and his voyage from his home puddle up through the threshold of the water's surface (the "sky"). Through this spatial movement, "Surface Tension" proves to be the inverse of Jules Verne's *20,000 Leagues under the Sea*, involving a supermarine ship that voyages up into the sky instead of a submarine ship that voyages into the depths below.

The story focuses on three key surfaces: the Bottom, the thermocline (which children can "sled" down), and the sky—a seemingly impassible barrier relative to the colonists' microscopic size. In one scene, Lavon attempts to see if he could "climb" a plant stalk and pass beyond the sky, even though its surface tension prohibits a being of his size to pass through. Yet for microscopic Lavon, the surface of the puddle water "seemed to give slightly, with a tough, frictionless elasticity."[22] Matters of scale are key to the action in the story: whereas macroscopic humans can easily place a hand through the water's surface, microscopic humans are not massive enough for a hand to break through the hydrostatic forces at work in the water's surface tension—which only can "give slightly." The interface's properties are an effect of the scalar relationship between interface and embodied subject. Through dramatizing the physical properties of the water's surface tension, Blish shows how an interface is relative to the size and scale of particular subjects.

The geographical interface of air/water sets up the narrative action to cross or transcend that very interface. The surface of the water is thus a kind of "chronotope," a term that Mikhail Bakhtin defines as a spatial figure in literature that also structures a particular experience of time. A road, for example, can be both a physical meeting place for characters and a plotline that structures chance encounters. Margaret Cohen writes that chronotopes can also involve bodies of water such as rivers, open water, the shore, and islands, environs that help advance the action of the story and convey its theme and content.[23] What makes the interface of the sea/sky a compelling chronotope in "Surface Tension" is the way that it sets up the action in the story to center on pushing against and, ultimately, transcending that which the interface delimits. In this way, Hookway's theorization of the interface may be seen not only as a spatial condition (a surface between two fluids) but also as a narrative (and thus time-based) effect. The sea/sky is able to function as a meaningful boundary in this way in large part because of the scale of the engineered human colonists, too small to transcend the boundary between sea/sky without technological intervention.

The chronotope of the sea/sky interface sets up a narrative pattern that is sometimes about crossing thresholds and sometimes about running up against limits. For example, after Lavon's attempt to cross the sky—which works momentarily but throws his body into shock and then hibernation—he decides to build a ship that will be able to safely break through the surface tension and voyage into the beyond. When the supermarine ship does break through, one person notably exclaims, "I can see the top of the sky! From the other side, from the top side! It's like a big flat sheet of metal. We're going away from it. We're above the sky, Lavon, we're above the sky!"[24] The imagery of the sky as a "flat sheet of metal" echoes an earlier moment in the novella that has to do with writing and the difficulty of preserving information in aquatic environments.[25] Blish's original colonists imagine that history could be preserved on a "set of corrosion-proof metal leaves, of a size our colonists can handle conveniently."[26] It is significant, then, that the character Shar describes the sky in the same terms as the only survivable medium for history: metal leaves. Although the imagery of the sky as a "metal sheet" suggests that the microscopic humans are impossibly encased in an impassible enclosure, it also suggests that the sky might be a legible surface of writing, or interface between worlds that must be "read" (to follow Drucker and Galloway). In this figuration, the sky is both their past history (where they came from) and their future (where they are attempting to go), a medium of destiny.

Yet whereas the sky is something that can be pushed against and transcended, the people of Hydrot struggle with a lack of tangible interfaces underwater that would make scientific experimentation possible. In one scene, Shar tells Lavon, "We live in water. Everything seems to dissolve in water, to some extent. How do we confine a chemical test to the crucible we put it in? How do we maintain a solution at one dilution? . . . We're thinking creatures, Lavon, but there's something drastically wrong in the way we think about this universe we live in. It just doesn't seem to lead to results."[27] To the extent that scientific experimentation depends on processes of purification and isolation, the freshwater environment clearly challenges their progress.[28] In addition to experiencing difficulty in isolating chemicals for experimentation, the microscopic humans find that they cannot control heat, which is "carried off as rapidly as it's produced."[29] Something about human thought—originally evolved to problem-solve on land—seems to persist in the engineered microscopic humans. Indeed, it seems that the drive toward tool use and experimentation is part of a Jungian ancestral memory (a possibility noted by one of the original colonists early in the story). Despite their physiological adaptation to an aquatic environment, the microscopic humans have retained certain habits of thought that belonged to terrestrial humans. Shar concludes, "Our unfitness to live here is self-evident."[30]

Although the most geographically significant interface in "Surface Tension" is the "sky" or water/air interface itself, there is another interface that is equally important but somewhat ignored. Early in the story, when the original colonists are deciding how to engineer microscopic humans, they decide to give them arachnid-like book lungs and webbed extremities to aid them in their new environment: "[The lungs] are gradually adaptable to atmosphere-breathing, if it ever decides to come out of the water."[31] What this implies is that to transcend the surface of the "sky," the microscopic humans would need to reverse-evolve their lungs to breathe air. However, we are left without enough physiological detail to imagine how this would occur; "Surface Tension" shies away from exploring the implications of the lungs as interface in favor of a more obvious poetics of the interface as surface between two fluids.

As we will see in the next section, a radically different sense of the interface emerges once the lungs take center stage. Jacques Cousteau's autobiographical writings pick up where "Surface Tension" leaves off. Although both deal with matters of crossing geographical interface—toward the depths or sky, respectively—Cousteau gives a much more detailed account of the role that the lungs play as interfaces between self and world. Rethinking the interface through the lungs means considering the fluidity of gases and liquids together, the absorption of pressurized air into the body's tissues as a volume rather than a surface. Here, interior and exterior are folded into the flesh of the human body through the semipermeable membranes of the lungs.

Flesh Feeling What the Fish Scales Know

Jacques Cousteau is arguably the most recognizable figure of ocean exploration in the twentieth century and is famous for coinventing the aqualung in 1942 with Émile Gagnan. Cousteau produced a variety of films and

FIGURE 1.1 Still image from *Le monde du silence* (*The Silent World*), 1956.

TV specials—notably, *Undersea World of Jacques Cousteau* (1966–76)—that showed the public what it was like to dive among corals, through kelps, and even under icebergs (figure 1.1).[32] Yet rather than his films, I turn to Cousteau's autobiographical narrative *The Silent World*, cowritten with his diving friend Frédéric Dumas, for its detailed account of the phenomenology of diving. The text includes many episodes where Cousteau and his friends (Dumas, Philippe Taillez) hunt for fish, break depth-diving records, and go to the edge of—and in some cases beyond—the thresholds of safety. Through its meditation on the lungs, *The Silent World* presents an occasion to think through basic differences between the interface as a chronotope of the "surface" (a geographical perspective) and how it looks from the perspective of human physiology underwater.

One of the differences between how Cousteau talks about the lungs as an interface and how media theorists have theorized the interface has to do with the role of conscious interpretation. As we saw earlier, Drucker and Hoffman placed a premium on conscious interpretation of interfaces that foregrounded the role of vision. Cousteau's intention for the prosthesis of scuba gear—what he first called the "aqualung"—placed an emphasis on nonconscious and somatic awareness. While living in Nazi-occupied southern France in 1942, Cousteau had asked his friend Émile Gagnan, an expert on industrial-gas equipment, for help designing a device that would be independent of connection to the surface via tubes. "I wanted an auto-matic device that would release the air to the diver without his thinking about it, something like the demand system used in the oxygen masks of high-altitude fliers."[33] Whereas a hand valve required the diver to physi-cally adjust the pressure of air delivered for breathing, Cousteau wanted an apparatus that would *automatically* deliver air at the ambient atmospheric pressure, where the diver would not have to calculate or think about the correct pressure.[34] This automaticity of air delivery, over conscious con-trol, is one of the hallmarks of scuba technology. Cousteau described the experience of breathing with the aqualung in the following way:

> The aqualung automatically fed me increased compressed air to meet the new pressure layer. Through the fragile human lung linings this counter-pressure was being transmitted to the blood stream and in-stantly spread throughout the incompressible body. My brain received no subjective news of the pressure. I was at ease, except for the pain in the middle ear and sinus cavities. I swallowed as one does in a landing airplane to open my Eustachian tubes and healed the pain.[35]

Cousteau's description of the aqualung differs from mainstream interface theorizations in that it operates in a *primarily nonvisual* and *nonconscious* manner. For example, Cousteau writes, "My brain received no subjective news of the pressure," and "We were acquiring an extra sense of the sea, a sort of *autodiagnosis of depth*. We meditated on our feelings, trying not to imagine symptoms that were not there."[36] Here, diving does not entail reading an interface in its visual signs and symbols but rather feeling the right balance of pressure between world and the interior of the self (blood, lungs, ears)—"autodiagnosis." Cousteau's desired requirements for the prosthetic of scuba technology suggest an interface that is not a matter of conscious interpretation so much as a matter of nonconscious proprio-ceptive feedback—an awareness of the body's position, movements, and internal state, independent of vision.

The importance of proprioception also emerges in Cousteau's poetic description of knowledge underwater. Upon successfully testing the aqua-lung, Cousteau reflected, "From this day forward we would swim across miles of country no man had known, free and level, with our flesh feeling what the fish scales know."[37] This formulation of a sensuous epistemics—flesh feeling what the fish scales know—places emphasis not on visual/conscious knowledge but on the body as a precondition for knowledge in relation to the tactile reciprocity of the ocean environment. If what fish do naturally is move underwater, then to feel what the fish scales know is to become partially fish—or the posthuman category of "menfish," as Cousteau liked to say.

In Cousteau's picture of the lungs as interface, air is not only the medium of human survival underwater but also part of the technical interface of scuba diving itself—filling the lungs and emptying from them, each breath a slight alteration in the buoyancy of the diver. Human lungs are like balloons in their ability to be inflated with air. Yet whereas balloons hold a fixed amount of gas steadily over time (except the small bit that leaks out through their one opening), human lungs absorb the oxygen they come in contact with, passing it (and other elements like nitrogen) into the bloodstream. In fact, the higher the air pressure one breathes, the more gas one absorbs into one's body through the interface of the lungs. This transcorporeal process of gas exchange marks the lungs as a very different kind of interface than balloons, whose rubber forms a solid boundary (like the screens of digital technologies) that gasses do not pass through.[38] Such fundamental porosity characterizes Astrida Neimanis's feminist view of posthuman being, which explores the implications of starting with a conception of human being that is always already open to watery material flows.[39]

This posthuman openness, however, carries with it a degree of vulnerability. In several episodes in *The Silent World*, Cousteau shows how the human body is its own measure of how long it is safe to remain underwater. To borrow Maurice Merleau-Ponty's term, the body in diving is a "measurant of things" that gives the flesh "its axes, its depth, its dimensions."[40] The submerged body of the human observer is a measurant of the depths, sensitized to the milieu-specific conditions of the distributed interface of air, rebreather, lungs, body. In one scene, Cousteau gestures toward the physiological effects of breathing pressurized air, specifically the way that the diver's bloodstream takes up the pressurized air breathed.

When the diver rises into lesser pressure, the nitrogen comes out of compression and becomes froth, on the same principle as opening a bottle of champagne. The CO_2 in champagne, which has been under pressure by the cork, expands theatrically when liberated. So does the nitrogen of the diver's body when he passes into the lighter water pressure. In mild cases the froth gives him pains in the joints. In severe cases the nitrogen bubbles can clog the veins, cut off the spinal ganglia or cause instant death by heart embolism.[41]

In this stereotypically French example ("opening a bottle of champagne"), Cousteau teaches that the longer the diver is underwater at the depth, the more gas the diver absorbs into their bloodstream.[42] If the diver rises out of the water too quickly without a safety stop, they risk getting "the bends," as free divers sometimes do. Tissue saturation defines the experience of the interface in diving, determining the feasibility of safely leaving the water. This positions us to see the interface is not just a surface (the lungs) but a volume (the whole body saturated by breathing compressed gas) that is negotiated through time-sensitive gas absorption.

Cousteau's experiments with breathing different gas mixtures point to the importance of proprioceptive feedback as an index of pain. These early diving experiments involved uncertainty about what constituted human physiological limits—or what we might call the nature of the durational interface between human body and breathed gas. In one anecdote, Cousteau experimented with breathing pure oxygen (rather than compressed air, which is primarily oxygen and nitrogen), a highly dangerous practice because it causes poisoning when breathed at high concentrations.

> I dived to the boundary of oxygen. I went down with ceremonious illusion. I was accepted in the sea jungle and would pay it the compliment of putting aside my anthropoid ways, clamp my legs together and swim down with the spinal undulations of a porpoise. . . . I borrowed the characteristics of a fish, notwithstanding certain impediments such as my anatomy and a ten-pound lead pipe twisted around my belt. . . . Then my lips began to tremble uncontrollably. My eyelids fluttered. My spine bent backward like a bow. With a violent gesture I tore off the belt weight and lost consciousness. The sailors saw my body reach the surface and quickly hauled me into the boat. I had pains in neck and muscles for weeks.[43]

In "putting aside my anthropoid ways" and borrowing "the characteristics of a fish," Cousteau adopts an amphibious posture of movement to swim effectively but at the expense of his physiological attunement to the surface. However, the experience was curtailed by the sudden trembling of his lips and loss of consciousness—indicative of oxygen poisoning. In this case, the distributed interface composed of human-compressed air-scuba

FIGURE 1.2 Char Davies, *Osmose*, 1995. Digital still of tree and pond captured in real time through HMD (head-mounted display) during live performance of the immersive virtual environment *Osmose*.

apparatus is a durational effect, *conditional upon time spent underwater* and at specific depths traveled. Cousteau only knew that he had reached a physiological threshold when he experienced pain and nervous system dysfunction. Thus, rather than a visual hermeneutics of "reading," diving asks that we think about interface in relation to proprioception—of feeling how the body responds to the technologies of air that enable and support underwater immersion, producing a sensuous epistemics indexed to time.[44]

Scuba diving's nonvisual interface has inspired digital artworks like Char Davies's acclaimed virtual reality (VR) artwork *Osmose* (1995) (figure 1.2). Linking movement to the user's breathing, *Osmose* invents a way to move through virtual environments ("natural" spaces of forests and the deep sea, for example). By linking movement to the user's rate of breathing, the interface in *Osmose* makes the "immersant" (participant) more aware of their body, departing from the ocularcentrism of VR that has continued from the 1990s into the twenty-first century. Mark B. N. Hansen suggests that *Osmose* catalyzes a shift from "a predominately visual sensory interface to a predominately bodily or affective interface."[45] Such an experience constitutes "a non-representational and nonvisual affective and proprioceptive experience of the body" that illustrates "how the living body exceeds the boundaries of the skin and encompasses parts of the environment."[46] In a different interpretation of *Osmose*, Frances Dyson counters that instead of dissolving the essential mediation between body and technology, *Osmose* only *simulates* this blurring between self and world, using digital technology to efface its own mediations. In other words, *Osmose* presents the illusion of blurring body and technology while allowing them, on a material level, to remain distinct, since no molecular gas exchange occurs. As an alternative, Dyson suggests reading Davies's work through aurality, "to look at breath and balance from the perspective of listening. The inner ear is after all the seat of balance, while the breath incorporates and is incorporated by that most affective, most troubling bodily production—the voice."[47] Whether one agrees with Hansen or Dyson depends on whether one views technical extension as mainly affective (as when one is moved by a digital simulation) or whether it needs to be material (as in gas exchange in diving).

One contradiction, however, is that *Osmose* does not involve the material osmosis (molecular exchange of gas) that real diving is predicated on, and breathing remains a safe form of navigation.[48] As we will see in the next section, cases of oxygen poisoning, the bends, and nitrogen narcosis—moments when the diver falls *out of immersion* with both scuba prosthetics and ocean environment—are painful and harmful transgressions of the physiological limits of human descent underwater that arise with gas saturation of bodily tissues. These conditions of real risk and pain show how the interface in scuba diving is indexed to proprioceptive feedback, where pain and discomfort give important nonvisual cues that alert the diver to potential danger (for example, sinus pain during descent indicates that the diver should equalize the pressure in their Eustachian tubes by pinching their nose while exhaling). Such signals show that the volumetric interface that the diver experiences as self is perhaps out of balance, or at the point of causing intoxication or harm. It is also importantly, as we will see, an effect of the ocean being a milieu of differential pressure.

Raptures of the Deep: On Tissue Saturation

Some of the more memorable moments in *The Silent World* involve Cousteau's accounts of nitrogen narcosis, or "rapture of the deep." Physiologically, nitrogen narcosis is "a condition that occurs in divers breathing compressed air. When divers go below depths of approximately 100 ft, increase in the partial pressure of nitrogen produces an altered mental state similar to alcohol intoxication."[49] The *Oxford English Dictionary* (OED) defines it as "a state of euphoria and disorientation in a diver," linking it not only to a feeling but also to the impairment of navigation and orientation.[50] Cold, stress, fatigue, and CO_2 retention can increase the effects of nitrogen narcosis as well. Cousteau writes that the first stage of nitrogen narcosis is like "a mild anesthesia, after which the diver becomes a god."[51] While Galloway might interpret nitrogen narcosis as an interface effect, the circumstances of deep diving challenge conventional understandings of the interface in terms of visuality and reading, and instead suggest that diving the interface underwater is a matter of duration. As we will see, nitrogen narcosis involves a meaningful physiological boundary or interface that exists not only at the surface but at a particular threshold of pressure indexed to time.

Like other forms of consciousness-altering drugs, nitrogen narcosis — also called "rapture of the deep" or, more colloquially, being "narked" — affects people differently. Cousteau writes, "I am personally quite receptive to nitrogen rapture. I like it and fear it like doom. It destroys the instinct of life."[52] In another episode, Cousteau writes of how his friend and diving partner Frédéric Dumas (nicknamed "Didi") succumbed to it first and began acting "drunk," and Cousteau had to help pull him to the surface. Such a differential is not unusual: "Tough individuals are not overcome as soon as neurasthenic persons like me, but they have difficulty extricating themselves. Intellectuals get drunk early and suffer more acute attacks on all the senses, which demand hard fighting to overcome. When they have beaten the foe, they recover quickly."[53] Yet unlike being drunk, one can alleviate the symptoms of nitrogen narcosis simply by traveling up to a shallower depth (typically above ninety feet). The reason for this is that a diver's regulator is designed to deliver air to them at precisely the ambient water pressure, because any pressure differential between air cavities and water pressure would result in pain. As a result, divers breathe more pressurized air at deeper depth (meaning more of that air becomes dissolved in their blood) and less pressurized air at shallower depths. In this way, nitrogen narcosis is a physiological phenomenon that trains us to see the ocean not only as a milieu of saltwater but, importantly, as a milieu of depth-dependent pressure.

Episodes in *The Silent World* show how Cousteau and his friends tested the physiological limits of deep diving before there were guidelines, often to the point where one or more divers would experience nitrogen narcosis. One of Cousteau's experiments that tested how deep a diver could descend offers a memorable description of narcosis. Following a carefully marked line with depth markers, Cousteau carried ten pounds of scrap iron to counter his buoyancy and descend; when he experienced discomfort he stopped, dropped the weight, and held onto a rope line. Boards were attached the line every five meters so that he and other divers could write a sentence describing their sensations.

> At two hundred feet I tasted the metallic flavor of compressed nitrogen and was instantaneously and severely struck with rapture. I closed my hand on the rope and stopped. My mind was jammed with conceited thoughts and antic joy. I struggled to fix my brain on reality, to attempt to name the color of the sea about me. A contest took place between navy blue, aquamarine and Prussian blue. The debate would not resolve. The sole fact I could grasp was that there was no roof and no floor in the blue room. The distant purr of the Diesel [engine] invaded my mind—it swelled to a giant beat, the rhythm of the world's heart. I took the pencil and wrote on a board, "Nitrogen has a dirty taste."[54]

As Cousteau recalls the effects of experiencing nitrogen narcosis, note the difference in detail between what Cousteau writes on the board while under rapture—"Nitrogen has a dirty taste"—and the detail of the rest of the paragraph, retrospectively remembered. Reflecting on the experience later, Cousteau says, "I could not write what it felt like fifty fathoms [actually less, about 270 feet] down."[55] Immediately after the dive, he notes that he could not even recall the act of writing: "When they hauled in the shotline I found that some imposter had written my name on the last board."[56] They all had headaches after; "none of us wrote a legible word on the deep board."[57] This suggests a disjuncture between the ability to speak, write, and describe in the moment of narcosis and the flurry of detail Cousteau recalled later upon reflection. Indeed, it is notable that today, the recreational limits of diving with regular compressed air are considered to be 120 feet—not 200!—and that one can expect nitrogen narcosis anywhere between 90 and 120 feet. In scuba diving, the interface is not only durational (according to time spent underwater) but also spatial (its physiological effects dependent on how deep one has dove) because the ocean is a milieu of pressure. Yet as the existence of the text indicates, Cousteau was later able to recall many more details in writing (the words he imagined for the color of the water, the purr of the diesel engine above, the unbounded spatiality of the "blue room").

Nitrogen narcosis changes the general conception of an interface as "a surface between two fluids" to a condition of tissue saturation, indexed to time. Saturation, according to the OED, is the condition of being "thoroughly soaked," or alternately, being charged to a "limit capacity" as in saturation diving: "The retention by the blood of the greatest amount of inert gas possible under the given pressure."[58] In a forthcoming essay collection I coedited with Rafico Ruiz, *Saturation: An Elemental Politics*, we theorize saturation as a material heuristic that "directs us toward the volumetric capacities, the spectrum of visual opacity and clarity, and suspended states of objects-subjects relations that are modeled by the lifeworlds of bodies of water," a spatial focus that "highlights saturation's ability to articulate terrestrial space as not just a container, but rather as a volumetric thickness."[59] This holds true in diving, where saturation indicates a fluid situation in which a limit is spatially figured as a volume rather than as a surface or interface. Yet saturation also involves a factor of time: time for gasses to dissolve in the bloodstream. Nitrogen narcosis necessitates a more complex spatial and temporal theory of the interface not only as a surface but as a time-dependent condition of tissue saturation.

The condition of saturation in diving suggests a way of seeing limits in terms of volumes and durations. Cousteau's goal to "find the limitations of the lung" ambiguously refers to both the human lung and the technology of the Aqua-Lung.[60] When at play, and not pushing the boundaries of dive limitations, according to Cousteau, "one realized the privilege of crossing the barrier, that molecular tissue which is actually a wall between elements. If it was difficult for men to break through the wall, it was more difficult for fish, which told us with their brief awkward leaps into the air how alien were air and water."[61] Here, that "molecular tissue" more difficult to break through than a wall is the human lung, which facilitates gas exchange between breathed air and the bloodstream. In this physiological context, a limit is not just a flat threshold (like the skin of the water in "Surface Tension") but also a matter of tissue saturation, beyond which cognitive functioning becomes impaired and the risk of physical injury increases. Saturation, then, figures the limit in terms of chemistry and volume.

Greg Egan's Hugo Award–winning novella, *Oceanic*, develops a science fictional take on "rapture of the deep" and illuminates the way that saturation emerges as a condition of interface.[62] "Oceanic" takes place on a planet called Covenant, set at an unspecified date in the future after human beings achieve both space travel and the ability to live forever without material bodies. The mythic "crossing" had taken place long enough ago that the people of Covenant no longer know much about why the "Angels" chose to incarnate into material bodies again, nor why there was a significant decrease in technology soon after they terraformed Covenant. The story begins with the protagonist Martin slowly falling asleep on a boat to the rhythm of the waves. Martin's brother Daniel suddenly asks him if he believes in God, admitting that he has joined the Deep Church and taken literally the following piece of scripture: "'Unless you are willing to drown in My blood, you will never look upon the face of My Mother.' So they bound each other hand and foot, and weighted themselves down with rocks." The way to acquire true faith, Daniel insists, is through immersion deep in the ocean, for, "in the water, you're alone with God," an experience of rapture that returns one to a feeling of originary spiritual unity.[63] In a religious sense, one might be saturated with faith, a water metaphor that dovetails with the ocean as a site of baptism.

The spiritual unity enabled by deep ocean immersion in "Oceanic" alludes to the "oceanic feeling" coined by Romain Rolland and popularized by Sigmund Freud. In *Civilization and Its Discontents*, Freud begins with Rolland's description of the oceanic feeling, which he does not feel himself, and goes on to relate it to the unbounded feeling of the ego's original unity with Nature and the maternal body.[64] Martin's description of his own immersion echoes the language of Freud's oceanic feeling: "Suddenly, everything was seared with light . . . as if I was an infant again and my mother had wrapped her arms around me tightly. It was like basking in sunlight, listening to laughter, dreaming of music too beautiful to be real."[65] This moment of oceanic feeling—from which "Oceanic" likely draws its title—merges the spiritual and the physical, taking the ocean as the site or wellspring of religious feeling and faith. The divine Mother (God) and the mother ocean are taken as one, where Martin is able to both feel the immenseness of the universe and, ecstatically, experience himself as inseparable from it. In this tale, Egan both literalizes and fictionalizes Freud's oceanic feeling, imagining a religion in which a drowned and resurrected Beatrice figures as Jesus, and in which religious feeling is experienced most intensely during and after a brief baptism in the depths of the ocean. Yet the idea that submergence in the deep ocean produces this ecstatic intensity of feeling is also evocative of nitrogen narcosis, or "rapture of the deep." Rapture, after all, has strong associations with ecstatic feeling or a "transport of mind, mental exaltation or absorption, ecstasy."[66] Whereas Cousteau's explanation of rapture of the deep (nitrogen narcosis) has to do with tissue saturation from breathing compressed gas below 120 feet, Egan fictionalizes a different "rapture" from being submerged: a religious rapture, or spiritual union with the holy Beatrice.

The main conflict of the story revolves around Martin's disenchantment with the Deep Church once he begins studying science. His work on Covenant's pre-Angelic fauna (before the arrival of human colonists) suggests that "rather than rain bringing new life from above, an ocean-dwelling species from a much greater depth had moved steadily closer to the surface, as the Angels' creations drained oxygen from the water."[67] Ecopoeisis—another name for terraforming—creates conditions that end up being favorable to a specific kind of benthic microbe: "Unwittingly or not, the Angels had set in motion the sequence of events that had released it [Zooytes] from the ocean to colonize the planet."[68] Covenant's human modifications led to a parallel set of planetary changes put into effect by the benthic microbes.

This discovery threatens to demystify the true cause of the oceanic feeling by pinning it on microbes rather than a relationship with holy Beatrice. After Martin attends a conference and notices one of the paper titles, "Carla Reggia: 'Euphoric Effects of Z/12/80 Excretions,'" he realizes that this microbe could be responsible for religious feeling by excreting an amine that was "able to bind to receptors in our Angel-crafted brains," an effect "almost certainly undesigned, and unanticipated."[69] This information places the "oceanic feeling" in an entirely new context: Martin was not simply drowning in the holy love of Beatrice; he was drowning in—saturated with—the potent drug of Z/12/80 excrement. In this reformulation, the source of religious feeling moves from the sacred to the profane, a matter of absorbing abject products from ocean microbes rather than divine love. Such a conclusion shakes Martin's faith in the reality of Beatrice, now explainable as a physical phenomenon like the warmth of sunlight on skin. Yet by the end of the story, Martin recognizes that, despite being knowable scientifically, Covenant's microbes still play a role as coproducers of "oceanic feeling"—a relational, multispecies, and transcorporeal phenomenon.

"Oceanic" dramatizes the religious crisis that occurs when the ocean depths cease to signify a holy, mysterious connection to Beatrice and instead become knowable through the pharmacological effects of indigenous microbes. Instead of the experience of tissue saturation by excess gas (as in nitrogen narcosis in *The Silent World*), this religious experience occurs through the tissue saturation of one particular rapture-inducing amine. As in *The Silent World*, saturation in "Oceanic" emerges as a condition of the interface between submerged human body and oceanic environment, a volumetric interface rather than a surface (or surface tension). Saturation shows how interface effects like nitrogen narcosis are dependent not only on contact between surfaces but also on the material conditions of specific environs—in this case, the ocean as an environment of pressure, which increases with depth. By attending to the physiological, chemical, and physical conditions of diving in this way, we can see milieu-specific interface effects.

Surface and Depth Reading

Such close attention to the milieu of the ocean in fiction and nonfiction has implications for debates about interpretation in literary theory that draw on spatial metaphors of surface and depth, where the text is a kind of surface through which the reader searches for a deeper meaning. Consider the 2009 issue of *Representations* that sought to outline "surface reading" practices as alternatives to the "hermeneutics of suspicion" or "symptomatic reading" promoted by Marxist and psychoanalytic theories. In contrast to the way that symptomatic reading "took meaning to be hidden, repressed, deep, and in need of detection and disclosure by an interpreter," Stephen Best and Sharon Marcus pose a key question about how to deal with violence that is explicit and spectacular (such as the torture at Abu Ghraib, or destruction wrought by Hurricane Katrina). In their view, the surface is "what is evident, perceptible, apprehensible in texts," "what, in the geometrical sense, has length and breadth but no thickness," and, importantly, "what insists on being looked at rather than what we must train ourselves to see through."[70] Their emphasis of the preposition "at" rather than "through" is a notable metaphorization, suggesting an optics of clarity over opacity.

The "Surface Reading" issue of *Representations* has spurred a number of generative discussions about literary interpretive practice, including the ways in which literary criticism itself aligns with forms of genre. In her contribution to this issue, Margaret Cohen uses the example of sea fiction to show how the work of "practical problem solving" that such genre fiction dramatizes (navigating, fishing, weathering storms) "is qualitatively different from plumbing the novel's hidden depths in search of revelation and truth," which she compares to detective fiction.[71] Other contributions to "Surface Reading" aim to complicate Freud's model of the unconscious with the position that not everything unconscious is repressed or accounts for the politics of what is or is not noticed in plain sight. Anne Cheng powerfully observes, "Sometimes it is not a question of what the visible hides but how it is that we have failed to see certain things on its surface."[72]

Nonetheless, forms of surface reading still share something in common with a hermeneutics of suspicion, which is this: a terrestrially inflected model in which a human interpreter remains on the "surface" of a text and chooses to either look at the surface or peer into its depths. The observer in literary interpretive models outlined here is never thought of as being submerged in the depths, or looking up at the surface, or envisioning more diffuse, gaseous, or saturated conditions of textual interface. This is where the oceanic and physiologically inflected models of the interface that I have outlined in this chapter have something to contribute. By complicating the notion of the interface as a surface—and demonstrating the importance of "saturation" as a complementary heuristic—*The Silent World* and "Oceanic" open to spatial models of interpretation beyond a strict surface/depth binary. Thinking with actual oceans opens the way for other kinds of physical factors to come to matter, such as chemical saturation and pressure. For example, accounting for the ocean as an environment of pressure indicates the importance of time and duration as conditions of interpretation; a human observer can only spend so long underwater. The physiology of diving, where the lung is as an "instrument of observation," to use Cousteau's phrase, necessitates a new hermeneutic model in which the observer might begin from a condition of saturation at depth rather than standing on the surface gazing into the depths, separate and apart. Oceanic conditions of observation presume an immersed observer, where the binary of surface/depth does not account for all the possible spatialities of interpretation; the observer might not just look into the depths, but venture down into them, experiencing tissue saturation as they go. By *thinking through* the ocean, we can begin to develop a sense of milieu-specific environments of critical practice that differentially implicate the human observer and their normative orientations to both literary interpretation and media theory.

The submerged human observer underwater suggests a kind of amphibious point of view, where terrestrial experience is brought into comparison with oceanic exploration. However, to see the critic as mobile between air and water is not without its limitations and conditions. As I show in the next section on Sylvia Earle's diving narratives, the amphibious perspective that emerges in diving is not about being equally comfortable on land or in the water but about experiencing alienation from one world as the price of venturing into the other.

A Conditional Amphibiousness: Passports of Air

Dr. Sylvia Earle's writings are a fitting complement and contrast to Cousteau's descriptions of the phenomenological experience of diving. Earle began her career as a phycologist studying marine algae and grew to become one of the most influential voices in ocean conservation. She was chief scientist of the National Ocean and Atmospheric Association (NOAA) and founded the organization Mission Blue to create a network of worldwide marine protected areas, or "hope spots." Nicknamed "Her Deepness" for spending more than one thousand hours underwater, she was also named a National Geographic "explorer in residence," and a set of Lego underwater explorers pays homage to her likeness. The descriptions of diving and care for the ocean in her memoir *Sea Change: A Message from the Oceans* offer an amphibious perspective that differs from Cousteau's *The Silent World*. If developing an amphibious perspective has always been conditional on who could or could not participate in diving, then one of the most obvious things about Earle's writings is how much gender played a role in shaping attitudes toward the ocean and its human exploration.

For Cousteau, becoming "menfish" (the name he gave to the human Aqua-Lung prosthesis) was a masculinized process tied into gendered practices of exploration and risk-taking that were voluntary, not out of economic or colonial compulsion.[73] Cousteau's early films feature all-male crews, and *The Silent World*'s focus on hunting prowess casts the ocean as a space of conquest. As Lorne Hammond writes, "Hand in hand with the first dives of Cousteau's 'menfish' or *mousquemers* (musketeers of the sea) came destruction. The book tells how Dumas bet he could spear his own weight in fish in an hour. He exceeded it, killing 280 pounds of large older fish to prove it."[74] Other early films like Hans Hass's *Under the Red Sea* (1952) fictionalize an intrepid female diver, only for her to encounter trouble and be saved by a brave rescuer (and love interest). Earle herself recounts trying to avoid "hassles" onboard predominantly male ships through hard work and humor—"even though a price is extracted in terms of bruised self-confidence, stomped-on tendencies towards leadership, and exclusion from being 'one of the boys.'"[75] Although Earle happily notes that there exists a long tradition of female-only freediving in Japan and Korea, and that she herself was mentored by diving legend Eugenie Clark (the "Shark Lady"), the picture of ocean exploration in the mid-twentieth century was very much a boys' club centered in the West.[76]

The construction of diving prosthetics for extremely deep dives also revolved around a normatively masculine body. In one chapter, Earle recounts her involvement using a deep-water diving suit called "Jim," a hermetically sealed suit for diving beyond recreational limits, where she set out to attempt "the deepest solo dive ever made without a tether to the surface" at 1,250 feet.[77] She humorously conflates the technology (the suit named "Jim") and its protective design with expectations of masculinity— the personification of toughness and impenetrability: "My first face-to-face meeting with Jim, at the Commercial Diving Training Center in Los Angeles, was not at all what I expected. From what I had heard Jim was rugged and reliable, the strong, silent type with a no-nonsense reputation for doing tough jobs in difficult circumstances underwater."[78] The description of the technology is simultaneously a description of masculinity, correlated with toughness, hardness, and strength. Whereas space suits can be soft and pliable in low- or zero-pressure environments, Earle notes that "Jim must be made of hard materials—metal, ceramic, or composites—to resist the pressure imposed by the weight of the water above. Whereas a fully outfitted astronaut's suit may weigh more than 100 pounds in air, Jim weighs about 1,000 pounds."[79] Further, "Jim is scaled for husky commercial divers who tend to be six feet or so tall and weigh in at 200 pounds plus."[80] In contrast to this picture of toughness, when Earle first "meets" Jim, he was "in pieces . . . both legs separated from the body, and one arm completely dissected," being adjusted to fit Earle's 5 foot 3 and 110-pound frame.[81] Jim was disassembled both literally and symbolically in Earle's presence, not looking so "rugged" and "strong" while lying on the floor. In this example, technological amphibiousness—like all good prosthetics—anticipates which bodies it is for, and here it is quite visible that the Jim suit was an interface designed with large men in mind. Because it was assumed that intrepid diving explorers would be male, diving prosthetics themselves were designed to be inhabited by normative male bodies.[82]

Gender also played a role in the composition of crews for long-term underwater exploration, such as the Tektite project.[83] In *Sea Change*, Earle recalls how she and thirteen other female scientists were chosen for the Tektite project initially based on the quality of their research proposals but also because there was anxiety about a mixed-gender crew. They were to spend two weeks in an underwater habitat, which would provide a home base to live in while diving to make research observations. Whereas Cousteau was framed as a daring and intrepid explorer, media coverage of Earle consistently downplayed the element of risk and highlighted her gender identity as a woman and mother. In *Sea Change*, Earle highlights a few memorable examples.

BEACON HILL HOUSEWIFE TO LEAD TEAM OF FEMALE AQUANAUTS

ALL GIRL TEAM TESTS HABITAT

BRAVE MOM'S HISTORIC DIVE TO BOTTOM OF THE WORLD[84]

The first two titles refer to Earle's participation in the Tektite project (1970) and the third to Earle's record-setting deep dive in a special waterproof suit. What these article titles have in common is their use of the gendered terms *housewife*, *girl*, and *mom* (along with accompanying pictures of her "dripping wet") to downplay the risk involved in Earle's explorations through references to domesticity. Earle writes that she guffawed at being called "girl" at a time when she already had three children. As feminist theories have long pointed out, "woman" is the marked category while "man" has the privilege of going unmarked—an "aquanaut" rather than a "female aquanaut," simply an explorer rather than a "brave mom." In wry retaliation, Earle recalls, "We even had fun rewriting some of the headlines giving the words a fresh twist, such as 'Beacon Hill Husband Leads Team of Male Aquahunks.'"[85] Earle negotiated an existence within masculinist structures of power and prosthetics, like the Jim suit, doubly aware of being out of her "element"—out of the norms of terrestrial habitation, as well as where society expected women to go.

Yet it was within the temporary female collective of the Tektite project that Earle made key insights about the relation of saturation to interface, which shows how the ocean is not only a saltwater environment, but also an environment of differential pressure. The Tektite project combined living in an underwater habitat with unlimited diving excursions (saturation diving) that could be made from the home base of the habitat (figures 1.3 and 1.4). In all, Earle would have to spend 21 hours decompressing in order to have 336 hours of continuous underwater time, a sacrifice she was willing to make for the freedom it allowed, unlike normal, or "stopwatch," diving.[86] Earle recounts how "saturation diving using the Tektite habitat approached the rules in a different way, providing unlimited time at the depth of the laboratory at 50 feet, with generous excursion time downward to at least 100 feet and upward to within 20 feet of the surface."[87] The end of the trip would involve a special diving bell, pressurized to bring them up to begin a long process of decompression. By spending continuous time underwater, she would get to know the fish "whose habits become as familiar as those of neighbors," taking advantage of an "extended passport."[88]

The word *passport* is a fitting description for the conditional belonging involved in diving into the ocean that refigures how theorists think about amphibiousness—not necessarily as belonging to two worlds but as acclimatizing to one world at the cost of temporarily excommunicating oneself from the other. In one recollection of the Tektite project, Earle describes the stakes of saturation diving, where one cannot return to the surface immediately if something goes wrong on a dive.

Of special interest was the incident I related concerning what happened when a sand-clogged regulator and a faulty reserve valve left

FIGURE 1.3 Still image from *The Tektite Documentary*, 1970. Members of the all-women team of Tektite II enter the water.

FIGURE 1.4 Dr. Sylvia Earle displays samples to aquanaut inside Tektite. *National Geographic*, August 1971. NOAA Photo Library.

me without an air supply more than 1,000 feet from the habitat. Sunlight and air were only 71 feet away—overhead—but I was separated
from them by a physiological barrier as effective as a brick wall. Racing
for the surface for air with my tissues saturated with compressed gas
would spell swift disaster: bubbles in my blood, pain, possible paralysis,
even death. My options were limited to a long swim back to the habitat sharing air with my buddy, the engineer Peggy Lucas, or activating
an emergency pinger to alert shore-based safety divers to try to find us
and drop spare tanks.[89]

Just as Cousteau described the lung as a "molecular wall" between elements (ocean/air), Earle describes her own tissue saturation as a "physiological barrier as effective as a brick wall," not to be crossed without
penalty of the bends—the colloquial name for decompression sickness
resulting from rising too quickly from a high-pressure to low-pressure environment. The longer one breathes air at the ambient pressure of the
ocean, the more saturated one's tissues become and, thus, the more alienated from the surface one becomes. This alienation is perhaps best articulated by early diving pioneer Robert Stenuit, whom Earle quotes at
length: "I have returned from a strange journey in an alien world. . . .
Living in the depths, I have become in certain ways a creature of those
depths, adapted to their pressures. Now the human environment is temporarily intolerable to me. I need pressure. . . . I must wait inside this life
saving prison of a decompression tank until I have been slowly weaned . . .
and made once more fit to live on Earth."[90] Earle's and Stenuit's descriptions of the physiology of diving show how the process of tissue saturation in diving is a process of becoming excluded from land—in Stenuit's
case, specifically in the maternal imagery of incubation and language of
rebirth. The decompression tank serves as the "life saving prison"—read,
womb or matrix—from which the human-amphibian can regain terrestrial passport, "slowly weaned" from the "alien world" of the depths. The
accumulation of gasses in the blood changes one's status of belonging;
no longer a creature of the land, one is more and more of the sea. If diving offers a form of amphibiousness, it is not a kind of universal passport
that allows us to go from land to sea but a process of alienating oneself
from the land at the very moment that one becomes more accustomed to
breathing air underwater.

Earle's picture of conditional passport concerns physiology in a way that resonates with the media concept of "excommunication," a term that Alexander Galloway, Eugene Thacker, and McKenzie Wark use to think about the conditions of possibility for communication. The three write, "We contend that excommunication was always part and parcel of any communication theory, that non-media always lurk at the threshold of media."[91] In the context of submerged human bodies underwater, we might appropriate excommunication as a term for addressing what happens when breathing pressurized air: becoming more adjusted to the depths at the price of being unable to safely return to the surface (until allowing time for decompression). In diving, the human is excommunicated from the surface world the longer they reside at depth, and can only return after allowing for the duration of decompression (dependent on the depth and length of the dive). If the body saturated by gas is a volumetric interface that modulates safe movement underwater, then exhalation of carbon dioxide (nonmedia) is vital to the process of being underwater. In this way, excommunication describes the ontological condition of amphibiousness.[92]

Yet for Earle, the position of temporary underwater passport and surface excommunication lends itself to a unique point of view. One recurring narrative pattern in *Sea Change: A Message from the Oceans* is Earle's adoption of the perspective of an alien visitor relative to the ocean, a position she sees as conducive to developing a sense of respect and care. Regarding her first experience diving, she writes, "I was supposed to be the watcher, but found myself the watchee, the center of attention for a bunch of curious fish, apparently mesmerized by the strange bubbling being that had just fallen through their watery roof," finding pleasure in being seen by the fish.[93] In *Sea Change*, Earle asks the reader to imagine the scientist as an alien visitor: "To appreciate the difficulties faced by explorers perched on the deck of a ship rolling through slate-green waters, imagine alien explorers flying a rocking craft slowly over New York City during a storm. . . . What could aliens conclude about the nature of life below from a random trawl sample?"[94] Earle suggests that the lucky few who do get to witness the sea's creatures should be responsible for sharing their experiences: "Like astronauts, charged on behalf of humankind to bear witness to sights not yet within the reach of most, it seems to me that those who travel into the deep sea also have significant news to share."[95] Underwater exploration through scuba and other diving techniques will have "permanently transformed human perspective, forcing those who have tried it to look at the earth—and themselves—with fresh eyes."[96] In another scene, Earle shows how diving can also be a science fictional strategy for moving across time. She pays homage to H. G. Wells's *The Time Machine* by imagining a magic submersible that would "descend through the eons" to "get a better feel for the place of humankind in the greater scheme of things and for the significance of swift changes now taking place."[97] Time travel is like diving: "Perhaps, after returning from a visit far back into the history of the planet, certain creatures would be treated with more respect. . . . Perhaps complex natural systems would be understood for what they are: the distillation of the processes of all preceding time, and the source of the ingredients required for human survival and well-being."[98] Here and later in the text, Earle uses the watery word "distillation" to describe processes unfolding over time, evoking the metaphor of time as a form of water.[99] As in the work of pre-Socratic philosopher Heraclitus, time is water; yet instead of stepping into its ever-changing stream, Earle imagines time as a distilled and vital ingredient for human survival. However, the human trespasser is the liminal figure that can only temporarily belong to the ocean before physiological conditions of tissue saturation take away their temporary passport. For Earle, the temporary quality of having an oceanic passport creates the sense of unbelonging that promotes care of the (oceanic) other. In this way, scuba diving is a technology of perception that positions the diver as a temporary alien visitor, promoting an epistemic humility that may lead to a greater sense of care.

Other works also utilize the human-as-alien viewpoint as a particular kind of tactic for reenchantment with the ocean environment. In *The Edge of the Sea*, Rachel Carson writes of the experience of seeing a ghost crab at night and feeling like she was the alien seeing the crab in its world for the first time.[100] Werner Herzog's science fiction fantasy *The Wild Blue Yonder* positions the viewer as the alien, looking at Earth from afar as a way of cultivating care. The alien visitor, played by Brad Dourif, comes to Earth after his planet's ecology has collapsed and narrates his shock at later seeing video footage of human astronauts land there looking for an alternative world to live on. The ironic twist is that the footage of the "alien" planet is actually footage from under the ice in Antarctica, featuring "alien" jellyfish and siphonophores. Thus, the alien's longing for his home planet was always already about longing for Earth itself; and perhaps it took the distance of imagining Earth as alien in order to long for it, at all. *The Wild Blue Yonder* offers cinematic reenchantment with our home planet through this kind of double vision of the Earth as both otherworldly and home. It is not that the ocean possesses alien creatures of exceeding strangeness but rather that human beings are temporary visitors to the worlds of marine natives, dependent on the saturation of air. Because of this dependence on air, we can only ever be partially successful amphibians, doomed to excommunicate ourselves from the pressure of the surface so as to better fit the pressure of the depths—and vice versa when we wish to return.

The picture of amphibiousness that emerges in Earle's reflections of scuba diving of a limited passport between the elements is contingent on the process of temporary alienation from the land as a condition of possibility for being underwater. Divers must negotiate the gradual process of tissue saturation, a transition that determines the bounds of safety in crossing from world to world. Tissue saturation may start at the lungs but fully involves the body as a form of biomedia. In this picture, it is not that human users exercise control across an interface but the embodied observer must also negotiate *being* an interface. One must learn to care for their interface and the world as interface—a perspective possible to cultivate from a subject position of science fictional alienation.[101]

Fathoming the Interface

If diving engenders a distinct kind of subject position involving temporary alienation from the land, then perhaps it also provides the preconditions for an ethics of care. Earle points out that the word *fathom* comes from "the Old English faethm, meaning 'the embracing arms.' It was once defined by an act of Parliament as 'the length of a man's arms around the object of his affections,' and later became a nautical term for six feet. As a verb, 'fathom' means to plumb the ocean depths, to probe their mystery."[102] It is telling that the etymological history of *fathom* has to do with measurement by way of a human embrace, highlighting the way that fathoming as understanding or knowledge requires an intimate measure. Although in one sense fathoming figures as a kind of penetrative probing of the depths, in scuba diving, fathoming is flipped: the observer is embraced by the water, immersed in the ocean element they are measuring—a true oceanic feeling. To fathom is to measure oneself as an observer against new conditions of immersion. This does not position the human at the center in terms of the Renaissance idea of man as the measure of things but as a participant in a buoyant, watery, and pressurized milieu. The diver is constantly aware of how their air cavities (lungs, ears) feel, an important index of safety and a sensuous measure of "flesh feeling what the fish scales know." If one of the goals of feminist science studies has been to critique the disembodied observer as the standard of objectivity, then the process of fathoming the ocean through scuba diving opens an environmentally responsive, vulnerable practice of generating partial perspectives.

Fathoming the interface in diving necessarily begins, as we have seen, with the lungs. The lungs serve as a ballast and breathing technology, bringing life-giving air to needy tissues. In diving, the lungs, regulator, and air become articulated as media within the vital process of breathing.[103] This involves the lungs not only as a meaningful surface of control but as the membrane that leads to a much larger volumetric interface of gas-saturated tissues. The lungs make it difficult to generalize a single, overarching theory of the interface as simply a computer screen or HCI, as something we read, as everything semiotically meaningful in one's environment, or even more basically as a surface between two fluids. What an interface is, and how it functions, depends on the specificity of an embodied observer in a particular milieu—requiring consideration of physiological and ecological dimensions. This milieu might be composed not only of qualities related to the common imagination of materiality—wateriness, saltiness, viscosity—but also other physical properties that may not be as intuitive to a terrestrial observer, such as pressure or heat.[104]

For the human lungs in diving, the interface is a mobile threshold of durational effects, indexed to time and pressure. Attention to the physiology of tissue saturation from breathing pressurized air shows how the interface does not stop at the lungs but instead comprises the volume of the body. For the diver to safely emerge back to air, enough gas needs to have precipitated out of bodily tissues such that dangerous bubbles do not form in joints or other sensitive areas that could affect the heart or brain. Under these conditions, the interface of body/air is something that emerges through the duration of continued breathing, a temporal effect rather than merely a spatial one. In addition, the diver's modulation of their air cavities through breathing and equalization places emphasis not on visual interpretation of the interface but on interpreting interface through proprioceptive knowledge, attuned to the body's inner state and orientation. In this way, diving reformulates how we think about the interface in relation to control, since the user is the interface. Yet self-control involves elements of risk and temporariness, of excommunication from the terrestrial atmosphere into the pressures of new depths.

The Blue Lungs of the Planet

If we take this core insight—that diving asks us to rethink the interface through the lungs, and the interface is a matter of gas exchange—then what we have is a means of tracing a complex ecology of air that moves between atmosphere, ocean, and self, an interface that is about the interpenetration of selves and world.[105] Indeed, the ocean does not exist in isolation but interacts with the atmosphere as a single fluid system—a fact registered by the name of NOAA (quite an appropriate reference to the flood story). In a stunning analogy to the human body, ocean advocate Kristina Gjerde reflects, "Often referred to as the blue heart of the planet, the global ocean is vital for maintaining life as we know it on Earth. I prefer to call it the blue lungs of the planet, for ocean phytoplankton supply fifty percent of the oxygen we breathe."[106] This is a common refrain echoed by Earle and others, who draw analogies to human physiology in order to make clear how the ocean supports life on Earth. Working from the condition of the submerged human being may seem anthropocentric on first glance; however, once we learn to see interfaces not only as meaningful surfaces but as saturated volumes with durational effects, then "interface" opens to much broader ecological possibilities of interpretation and fathoming.

Let us take, as a final example, the 2009 "underwater cabinet meeting" staged by then-president of the Maldives, Mohammad Nasheed—a leading climate change activist—and consider what interface refers to in this context. The Maldives is an archipelago in the Indian Ocean with centuries of cultural history, and a maximum height of seven feet above sea level. When former president Nasheed took office in 2008, he prioritized making anthropogenic sea level rise an international issue at the UN Climate Change Conference in Copenhagen and at subsequent meetings, working with other small island nations to gain visibility for the anthropogenic threat to their national sovereignty. One of the more imaginative tactics to emerge from President Nasheed's office was the underwater cabinet meeting—an instance of what I call elsewhere "performative science fiction" through its staging of a possible future.[107] True to its name, the entire presidential cabinet donned scuba gear and took a plunge fifteen feet underwater, gathering around preset tables with name tags to sign a document pledging the Maldives to become carbon neutral (plate 3). Through such terrestrial staging—a very literal example of displacement— the event symbolically "inverted" the closure of the governmental "cabinet," spilling it into the open vulnerability of the ocean.

In video footage of the event, the underwater cabinet meeting almost seems to have come out of a science fiction movie: bubbles stream up from the mouths of prosthetically augmented beings, as they struggle to retain their terrestrial habits by "sitting" around tables underwater, a profoundly unnatural posture in the ocean. If we were to describe the nature of the interface in this scene, we might begin, conventionally, with the scuba technology—the regulator is the interface between human being and air tank—or even the air/water interface, whose rising poses a threat to coastal life. Yet as we have seen in this chapter, the lungs are part of a more distributed and volumetric interface, which includes both air tanks and the saturation of human tissues.

However, we may consider not only the ecological conditions of sea level rise but how gas exchange works on a global ecological scale. Like human tissues, the ocean itself absorbs gasses from the atmosphere such as carbon dioxide, the well-known byproduct of fossil fuel emissions, resulting in a phenomenon called ocean acidification. As more carbon dioxide dissolves into the ocean, it produces carbonic acid, occurring on such a large scale as to measurably lower the pH of the entire ocean and threatening to dissolve the calcium carbonate shells of animals that function as important elements of the food chain—thus earning ocean acidification the nickname "climate change's evil twin."

If the ocean really is the "blue lungs of the planet," as Gjerde and others write, then it is just as vulnerable to tissue saturation as human bodies. It is thus possible—and necessary—to see the event of ocean acidification as a matter of interface. The human interface with the ocean does not start or stop with etched lines on maps; the human interface with the ocean is also a matter of saturation. What this suggests, to follow Stacy Alaimo, is "a trans-corporeal conception of the human as that which is always generated through and entangled in differing scales."[108] Theorizing the interface in ocean acidification requires a kind of posthuman ethics shared by Alaimo, Neimanis, Karen Barad, and other scholars in feminist science studies, where observer/observed is no more separate than user/interface.[109] Indeed, the separation of user/interface is a fiction we inherit from a terrestrial media studies that is not adequate to capture situations where water is involved, be it the human body or the global ocean.

Nonetheless, I want to keep the term *interface* because it performs the critical work of identifying zones of intra-action, where surfaces may give way to co-saturating volumes and may allude to conditions of vulnerability through temporarily inhabiting a new environment. Theories of mediation prompt us to understand and qualify the ways we come to know the ocean through prosthetic tools and sensing devices, which sometimes then teach us just how already entangled with the ocean we are. Alaimo echoes this condition in her discussion of ocean acidification visualizations, which frequently portray the slow dissolve of spiraling shells. Such images call on viewers to contemplate "a fleshy posthumanist vulnerability that denies the possibility of any living creatures existing in a state of separation from its environs," making it harder to "imagine we are less permeable than we are" and, instead, to dwell in the dissolve.[110] We are all caught up in the saturations of a carbon economy.

What holds true across scales is that ocean acidification and diving are both forms of pneumatic media—one at the scale of the human, or the multispecies planet—that involve ecologies of air and absorption. The valence of "interface" required by pneumatic media is one that moves away from the user/interface split, away from surficial exercises of control, and away from a dominant sense of visuality. Instead, speculative performances like the Maldives's underwater cabinet meeting offer a shared experience of vulnerability and exchange that dramatize the interface as a condition of saturation, helping us better visualize the differential effects of climate change and create performative responses. Rather than transposing a sense of interface inherited from computational media into aquatic situations, the human diver's submergence in the ocean gives rise to a new saturated sense of the interface that we can then recognize in broader ecological phenomena beyond the human. In this way, ocean-specific theories of mediation—even if they begin from an anthropocentric point of view—can contribute to better accounts of climate change and the broader struggle for environmental justice.

This expanded vocabulary of media emerging from oceanic contexts (saturation, the dissolve, and even pressure) suggests a picture of oceanic materiality that challenges another key term in media studies: inscription. If inscription is predicated on the ability to create a mark or cut on a given surface, then to what extent does it make sense to talk about inscriptive processes of mediation in an underwater context? Developing this question will require us to go even deeper and to speculatively switch bodies, following Vilém Flusser's strange fable about the vampire squid into the darkroom of the abyss.

CHAPTER TWO

INSCRIPTION / Vampire Squid Media

Vampire squids are useful to think with. Combining the figure of the vampire with the tentacular body of a mollusk that lives in the deep ocean,
the vampire squid provides a potent form for imagining configurations
of power, communication, and the opening or closure of freedom (figure
2.1).[1] We might look to Matt Taibbi's *Rolling Stone* article that calls the investment bank Goldman Sachs a "great vampire squid wrapped around
the face of humanity, relentlessly jamming its blood funnel into anything
that smells like money," conjuring an image of the vampire-as-rapist, one
associated with Bram Stoker's nefarious Count Dracula.[2] Critiques of im-
perial, colonial, and corporate entities often find analogy in cephalopod
bodies, which are often used in political cartoons to depict unchecked
power, greed, or libidinal energy.[3] Cephalopods and tentacled creatures
also appear in science fiction, from the Kraken in Jules Verne's *20,000
Leagues under the Sea* to the tentacled, salt-sucking femme fatale in the first
episode of the original *Star Trek* ("The Man Trap"). The vampire squid
seems a ready-made villain, transporting mundane forms of power and
control into the realm of fantasy and horror.

    In contrast, other figurations of the cephalopod body speak to the abil-
ity of individual people to connect with one another in terms of move-

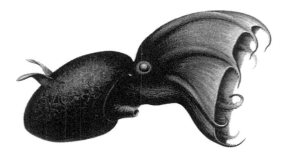

FIGURE 2.1 Carl Chun, illustration of *Vampyro-teuthis infernalis*, 1910.

ment, communication, and the erotics of touch.[4] For example, the pre-paid card in Hong Kong that enables one to ride public transportation (metro, ferry, bus, minibus) or to make purchases at grocery and conve-nience stores is called an "octopus card" (八達通), where rail lines radi-ate from the center of the transit map like tentacles.[5] Tentacles also sug-gest the flows of interspecies sexuality, from the Japanese painting *Dream of the Fisherman's Wife* to the anime/manga genre of hentai.[6] Hsuan Hsu points out that both Occupiers and hipsters have claimed the octopus to connote the values of interconnectivity and flexibility in social media.[7] Then again, so has the U.S. National Reconnaissance Office (NRO), which adopted an octopus logo with the motto, "Nothing is beyond our reach" (figure 2.2).[8] In a more visionary manner, Donna Haraway's alternative to the Anthropocene—the "Chthulucene"—adds an "h" to the Lovecraftian figure of "Cthulu" (the abyssal, tentacle-faced monster) in favor of evok-ing processes of world making with subterranean beings.[9] In these varied examples, the cephalopod drifts between opening and closing channels of communication and surveillance, a potent figure for conceptualizing networks and infrastructures.

Vilém Flusser's unique tale *Vampyroteuthis Infernalis* or "the vampire squid from hell" imagines what media might look like *for* the vampire squid, exploring the relationship between physiology and environment in a genre of writing that I will call, here, the media fable.[10] Usually academic writings about media aim for clear communication, adopting the genre of the essay and its formalities to signal to the reader that they are meant to be interpreted literally, even if they discuss the complexities of form and genre in media artworks, film, data visualizations, hardware, and other objects of interest. In contrast, Flusser dives into the phenomenological

FIGURE 2.2 Mission "patch" of
NROL-39: an octopus grabbing
the Earth's globe, labeled
"Nothing is beyond our reach."
National Reconnaissance Office,
U.S. government, 2013.[11]

world of the vampire squid, paying attention to the differences of embodiment and environment between vampire squid and human and speculating how these differences might reflect different perceptions of media. *Vampyroteuthis Infernalis* opens a way for elaborating a theory of mediation that takes seriously the conditions of seawater as a space for communication and relation, including liquid media (ink clouds, skin paintings), but always with a particular reader or interpreter (another vampire squid) in mind. As a fable, *Vampyroteuthis Infernalis* enables Flusser to displace the anthropocentrism of media theory by imagining "for whom" and "under what environmental conditions" media exist as such—a multispecies and milieu-specific question that sees media as a matter of relationality.[11]

Part of Flusser's innovation in the media fable is to take the abyss as a speculative environment, constructing a "molluscan point of view" to imagine how an intelligent aquatic organism would develop different concepts to orient itself to its world than those familiar to the dry landscapes of human thought.[12] The abyss dramatizes the ocean's condition of ephemerality, where inscription on paper or even stone tablets would eventually be eroded by seawater or encrusted with growth. Because the vampire squid lives in a milieu where not all of our vocabulary or figurative language works smoothly, it pushes us to consider more ocean-specific conditions of mediation and a vocabulary that would be adequate to the abyssal environment.[13] Through a consideration of the vampire squid's liquid media in the benthic environment of the deep sea, I show how a terrestrial bias persists not only through media theory's choice of objects of analysis but also through descriptive language and naturalized metaphor. *Vampyroteuthis Infernalis* exemplifies how thinking with the ocean requires a method that focuses on both the materiality of the environment and the perceiver attuned to it as conditions for thought. Flusser thus offers a comparative epistemology between human and vampire squid, a creature providing "enough distance from the human condition to be able to observe it" but whose point of view is "not transcendent."[14]

As a media fable, *Vampyroteuthis Infernalis* demands to be read both literally and allegorically at the same time, where one must keep in mind the benthic world of the vampire squid and, as we will see, the terrestrial world of photography. Fables tell a story about an animal (or animals) as a pretext for presenting a lesson to human readers, and this is precisely what we find in *Vampyroteuthis Infernalis*. Flusser describes his fable as both "scientifically exact and mad fantasy (*fantasia essata*)," musing that such a "philosophy of fantasy" could become a "discipline as rigorous as phenomenology."[15] His introduction to the fable concludes with the caution *De te fabula narratur*, footnoted with a reference to Horace translated as "change but the name and of you the tale is told."[16] Flusser confirms his intention at the end of the tale, writing that the purpose of every fable is to "contemplate this mirror [the vampire squid] with the aim of recognizing ourselves in it, and with the aim of being able to alter oneself thanks to this recognition."[17] Literary critic Darko Suvin describes the mirror of science fiction in a similar way, where it is not only reflective but transformative, a "virgin womb and alchemical dynamo: the mirror is a crucible."[18] The nature of this transformative mirror depends on the reader's capacity for not only the recognition of similarities between vampire squid and human, but also the recognition of the tale as an allegory for photography.[19]

As I show later in this chapter, Flusser uses the vampire squid as a pretext for considering photography as a medium that marks a transition in society from valuing objects (like individual photographs) to the information transmitted (the film negative). Flusser imagines that the recording of history—if it were to take place at all—would have to occur via inscription on subjects, or other vampire squid, rather than on external objects, through ephemeral media such as the squid's skin (like photographic paper, "a medium for colorful messages").[20] Here, the deep sea models both the primordial past through the ancient vampire squid, and an emerging future—or what Flusser calls "post-history"—where photographers create images that inform the behavior of future viewers such that "society is in a feedback relationship to the camera."[21] If fantasy is always a scene, we might say that the deep sea is a kind of darkroom where Flusser develops his thoughts on photography (and information society) through the negative image of the vampire squid. Yet as I show in this chapter, even the vampire squid's glandular media still channel a kind of terrestrial bias, leaving us adrift with the open question of how to think about recording and inscription in the abyss.

While the vampire squid may seem an unusual vessel for media and cultural theory, Flusser's biographical history sheds some light on the key issues informing its genesis.[22] Vilém Flusser was born in Prague in 1920 into a family of Jewish intellectuals. He studied philosophy at the Charles University in Prague and in 1939 immigrated with his wife, Edith, to London to continue his studies on communication and language. Within the next year, his remaining family in Prague was deported to concentration camps and murdered at Buchenwald, Auschwitz, and Theresienstadt. In 1941, Flusser and his wife left London and moved (migrated, escaped, fled) to São Paulo, Brazil, where they stayed for the next few decades. The violence of the Holocaust, the abrupt loss of his family, the sudden need to learn Portuguese, and the process of adapting to Brazilian culture would inform his later writings. These challenges appear explicitly in *Freedom of the Migrant*, in which Flusser explores the simultaneous suffering and positive openness to change available to the emigrant: "to be unsettled, one first has to be settled."[23]

The questions that arise in Flusser's media theory—technology and possibilities of freedom, the historical shift between writing and technical images (or history and what he calls posthistory)—respond to some of the worst events of the twentieth century, involving fascism and genocide as well as the power of early communications systems such as radio and film. Sensitive to future changes in the global possibilities of communication, Flusser's writings consider how technological shifts in communication might change the possibilities for human relationships: in the best possible world, media would cease to be a one-way, totalitarian system, emanating from a single source to a silent receiving audience, and would instead facilitate dialogue between receivers and senders.[24] As we will see, *Vampyroteuthis Infernalis* considers how information might be preserved underwater through the inscription of memories on subjects rather than externally on technical recording media—a move that channels Flusser's concerns about the future of media.

The milieu of the deep sea challenges the way that inscription has been traditionally discussed in media theory as a legible mark or cut. As Katherine Hayles writes, "To count as an inscription technology, a device must initiate material changes that can be read as marks. Telegraphy thus counts; it sends structured electronic pulses through a wire. . . . Additional examples include film, video, and the images produced by medical devices such as X-rays, CAT scans, and MRI."[25] In these examples, some kind of hard and permanent substrate preserves a certain arrangement of marks, impressions, or electric polarities, in order to make them available for future viewing. The *Oxford English Dictionary* adds that inscription can refer to "a set of characters or words written, engraved, or otherwise traced upon a surface; esp. a legend, description, or record traced upon some hard substance for the sake of durability, as on a monument, building, stone, tablet, medal, coin, vase, etc."[26] Yet as we saw in the previous chapter's discussion of "Surface Tension" by James Blish, aquatic environments present major challenges to the possibilities of creating inscription technologies, or recording information underwater.[27] Hard surfaces might become worn and illegible from the movements of water, or unwanted life might grow upon and cloud recording surfaces.

This begs the question: could inscription technologies exist in an underwater environment for aquatic beings, enduring past aquatic forces of erasure and data corruption? In addition to this materialist inquiry, what might we recognize in the mirror of the ocean that has something to say about inscription technologies? To begin, let us imaginatively plunge with Flusser into the abyss and imagine what it means to orient to the world with our mouth surrounded by eight arms, buoyant and suspended in the three-dimensional space of the water column. From this science fictional and cognitively estranging position, we are challenged to imagine: under what conditions have terrestrial knowledge structures evolved, and how would these knowledge structures appear radically different in an aqueous environment from the perspective of the vampire squid?

Diving into *Vampyroteuthis*

Vampyroteuthis Infernalis can be read as speculative fiction that imagines how the culture, science, and media of the vampire squid would have developed in relation to the dual influences of its molluscan physiology and the deep sea environment. However, what is unique about *Vampyroteuthis Infernalis* is the way that Flusser qualifies this speculation as emerging from a human vantage point: "There is no 'general world' or 'objective universe' which is common to both [human and vampire squid]. Such an abstract world of science does not exist. If we find Vampyroteuthis, it is within our world that we find him. We do not find him as existence, but as object."[28] Flusser draws attention to the epistemological question of how we come to know about the vampire squid from the particular constraints of our human embodiment in a terrestrial environment. With this self-reflexive consideration in mind, he writes:

> We shall not dive into the depths with the aim of explaining anything, but with the aim of implicating ourselves in the vampyroteuthian situation. As we cannot observe the depths through phenomenological methods (we do not know how to dive into the oceans), we shall aim to do it by an intuitive method (diving into Vampyroteuthis). And as we assume, therefore, his point of view upon his habitat that is planet Earth, at the end, we shall be surprised to observe that Earth becomes even stranger than Mars or Venus.[29]

"Diving into Vampyroteuthis" is a methodology for estranging our view of Earth and terrestrial habitation, a vicarious attempt to inhabit its orientations to the abyss. Recognizing that the vampire squid is "literally facing a different world" allows us to "see with his eyes and grasp with his tentacles."[30] Flusser asks us to keep track of what surprises us about the vampyroteuthic world compared with our own terrestrial experience: "We are leaping from a habitual world to a fabulous world. It is a world that is not apprehended and comprehended by hands, as is ours, but by eight tentacles."[31] Here, Flusser speculates that differences in bodies (vertebrate, mollusk) would lead to different intuitions of the world—different habits of moving and gravitating to things.

The vampire squid's alterity, then, arises from both its alternate body plan and its alternate environment, and suggests a different philosophical perspective on the world. Comparing the ocean with land, Flusser infers that the vampire squid would have a volumetric rather than planar experience of space. In humans, Flusser writes, "Bipedal stride, with both arms like pendulums, divided the world into past, present, and future."[32] Spatial theorists like Yi-Fu Tuan have also commented on the way the human body provides a reference point for spatial intuitions, dependent on front, back, and sides.[33] Yet whereas our vertebrate physiology is like that of a "coat hanger," with shoulders and spine standing up in response to gravity, Flusser explains that "the spiral is the fundamental theme of the molluscan organism," a position responsive to a buoyant liquid environment.[34] As vertebrates, "our dialectic is linear," while the vampire squid's "is coiled. We think 'straight,' and he thinks 'in a circle.' . . . That is because our world is a plane and his is a volume."[35] Further, vampire squid are "whirlpool animals" with "coils that tend to uncoil. They are springs that tend to stretch, fists that tend to open up into flat palms. . . . As they uncoil, they release the accumulated energy of the spring. This may explain their extraordinary ferociousness."[36] The vampire squid's experience of space would not be Cartesian but "a twisted tension sustained by an external spiral shell."[37]

These differences in physiology might result in entirely different conceptions of spatiality. Flusser writes, "It would be a mistake to think that we exist on the 'same Earth.' We exist on an Earth that is a habitable surface. He exists on an Earth that is a habitable hole."[38] Human senses of space proceed from surface habitation, while vampyroteuthic senses of space emerge from life in a volume; the vampire squid "perforates the third dimension just like a screw."[39] Comparing the way "we think in a line" with how the vampire squid "thinks in a circle" or moves in a spiral should remind us of Flusser's schema for history (line) and posthistory (broken line, programming), which I will elaborate in the next section.[40]

Flusser also connects the vampire squid's physiological posture (consider a bulbous body on top of a thin umbrella of skin) to different behavioral and cognitive tendencies, such as the predisposition for aggressive movement. Running through every chapter in *Vampyroteuthis Infernalis* is a deep fascination with psychoanalysis, of the vampire squid's unconscious as the photographic and moral negative (Other) to ours. Take the following passage: "Our conscience is the vampyroteuthian unconscious, and vice versa. This is reflected in our respective postures: the position of our head corresponds to the position of his belly. If Vampyroteuthis analyses the world, he is doing 'depth analysis,' and if he analyses his own being in the world, he is doing a 'critique of reason.' His Newton is Freud and his Jung is Einstein."[41] This surrealist image—that our heads are anatomically in the place of the squid's belly—may remind us of the famous cover of Georges Bataille's *Acéphale*, evoking the way in which the human subject of analysis thinks and/or acts according to the belly/libidinal zone.[42] Through inversions such as this, Flusser positions the vampire squid as a kind of photographic negative of the human, the image that makes the human appear under the chemical fixing fluids of fiction.[43]

However, it is not just that the vampire squid has a different physiology than human beings; this physiology is tied into different dispositions, affects, and habituations of orienting within the world. Eduardo de Castro's account of Amerindian "perspectivity" offers an important clarification of what is at stake in imagining the world from the point of view of animal others. De Castro carefully traces Amerindian myths that "tell how animals lost qualities inherited or retained by humans."[44] Animals are not wholly other but are "ex-humans," and thus "what is blood to us is manioc beer to jaguars, a muddy waterhole is seen by tapirs as a great ceremonial house."[45] Here, objects have an "ambiguous ontology" because it matters *to whom* an object exists in relation. This relationality—to the environment and to other entities—characterizes how de Castro understands bodily difference as something separate from physiology.

> [By bodily difference] I am not referring to physiological differences—Amerindians recognize a basic uniformity of bodies—but rather to affects, in the old sense of dispositions or capacities that render the body of each species unique: what it eats, how it moves, how it communicates, where it lives, whether it is gregarious or solitary. The visible shape of the body is a powerful sign of these affectual differences, although the shape can be deceptive, since a human appearance could, for example, be concealing a jaguar affect.[46]

De Castro offers an important nuance to my reading of Flusser by clarifying the difference between "physiology" and "dispositions or capacities." Whereas physiology implies body plan, affects, dispositions, and capacities include the environment. Organisms develop in the irreducible complexity of actual lifeworlds, where acquiring food, avoiding predators, moving around, and communicating all take place within the specific constraints of particular milieu. Habits for both humans and animals thus form through the relation of body and environment, through active orientations, and, as we will see in the next section, become folded into language.

Metaphor in the Ocean

The ocean is an environment where many of our intuitive ways of speaking about the world simply do not work, since our senses and media are attuned to the terrestrial surface. In *Vampyroteuthis Infernalis*, the vampire squid's body and environment position it to consider the world from a perspective almost opposite to ours. Such speculations about the relationship between physiology, environment, and worldview are common to science fiction, in the ocean as well as other environments. The short story "The Author of Acacia Seeds" by Ursula Le Guin shares much in common with *Vampyroteuthis Infernalis*, imagining the ways we use language to orient to a particular environment as exemplified by the writing of underground ants. A team of therolinguists (studying animal languages) stumbles upon a series of fragmentary messages written by an ant through glandular exudations.[47] The therolinguists have difficulty interpreting the meaning of the phrase on one seed, "Eat the eggs! Up with the Queen!" until they think beyond conventional human understandings of the word *up* and remember that ants live underground. Although located in the subterranean earth, the story performs similar metaphorical estrangements as if it were set in the deep ocean.

> To us, "up" is a "good" direction. Not so, or not necessarily so, to an ant. "Up" is where the food comes from, to be sure; but "down" is where security, peace, and home are to be found. "Up" is the scorching sun; the freezing night; no shelter in the beloved tunnels; exile; death. Therefore we suggest that this strange author, in the solitude of her lonely tunnel, sought with what means she had to express the ultimate blasphemy conceivable to an ant.[48]

Like the ocean abyss, Le Guin's subterranean milieu teaches us to rethink the ways we subconsciously value orientations through the metaphoric use of prepositions. Understanding the message of the ant requires understanding how certain orientations (up, down) have emotional connotations that would be specific to the lifeworld of ants. Consider all the con-

PLATE 1 Digital photograph taken inside a shipwreck. Photo by author, July 2014.

Radio for Everybody pages 298, 304
358

SCIENTIFIC AMERICAN

The Monthly Journal of Practical Information

35¢ a Copy   MAY 1922 $4.00 a Year

WITH WATERPROOF PAINTS AND CANVAS: PAINTING A SUBMARINE SCENE AT FIRST HAND.—[See page 319]

Scientific American Publishing Co., Munn & Co., New York

PLATE 2 Cover of *Scientific American*, May 1922.

PLATE 3 Lou Gold, "Maldives Government Meets
Underwater," October 17, 2009.

PLATE 4 Monterey Bay Aquarium interactive exhibit
where guests can superimpose cuttlefish patterns on
their faces. Photo by author, August 2018.

PLATE 5 Sanna Dullaway, "Inverted Earth / Day and Night," August 12, 2012.

PLATE 6 Jason deCaires Taylor's "Silent Evolution."
Photo by author, July 2014.

PLATE 7 Jason deCaires Taylor's "Silent Evolution."
Photo by author, July 2014.

PLATE 8 Jason deCaires Taylor, face changes over time
in a sculpture from "Silent Evolution," 2009.

text required to understand Le Guin's example of "Up with the Queen!":
You have to know that the normative body and normative environment
are those of an ant underground rather than a human being walking
above ground. Furthermore, the "metaphors" of the sentence are subtle:
UP is danger/exile, while DOWN is security/home (the assumed conceptual metaphors that underlie "Up with the Queen," even though that sentence itself does not explicitly use the verb *is*).[49] Perhaps such a linguistic
habit, responsive to directional valuations, constitutes something like a
noninscriptive memory. The memory is not one of information written
down and retrieved but a preconscious tendency to orient in space in certain ways. Through the novum of ant writing (a form of imaginary media), Le Guin draws our attention to the ways human language is not
value neutral but encodes a variety of orientational relationships to the
Earth's surface and the normative milieu of our own habitation.

Both *Vampyroteuthis Infernalis* and "The Author of Acacia Seeds" exemplify the argument made in George Lakoff and Mark Johnson's seminal
linguistic study, *Metaphors We Live By*, which uses linguistic evidence to
show that the way we ordinarily speak is highly metaphoric, and these
metaphors both structure cognition and correspond to our embodiment
as human beings in the (terrestrial) world.[50] Part of Flusser's contribution
to milieu-specific analysis is to extend Lakoff and Johnson's theorizations
about human cognition and metaphor to the vampire squid in its aquatic
environment, providing the foundation for a comparative epistemology
between human and vampire squid and speculative technique. Contrary
to the belief that metaphor is merely ornamental language, Lakoff and
Johnson argue that metaphor is a matter of conceptual structure that "involves all the natural dimensions of our experience, including aspects of
our sense experiences: color, shape, texture, sound," and especially gravity.[51] Lakoff and Johnson's example of "orientational metaphors" is particularly useful to show how metaphors subtly structure the way that we
cognize the world, and suffuse everyday language.[52] Using English as an
example, Lakoff and Johnson discuss how the direction "up" tends to correlate with happy emotions and "down" tends to correlate with sad emotions. We might say, for example, "I'm feeling up" or "that boosted my
spirits" compared with "I fell into a depression" or "my spirits sank."[53] This
is not to say that embodiment and environment act in entirely determin-
istic ways—one can always think of counterexamples where DOWN does
not correlate to an undesirable state (such as "I'm down for dinner tomor-

row night," where DOWN is COMMITMENT), and such ways of speaking are "constantly being tested through ongoing successful functioning by all the members of our culture."[54] Our sensory-motor domains—the ways we orient in space from the reference of our own embodiment—often map onto other domains of social experience having to do with emotions and interpersonal relationships.

Yet it is precisely this class of orientational metaphors that take Lakoff and Johnson into science fictional territory, perhaps because orientation metaphors require an awareness of the embodiment of the speaker and their particular physical environment. In order to show the importance of our embodied interactions with the physical environment for cognition and language, Lakoff and Johnson give a brief example of a counterenvironment to human norms.

> UP is not understood purely in its own terms but emerges from the collection of constantly performed motor functions having to do with our erect position relative to the gravitational field we live in. Imagine a spherical being living outside any gravitational field, with no knowledge or imagination of any other kind of experience. What could UP possibly mean to such a being? The answer to this question would depend, not only on the physiology of this spherical being, but also on its culture.[55]

The example of a "spherical being living outside any gravitational field"—which may remind us of the vampire squid suspended in the ocean—seems to emerge straight out of the genre of science fiction, which has long concerned itself with the variety of ways that nonhuman beings might speak and cognize their worlds. The important part of the example is the insight that *our* metaphorical uses of "UP" would probably not make any sense (if translated) to such a spherical being; not only would the spherical being have a completely different embodiment, but it would also live in an environment within which "I'm feeling up today" would not make any sense. Lakoff and Johnson's invocation of science fiction shows how human ways of cognizing the world through metaphor (in any language) are not universal.

Like Flusser's squid and Le Guin's subterranean ants, Lakoff and Johnson's speculative example transports us out of our normative milieu of surface habitation (whether on land or on a boat) and denaturalizes our habits of using orientational metaphors. The challenge of attempting to imagine how a spherical being, vampire squid, or ants might speak about their world is that we are always working from a position of surface dwelling. As I discussed in chapter 1, forms of literary interpretation (like surface reading and the hermeneutics of suspicion) normally assume an interpreter positioned at the surface. However, interpreting from the surface not only has implications for spatial models of interpretation; it also shows a latent terrestrial bias through the ways we use orientational language and metaphor. The uses of "up" that Le Guin, Lakoff, and Johnson discuss focus on the *preposition*, that part of speech that assists with the orientation and location of nouns and pronouns. This is different from common examples of metaphor—following Aristotle—that tend to focus on the likeness between individual words or *nouns* (for example, "the unconscious is an ocean"). Rather than thinking of metaphor as purely a matter of substitution, of noun for noun, metaphor can occur at the level of the full sentence (what Paul Ricoeur calls the level of semantics) and often borrows from sensory-motor experiences in order to conceptualize abstractions.[56] The reason that sentence-level metaphor matters is because it indicates how speakers position themselves in space, which occurs not through nouns but via other parts of speech, like prepositions and verbs. Looking to preposition usage, then, is a key technique for identifying areas of terrestrial bias.

Metaphor and Science Fictions

One of the clearest articulations of the relationship between science fiction (SF) and metaphor comes from Darko Suvin's essay "Science Fiction, Metaphor, Parable, and Chronotope," reprinted in the 2016 edition of *Metamorphoses of Science Fiction* (1979). In this essay, Suvin argues that SF shares kinship with metaphor through the way that it shuttles between the reader's empirical world and another world of alternate norms.

> The famous SF statement and proposition "The door dilated" presupposes, to being with, that in this text's universe of discourse and possible world there are intelligent beings (psychozoa) who use sight, locomotion, and constructed edifices; and further, that these edifices incorporate building techniques not used in human history up to the writer's time and that the text's "otherwhere" locus is normal for the

implied narrator. . . . This sentence reassures the reader that the *cate-gories* of the visual . . . are relevant for understanding this universe: the species of dilating door may be unfamiliar, but the *genus* of door an-chors it again into familiarity. *Per species incognitam sed genus cognitum* seems to be the motto of most SF estrangement.[57]

Like Lakoff and Johnson's spherical being for whom "up" makes no sense, the "dilating door" makes no sense in our immediate universe. Yet because we are encountering this sentence as a science fiction, we know we are being asked to imagine a universe in which doors *can* dilate—suggesting the literalization of the metaphor "the door is an eye." Suvin writes that the estranging "language deviance" of metaphor results in "the percep-tion of a possible relationship which could establish a new norm of its own," rearranging the very "categories that shape our experience."[58] The special case of science fictional metaphor, then, has to do with setting up surprising new norms that may be continuous with our reality. Suvin ar-gues that metaphor is more than a poetical ornament, and instead has a powerful cognitive function, because metaphor "necessarily refers, among other things, to what a given culture and ideology consider reality."[59] Both metaphors and models possess a creative generativity to redescribe reality, acting as "*heuristic fictions* or speculative instruments mediating between two semantic domains."[60] However, Suvin points out that comparing metaphor and science fiction raises the question of scale. While meta-phor itself operates at the level of the sentence, the *metaphorical process* of bringing together two unlike things can still occur at the scale of a longer narrative. This metaphorical process can have the science fictional effect of "cognitive estrangement" through the way that it shuttles between the reader's "empirical norms" and the "new normative system" or "between the addressee's 'zero world' and the possible world of the SF text."[61] Here, the reader's empirical norms constitute the "absent paradigm" that the reader refers to when reading SF. Good SF, then, needs to find the "*optimal* distance between the reader's initial 'normal' paradigm and the new, not fully existent but sufficiently clearly suggested paradigm of the SF story."[62]

Theories of metaphor in literary theory and philosophy tend to use spatial metaphors to characterize metaphor itself, describing the tropo-logical in terms of the topological. Paul de Man writes that "tropes are not just travelers, they tend to be smugglers and probably smugglers of stolen goods at that."[63] Yet for Ricoeur, metaphor is not the reproduction of likeness but rather about "*new* predicative meaning which emerges from the collapse of the literal meaning."[64] Metaphor, then, has a certain navigational function: "What is most needed in this situation of uncertainty is orientation."[65] Metaphors, like maps, can assist with cognitive and spatial orientation. Michel de Certeau gives the example of how in modern Athens, public transportation vehicles are called *metaphorai*: "To go to work or come home, one takes a 'metaphor'—a bus or a train. Stories could also take this noble name: every day, they traverse and organize places; they select and link them together; they make sentences and itineraries out of them."[66]

Such a t(r)opological formulation not only links spatial orientation and metaphor but, importantly, shows how both are involved in the formulation of habits. Itineraries, going to work, and taking public transportation all suggest a set of accustomed pathways between distant places that become commonly linked. I am reminded of the metaphorical patterns that Lakoff and Johnson identify (life is a journey, theories are buildings, ideas are plants, etc.) as precisely such habitual routes of association that we draw on in ordinary speech. However, this does not mean that all metaphors are "natural," since they can also be culturally conditioned and then reified.[67] Nonetheless, Lakoff and Johnson's discussion of orientational metaphors has powerful implications for philosophy and critical theory, because through tracing them we see how ordinary language almost always assumes a human standing on Earth's surface as the normative condition for observation.

Flusser's speculative technique in *Vampyroteuthis Infernalis* of considering embodiment, metaphor, and cognition reformulates Thomas Nagel's classic philosophical problem, "What is it like to be a bat?"[68] Whereas Nagel focuses on "qualia" and whether we can really know the world of the bat, Flusser imagines the perceptual world of the vampire squid in order to develop an epistemic check on human objectivity. The end goals are thus quite different: for Nagel, to try to know the experience of the animal from the disembodied I/eye of science; for Flusser, to take the animal as a kind of critique of the disembodied I/eye, making human and terrestrially developed concepts seem strange from the animal's point of view. Le Guin's tale about the ant that writes, "Up with the Queen!" performs a similar estrangement, offering the viewer a window into the phenomenal world of the ant only to have the reader check the limitations

of their own point of view. Attending to the environmental and embodied conditions that have structured our cognition implies that human
categories of perception might not be the only ones, or the most adequate
ones, with which to understand phenomena in the world. Flusser calls
this skepticism "biological Kantianism," or the idea that each sensing organism might have its own set of "categories" through which it perceives
the world.

   "Biological Kantianism" is strikingly similar to Jacob von Uexküll's
theory of *Umwelten,* or perception worlds, which takes individual animals
as loci of perception worlds that are qualitatively different from one another.[69] His strong claim is that "there is no space independent of subjects.
If we still want to cling to the fiction of an all-encompassing world-space,
that is only because we can get along with each other more easily with the
help of this conventional fable."[70] Rather than one world, we must now
consider phenomenal worlds in the plural. Although Uexküll argues that
the animal's environment is "only a piece cut out from its surroundings,"
which are "our own human environment," Flusser does not assume that a
human perspective is an adequate umbrella for appreciating the nuances
of all other animal worlds. In *Vampyroteuthis Infernalis,* he shows how human science is but one way of parsing animal lives: "Biology is itself a
product of the human 'web.' It catches everything in the categories of
theoretical reason, including reason itself, and not only the spider's web.
The biologically-biased Kantianism does not resolve the problem, it only
transfers it to another level."[71] That is, the study of biology (physiology,
morphology, marine science) provides the means of intuiting an animal's
Umwelt, but biology itself is created from (and according to) what humans
think to measure (and make sensible to themselves).

   Although Flusser sees no outside to this Kantian problem, the vampire
squid brings into relief the terrestrial conditions (gravity, planar space, reliance on vision) that inform specific concepts and points of view we take
for granted. However, sometimes these concepts can be read back into the
fable to show its own construction. As with Flusser's Kantian problem,
the fable shows us not absolute alterity but a refracted view of ourselves.
Perhaps what the genre of the fable most usefully does is preserve two levels of analysis: a materialist speculation about the phenomenology of the
vampire squid and its media (ink clouds, skin paintings) and an allegorical level at which we might see the vampire squid as a figure for thinking
about photography and what Flusser calls "post-historic images."

This oscillation, between the tale being literally about the vampire squid and allegorically about photography, demands more of the reader than typical instances of media theory (including this chapter). One might say that it requires a sort of amphibious vision, half-submerged in the abyss and half-thinking about terrestrial applications. As we will see in the next section, what began as a pure speculation into the perceptual lives of vampire squid—a kind of comparative epistemology between *Vampyroteuthis infernalis* and *Homo sapiens*—turns out to function allegorically as a fable about photography and genetics. To understand how this works, I will briefly explain how Flusser sees the relationship between media forms and forms of historical consciousness, and then move on to the details of the photographic fable.

Posthistoric Images, Genetics, and Media

Flusser argues that historical consciousness shifts with the emergence of two specific technologies of communication: the invention of writing (a shift from prehistoric to historic) and the invention of photography (a shift from historic to posthistoric). In this schema, prehistoric consciousness assumes a one-to-one relation between world and image. The function of the image is to refer to reality: "Prehistoric images (from cave paintings to proto-historical wall paintings) are maps that enable their addressees to orient themselves in their environment."[72] Historic consciousness emerges with the advent of writing, a linear technology that does not simply refer to a preexisting reality but shows how things came into being: "Linear texts explain images, they roll out their scenes into processes, and they order things into irreversible chains of causality. The environment can be causally explained and progressively manipulated."[73] Images like "church windows, columns, or oil paintings" also have an explanatory function, but are on the decline because "all models of perception and behavior can be found in texts."[74]

If prehistoric consciousness is static, and historical consciousness is linear, then posthistoric consciousness is the fragmentation of the line into a designed image. Flusser writes that photographs are "only the first of these posthistorical images," not surfaces but rather "mosaics" composed of "dot elements" like the molecules in silver compounds. Visualization refers to the ability to "turn a swarm of possibilities into an image."[75]

From a posthistoric point of view, creating photographic images involves a process of calculation rather than imagination, because the photographer must consider settings and adjustments of the apparatus. Thus, photographs (or "technical images") are not Platonic copies of reality but structurally "projects."[76] Although photographs are often considered part of an archive of the past, Flusser argues that photographs are future oriented because they are images ("models of perception") yet to be seen by viewers. To distill Flusser's argument, we might say photographers act science fictionally upon the present to "project a potentially alternative future."[77]

Part of what makes photography posthistoric, in this schema, is its future orientation. This perspective appears similar to the argument that Jacques Derrida advances in *Archive Fever*, where the archive is not about recording the past but is always already directed toward its future use: "The question of the archive is not, we repeat, a question of the past. It is not the question of a concept of dealing with the past that might *already* be at our disposal or not at our disposal, *an archivable concept of the archive.*"[78] To extend Derrida's argument in Flusserian terms, we might say that earlier archives (curiosity cabinets, libraries) are *also* posthistoric, directed to future viewers. Then again, Flusser's temporal schema of prehistoric, historic, posthistoric is itself a symptom of linear (read: historical) thinking, following a logic of sequentiality.

Despite this contradiction, Flusser's discussions of posthistory do important work to address the cultural practices emerging with cybernetics — a question of media and photography but also of biotechnology. In a series of letters exchanged with his close friend Milton Vargas in 1981, Flusser wrote that whereas evolution suggests a linear perspective on the emergence of species, genetic engineering "leaps over phylogenetic barriers and exchanges information from distant 'branches,'" and "it will end up creating organs and organisms" turning the phenomenon of life informatic and cybernetic.[79] Here, "the challenge is not biological but epistemological; to rethink evolution not in 'causal' terms or 'finalistic' terms, but in 'programmatic' terms."[80] Genetic engineering means rethinking evolution not as a line but in programmatic terms of splicing and reordering genes; a "program" is "a combination game with clear and distinct elements," a definition that allows Flusser to consider genetics, photography, and posthistory in the same language.[81]

In *Vampyroteuthis Infernalis*, the vampire squid embodies such a relation between genetics and media technology. Flusser views genetics metaphorically as a kind of combinatorial program, where human and cephalopod are both "variations of the same game played with the calculi of genetic information that programmes all terrestrial life."[82] Here, each individual is an actualization of one possibility of evolution. Flusser's view on genetics is thus similar to his writings on photography: each photograph is not the product of an artistic genius but merely one actualization of possible images configurable within the camera apparatus.[83] Yet the comparison between organism and photograph only goes so far: unlike the camera apparatus, the "genetic program" of organisms is not part of a closed system. For example, the entire field of epigenetics studies how extragenetic or environmental factors influence the development of an organism. Even given identical DNA, individuals develop differently over a lifetime.[84]

Evolutionary pathways are so important to this text that they shape the very form of the narrative. Specifically, *Vampyroteuthis Infernalis* adopts taxonomy as a storytelling structure for the vampire squid's fictional relationship to the human. Although it is a fable, *Vampyroteuthis Infernalis* has no traditional plot with rising action and a climax: the text reads like a scientific report about the vampire squid, which the reader can recognize as fictional mainly through oblique self-reference and hyperbolic content. Instead we could say the climax(es) of the fable are the moments when *Vampyroteuthis infernalis* breaks through as the refracted image of (1) humanity, (2) photography and the photographic apparatus, or (3) posthistory broadly. However, the fable requires that we consider in parallel the evolution of two different species, humans and vampire squid. Flusser writes, "Their conches are our fish, their snails are our birds, their cephalopods are our mammals, and the several octopi, edible or not, are our Neanderthals and Heidelbergenses."[85] In a move both serious and surreal, Flusser asks us to consider the evolution of intelligence in the molluscan phylum as parallel to that of *Homo sapiens* as the former moves from the conch to the snail, cephalopod, octopi, and finally—at the pinnacle or nadir, however you have it—the vampire squid. At this point, Flusser's use of taxonomy forces the critical reader to make certain choices about how to describe and address his treatment of the vampire squid as Other: does the vampire squid *reflect* a view of humanity, mirrored like left and right hands? Does it *refract* a view of humanity (to borrow Eva Hayward's optical and watery term), estranged but still recognizable?[86] Might we push the photography metaphor and say that the vampire squid figures as a kind of "film negative" of the human, that he develops in the abyss?

Whichever verb one chooses, it is clear that the vampire squid comparison is intentionally extreme, and serves to help highlight those elements of cameras and photographic practice that go unnoticed, naturalized, invisible. In this way, the vampire squid is a kind of "anti-apparatus" (to use Flusser's own term) against photography. The term *anti-apparatus* first emerges in Flusser's essay "Criteria—Crisis—Criticism" (1984), in which he discusses the possibility of a new kind of photography criticism that does not focus solely on selecting which photographs are good or beautiful. Rather, a new photography criticism is needed that *critiques the criteria* by which we judge photographs, as well as the camera apparatus's functions. Flusser writes, "Therefore, it is first necessary to invent an anti-apparatus" to photography that has to "critique the entire apparatus of culture and all its totalitarian tendencies, including the apparatuses that program us."[87] The vampire squid in *Vampyroteuthis Infernalis* is precisely such an anti-apparatus, used to make the cultural contexts of photography visible.[88] Ursula Le Guin's ant in "The Author of Acacia Seeds" performs a similar function as an anti-apparatus to human forms of speech, operating, like Flusser, in the mode of the fable.

Although there are many examples of animals serving as "anti-apparatuses" to human beings, what is unique about Flusser's fable is the role of the deep ocean. The abyssal environment that sustains the vampire squid—the environment in which it swims, eats, and makes its media, and environment whose liquidity, temperature, darkness, and pressure are so very different from our own—is also a form of anti-apparatus. John Durham Peters, in a similar move, has called the ocean an "anti-environment" that draws attention to what we have taken for granted on land. In *The Marvelous Clouds* (2015), Peters writes that

> McLuhan, who in his youth loved to sail, made piscine obliviousness famous, but was not original when he claimed: "One thing about which fish know exactly nothing is water, since they have no anti-environment which would enable them to perceive the element they live in." In fact, fish probably know lots about water's temperature, clarity, currents, weather, prey, and so on, but the point was that they did not recognize it as water. It was just background, the stuff that slides into infrastructural obliviousness. As McLuhan said elsewhere: "Environments are invisible." (His mission was always to provide an anti-environment).[89]

This passage brings to mind (but does not cite) David Foster Wallace's famous graduation speech at Kenyon College, "This Is Water." Water—whose differences from air are so obvious to us—is that which is taken for granted, invisible, and naturalized to fish. By considering what counts as simply "background" to fish, Peters prepares human scholars to think about the environment that they take for granted as the condition of possibility for media processes—recording, transmission, and storage. This is precisely the logic of Flusser's fable: he tells a speculative fiction about the deep sea in order to provoke the reader to think about what they have taken for granted (or what has been made invisible) about the conditions of mediation in human communities—a novel alternative to a medium-specific analysis of photography.

Photography in the Darkroom of the Abyss

The abyssal environment offers a compelling structural parallel with the photographic darkroom. Consider the similarities: the darkroom and the abyss are places of sensorial estrangement (for humans) where our visual modes of perception are compromised. In the darkroom, only a red/red-orange light illuminates space to avoid disturbing the sensitive photographic paper. From the shallow pools of chemicals rise the hellish smells of sulfur and vinegar. Negatives are brought to these pools—miniature scenes captured from the camera's world—which are then projected and affixed to photographic paper. After the paper is bathed in the pools of chemicals, images slowly reappear. There is something primordial about the darkroom and something vampyroteuthic about the way light and liquid chemicals combine to produce images. These images are themselves entirely structured by the apparatus of the camera and all its "glandular appendages": the lens; the chromatophore-like shutter, opening and closing to change how light and color reflect; the enlarger that flickers light onto chemically sensitized paper; the liquid baths that secrete photographs.[90] Looking at photography vampyroteuthically means seeing photographs not only as inscriptions of light but as the secretions or precipitate of the liquid bath itself.

The abyss presents the cognitively estranging conditions that enable Flusser to develop a theory of information beyond inscription of objects. In his chapter "Vampyroteuthan Art," Flusser considers how inscriptions on stone tablets would not last underwater but be gradually eroded away, or used by other organisms as a surface on which to grow: "This human trust in the permanence of the objective world seems derisory from the point of view of those who, like Vampyroteuthis, inhabit a liquid environment. From this point of view, the only material for information storage that is worthy of trust is the egg. Genetic information is *aere perennius* and will outlive not only all books, buildings, and paintings but also the species itself, although in mutated form."[91] Think about what seawater does to objects: it rusts metal, dissolves paper, and allows barnacles and other organisms to attach to hard surfaces like ships and stones.[92] The ocean is not a generic fluid but an environment of particular chemical composition, what Michel Serres (following Jules Michelet) calls "the soup" of life, full of microscopic organisms, larvae, detritus, and dissolved minerals. The ocean erodes external objects like "books, buildings, and paintings," countering trust in the "permanency of the objective world."[93] If information could last underwater, Flusser imagines, then the substrate or media would have to be genetic material—information storage at the level of the germ line rather than external media.

The subaquatic fable develops further, as Flusser describes the desires of the photographer and vampire squid in strikingly similar terms. Consider the following passage from *Towards a Philosophy of Photography*.

Photographers' intentions are first, to encode their concepts of the world into images; second, to do this by using a camera; third, to show the images produced in this way to others so that they can serve as models for their experience, knowledge, judgment and actions; fourth, to make these models as permanent as possible. In short: Photographers' intentions are to inform others and through their photographs to immortalize themselves in the memory of others.[94]

Compare such a perspective with the following passage from *Vampyroteuthis Infernalis*.

With this artistic creation [i.e., the squid's modulation of its skin pigmentation] we are able to distinguish between several phases. (1) Vampyroteuthis goes through a particular experience. (2) He searches in his memory for a suitable model in order to capture it. (3) He verifies the absence of this model: the experience is as yet unexpressed. (4) This arresting experience goes beyond his organism, is organised by the brain and then transmitted to the chromatophores. (5) The chromatophores transcode the experience into a "skin painting." (6) Such colouration never before seen provokes the curiosity of another Vampyroteuthis. (7) The sender uses the new colouration to seduce the receiver and copulate with it.[95]

The ways that photographers and vampire squid deliver information to the "other" share a similar process of first having a concept/experience, then desiring to transmit it, then encoding it in an image, and then transmitting it in order to immortalize the image in the memory of others. Drawing this parallel between *Vampyroteuthis Infernalis* and *Towards a Philosophy of Photography* suggests that the liquid media of the vampire squid— skin paintings and sepia ink clouds—stand in place of photographs, as nondurable images. Because this is a media fable (as opposed to philosophy alone), Flusser is at once able to develop a milieu-specific theory of media inscription underwater (occurring at the level of genetics rather than external surfaces), as well as a medium-specific theory of photography (through the homology between photographic and vampyroteuthic media). Flusser writes, "The act of photography is that of 'phenomenological doubt,' to the extent that it attempts to approach phenomena from any number of view points."[96] In a way, then, Flusser takes the vampire squid as a kind of "camera" of the deep to realize as many phenomenological viewpoints as possible from the vampire squid's standpoint (or better, floatpoint).

If Flusser's vampire squid is a camera, then its skin is photographic paper. "What fascinates the photographer," he writes, "is not the photographic paper, the object, but the information transmitted. The photographic paper is for the photographer what the skin is for Vampyroteuthis: a medium for colorful messages."[97] In this analogy, the vampire squid itself is thus both photographer (inscriptor) and photograph (medium), using its bodily tissues and fluids to produce deceptive images that fascinate other vampire squid. Although Flusser claims (in his chapter on Vampyroteuthan art) that the vampire squid models "directly on the other," not on objects, it is the squid's own body that facilitates the communication of messages via chromatophores, or skin pigment cells, and ink clouds.[98] This reflects a shift from a society of subjects who "imprint information on objects" to subjects who become information programmers, broadcasting their own content (via skin) directly to viewers.

Although unknown to Flusser at the time, there have since been a variety of scientific studies of cephalopod skin as an optical technology. One study of the California two-spot octopus (*Octopus bimaculoides*) found that it could sense light with its skin, without input from the central nervous system. Light-sensitive proteins called opsins (usually found in eyes) were found in the skin, whose chromatophores changed color when exposed to bright light.[99] This finding suggests that Flusser's analogy of squid skin as photo paper is appropriate for other species of cephalopods. Beyond photo paper, scientists have compared cephalopod skin to other artistic media such as a "canvas" or "mixed media palette" composed of chromatophores, iridiphores, and leucophores that evoke painting traditions of the mosaic or pointillism.[100] In *Other Minds*, Peter Godfrey-Smith imagines cephalopod skin as an even more dynamic medium, where the "passing cloud display" of a cuttlefish is "like movies played on the screen of a cuttlefish's skin."[101] The *Tentacles* display at the Monterey Bay Aquarium played with this aesthetic of skin as screen; not only did it interchange aquarium glass and screens throughout the exhibit, but it also included an interactive touch screen display where you could "swap your face" with cephalopods like the flamboyant cuttlefish (plate 4).[102] Cuttlefish can create such rapidly moving skin patterns that programmer Jaron Lanier proclaimed his "jealousy" of them, since they naturally perform what he calls "post-symbolic communication" with "images at the speed with which we can imagine them" rather than the slow bandwidth of verbal language.[103] Although the specific properties of cephalopod skin differ between species, these examples show how the skin operates as a complex optical technology for both hiding (camouflage) and being seen (communicating).

Unfortunately for Flusser, scientists now know that *Vampyroteuthis infernalis* does not change color like photo paper. Indeed, several of Flusser's speculations about vampyroteuthic media proved to be incorrect. Flusser wrote *Vampyroteuthis Infernalis* from 1981 to 1987, when not much was known about the vampire squid, and made significant errors in its characterization.[104] For example, the vampire squid grows to only about one foot in length, not (as Flusser erroneously writes) twenty meters.[105] It has both black and reddish-brown chromatophores but cannot change its skin color like other cephalopods can.[106] The vampire squid also does not secrete sepia ink to escape, as dark ink would be redundant in the abyss; instead it has light-producing organs called "photophores" on the tips of its webbed tentacles and produces a bioluminescent mucus (instead of an ink cloud), which it can excrete to distract predators. Had Flusser known of photophores, he might have considered these photo-graphic media (in the full sense of light-writing) to have offered a more compelling analogy with the camera.

However, the purpose of ephemeral media (ink clouds and skin paintings) appears secondary compared with how Flusser imagines the squid's ultimate goal of preserving its messages and memories. The vampire squid's single objective is to trick another vampire squid into becoming fascinated with its ephemeral media of coloration, in order to "seduce the receiver and copulate with it," a moment of contact where genetic messages may be inscribed on the egg, "the only material for information storage that is worthy of trust."[107] It is this trust in genetic storage that orients the vampire squid's use of ephemeral media like sepia clouds, which can fascinate and affect other *Vampyroteuthes* for the purpose of informing, altering, and imposing on them "particular information, knowledge, behavior and sensations."[108] That Flusser's vampire squid, the most intelligent animal in its phylum, would aim to "alter the other" and "impose" its own information on others of its kind should alarm us as a particularly violent form of depersonalization. Here it figures as a kind of "reverse" vampirism, of pumping a substance into others rather than sucking it from them. Especially disturbing, particularly because Flusser genders the squid as male, are the connotations of "raping the mind" that Joost Meerloo points to in his 1956 discussion of menticide and brainwashing: "[*Vampyroteuthis infernalis*] seeks to seduce and violate his mates so that these may store the information without critique."[109] Further, "in order to be informed it is the other that has to be violated. The other's memory is for Vampyroteuthis the same as stone and language are for us. . . . He hammers and composes the other."[110] The sexual politics of imagining—even in fable—that "genetic memory as information storage" would be modifiable only through the vulnerable moment of sex between squid, and that the sex of the inscriber is male (Flusser calls the vampire squid "he"), should not be let off the hook as a simple reflection of reality. We should ask why this model of sexuality finds itself reinscribed in Flusser's narrative rather than challenged and questioned.[111]

One way to address the gender politics in *Vampyroteuthis Infernalis* is to turn to the masculine gendering of photography in critical theory, as well as its alternatives. Here we might begin with Roland Barthes's phallic theory of the "punctum" in *Camera Lucida* to describe the way a photograph strikes and fascinates the viewer. Distinguishing it from the "studium" ("of the order of *liking*" a "vague, slippery, irresponsible interest one takes"), Barthes writes that "punctum" is the "sting, speck, cut, little hole—and also a cast of the dice. A photograph's *punctum* is that accident which pricks me (but also bruises me, is poignant to me)," often a specific detail of the photograph.[112] This formulation, predicated on a kind of visual injury, reminds us of the way the vampire squid also seeks to strike and fascinate the viewers of his skin paintings. Similarly, Flusser considers the camera as masculine agent in *Towards a Philosophy of Photography*: "If one observes the movements of a human being in possession of a camera (or of a camera in possession of a human being), the impression given is of someone lying in wait. This is the ancient act of stalking which goes back to the palaeolithic hunter in the tundra."[113] Flusser's gendered depiction of the vampire squid correlates with an existing tradition of critical thought connecting the camera with a masculine, penetrative logic. For example, in breaking down cinematic codes and normative conventions of looking, Laura Mulvey famously diagnosed the "male gaze" as a mode of depicting women from a male, heterosexual, perspective—rendering women as sexual objects through particular techniques, such as lingering.[114] Susan Sontag and Donna Haraway extensively discuss the parallels between guns and cameras as phallic objects that "shoot" subjects, and the similar "click" of a trigger in each.[115] Although other scholars have complicated gendered-looking relations in photography by exploring queer and feminist gazes, the camera apparatus often lends itself to a heteronormative, masculinist logic.

However, it was not inevitable for Flusser to have developed such an extreme diagnosis of masculine relations between photographic subject and photographer. In fact, one alternative theory of photography that he could have developed would begin from the history of cameraless photography and experimentation with photo-sensitive surfaces. If the camera has been characterized as the bearer of a particular gaze that penetrates a landscape or subject, then what to make of a practice like cyanotype photography (sometimes called "sun printing" or "blueprints"), where no camera is involved? The process of making cyanotypes was developed by John Herschel in 1842, and involves combining two chemicals (ferric ammonium citrate and potassium ferrocyanide) with water, and painting this onto paper in a dark room. Once sensitized, the paper is ready to use: the "photographer" then places objects directly on the paper in sunlight.

When the paper is developed in water, shadows appear as gradations of white, and sunlit areas appear blue. Appropriately, the first "book" of cyanotype photograph was made by Anna Atkins—*British Algae: Cyanotype Impressions* (1843)—where the medium (cyanotype) is well suited to the subject of seaweeds, seeming to cast them naturally in front of a blue ocean.

Now, think of what this process implies: instead of a camera separating object and onlooker, cyanotype printing places the "photographer" on the same side of the film as the objects themselves. In order to make the print, the photographer must physically *arrange* the objects on top of the photosensitive paper, actively touching and adjusting their positions relative to the source of sunlight. Cyanotype photography, then, necessitates a kind of proximity between photographer and object(s) photographed at the time that shadows are captured on paper, before their ghostly apparition under the developing fluid of water. The photographer does not so much "stalk" their object of interest and "shoot" it as carefully (and quickly) compose the position and orientation of the object(s) that they wish to print.[116] If photo-sensitive surfaces mattered more than camera apparatuses in defining photography, then Flusser could have dwelled even more deeply with the significance of squid skin as photo paper and explored the possibility of the photographer not as penetrator but as participating in an "ontological choreography" of arrangement and fluid fixation.[117]

The Vampyroteuthian Path

Flusser's vampire squid is, then, an ambivalent character of media futurity. Becoming vampyroteuthic means gaining a kind of individual agency against the surrounding climate of media by programming others, but the recovery of our individual agency comes at a cost—of belonging to a society where vampyroteuthic media are predicated on deception and lies. The question Flusser leaves us with is whether our future is one of vampyroteuthic media or not: "Our communicational structures are being fundamentally transformed, in the sense of becoming constituted by ephemeral and transient media that allow the other to be informed without the need for objects. It is as if humanity, after a multi-millennial turn through the objective world, had now reencountered the vampyroteuthian path."[118] In this vision, society becomes vampyroteuthic as human-made media move into an aquatic paradigm of informatic "flow" programmed to influence human behavior rather than inscribe objects. Indeed, "the society of the immediate future shall be a society of information consumption, less and less interested in the consumption of 'goods,' of objects. The interest diverted from economy to sociology. Intersubjective society: a society of Vampyroteuthes."[119] In this moment the "underwater media" specific to the vampire squid turn into a commentary about memory and an emerging information society. Flusser writes, "Vampyroteuthis is always a 'total artist,' that is, one who seeks to attain immortality through the epistemological, aesthetic and ethical modeling of the other"—a form of media focused on the transformation of subjects rather than objects.[120] Through its concern with inscription on the other, Flusser's art of the vampire squid is a fable about totalitarian media, of being forced to carry someone else's memory or experience like a tattoo.

The vampire squid thus embodies both a kind of totalitarian power (seeking to inscribe its memories on others) and resistance to this same power (taking the role of the inscriber/programmer instead of the inscribed). In a letter from 1988, Flusser's friend Vargas responds to *Vampyroteuthis Infernalis* by comparing it to Nazi fantasies of a possible superman (super-mollusk?) and *Star Wars*: "The fact is that both you and [Louis] Bec, as well as the TV producers, are on the trail of the primitive Nazis on the fantastic search for 'new forms of being.' For now, thank God, this is fantasy, but gene technology threatens to turn it into reality (concrete)." Vargas writes that *Vampyroteuthis infernalis* is like the "Emperor" or "Darth Vader," urging Flusser to think of "the biography of an animal as powerful as Luke Skywalker or Obi-something-or-other that has the light side of the 'force.'"[121] Flusser defends his organism, arguing, "when fantasy loses its exactness it becomes banal (I don't know Skywalker, but I imagine him to be a lot less fantastic than, say, the pseudo-social organization of ants)."[122] Ant colonies and the vampire squid interest Flusser because of the cognitively estranging forms of perception they offer—forms that participate in a broader epistemological project of depriviledging both human perspective and the "objectivity" of machines.[123]

For me, *Vampyroteuthis Infernalis* both succumbs to and sets up the conditions for a critique of the terrestrial bias of media theory and philosophy. Although it helps pluralize the points of view through which we might approach and develop concepts, it also imagines media in dry terms of inscription rather than the messy, turbulent movement of fluids. Flusser's most famous claim—that the program of the camera determines

the possibilities of the photographs produced—looks only at the apparatus producing the photographic negative, not the development of actual
photographs: "To every photograph there corresponds a clear and distinct
element in the camera program."[124] Yet in film photography, or cyanotype photography, every individual photograph depends on development
in liquid baths and the unpredictable vagaries of human error/artistry and
chemical fluidity. Why is it that Flusser ignores the liquid in his most extensive work on photography, only to set his estranged drama about photography in *Vampyroteuthis Infernalis* in the liquid world of the deep sea?

Liquid Intelligence and Noninscriptive Media

Part of the answer to this question about Flusser's ambivalent relation
to liquids may have to do with the errancy of water, which is what the
camera apparatus has historically sought to control and canalize. In Jeff
Wall's provocative essay "Photography and Liquid Intelligence," the "liquid intelligence" of water opposes "the glassed-in and relatively 'dry' character of the institution of photography."[125] Whereas liquids flow in turbulent and organic patterns, "the mechanical character of the action of
opening and closing the shutter—the substratum of instantaneity which
persists in all photography—is the concrete opposite kind of movement
from, for example, the flow of a liquid."[126] These elements (liquid and camera) play a role in Wall's photograph *Milk*, where he contrasts the ninety-
degree angles of the urban environment (brick building, cement) with a
man crushing a carton, causing milk to spray into the air (figure 2.3).[127]
In an otherwise intentionally ordered photograph, the liquid milk (and
the man's expression, turning away) constitutes the "incalculable" element in the photograph, compelling for the way it evades photographic
prescription and control.[128] Although water "plays an essential part in the
making of photographs, it has to be controlled exactly and cannot be per-
mitted to spill over the spaces and moments mapped out for it in the process, or the picture is ruined."[129] Thus water is "admitted to the process"
of making photographs but also "excluded, contained, or channeled by
its hydraulics."[130]

At the time he was writing in 1989, Wall speculated that digital photography would usher forth "a new displacement of water," which will
"disappear from the immediate production process" such that "the his-

FIGURE 2.3 Jeff Wall, *Milk*, 1984. Transparency in lightbox, 187 × 229 cm.
Courtesy of the artist.

torical consciousness of the medium is altered."[131] This portends an increasingly dry technical consciousness—one perhaps echoed in science
fiction film's imagination of future cities and highly sanitized space stations, where water is invisible beyond decorative functions. We might say
that the role of liquids in the production of photography never really goes
away but becomes channeled and canalized at earlier stages in the process (to produce, say, the electricity that it takes to power the camera).
Such a concern about the invisible agency of water in digital technologies
underlies Joanna Zylinska's recent work on "hydromedia," a framework
that examines how water is "involved in the production, transportation,
and usage of media devices," such as excavation of minerals for computer
parts, the cooling of servers, and even the content of water in human
bodies and brains.[132] From this view, all media might be understood as
hydromedia, where water "*literally saturates media ecologies*, binding media
subjects and media objects into a liquid dynamic of exchanges."[133] What
Zylinska clarifies is that liquid intelligence is not only involved in photog-

raphy but has to do with the production of digital technologies and media systems as a whole.

Wall's striking description diagnoses a latent hydrophobia in Flusser's writings. In *Towards a Philosophy of Photography*, Flusser describes posthistoric images in curiously "dry" terms: "Photographs are dams placed in the way of the stream of history, jamming historical happenings."[134] This is similar to how Wall writes that the opening and closing of the camera shutter is the opposite kind of movement to that of the liquid. Flusser's vampire squid also aims to control the flows of liquids for the purpose of making messages. The messy media of Flusser's vampire squid (sepia ink clouds, chromatophores, salivary glands, gelatin-secreting glands, and seminal fluid) would not seem to be conducive to encoding clear messages, but this is precisely how Flusser imagines them. Consider the vampire squid's skin paintings, which channel and control the glandular media of communication: an experience "is organised by the brain and then transmitted to the chromatophores" that "transcode the experience into a 'skin painting.'"[135] Flusser's imagination of ink clouds is also about recording a discrete memory: "The experience that Vampyroteuthis has just gone through must be expressed in the cloud, no longer with the intention to divert a hypothetical aggressor, but to store this experience in the memory of another Vampyroteuthis."[136] That the end goal is to "store" the experience "expressed in the cloud" in the memory of another Vampyroteuthis suggests precise control over the ink cloud, quite unlike Jackson Pollock's interest in the unpredictable behavior of fluids. All liquid media are tightly channeled by the vampire squid and thus compatible with inscriptive paradigms.

What we have in Flusser's media fable is, then, a strange tension between the portrayal of liquids at the levels of speculative fiction and allegory. In Flusser's speculative imagination of the vampire squid's ink clouds and skin paintings, liquidity plays a key role as an environment and as communication media. Yet at the allegorical level of reading (since fable is a species of allegory), Flusser thinks about photography in terms of a dry paradigm of inscription. Flusser presupposes that a single agent (vampire squid or photographer) has an idea or concept and that it "encodes" or inscribes in a medium that then conveys the message to another subject. In this way, Flusser's vampire squid artist suggests insemination over Derridean dissemination. Whereas "insemination" implies an originary moment of fertilization by a single agent, "dissemination" affirms the "nonorigin," suggesting the failure of mastery; it also alludes to the impossibility of prescribing a message. But if such a thing were possible, "dissemination is precisely the impossibility of reducing a text as such to its effects of meaning, content, thesis or theme."[137] In another context, Colin Milburn elaborates the fluid resonances of dissemination as the "movement and overflow of the semantic and seminal from within, the multiplication of essential meanings and vital fluids," the spillage, over-flow, flooding.[138] This is not the sense of media we see in *Vampyroteuthis Infernalis*, which concerns itself with message delivery rather than a more radical materiality of water. The vampire squid's desire to tightly control water and glandular media reflects on the institution and apparatus of photography, chained to terrestrially informed media theory based on a concept of tightly controlled inscription rather than the errancy that more materially relates to fluid media. Flusser's vampire squid thus floats suspended between the "dry" technology of the camera and the "wet" technologies of ink clouds and skin paintings.

As Wall points out, the history of photography itself has historically concerned the agency of fluid processes, suggesting that Flusser's fable could have turned out differently. Liquid chemicals used in photography recall older technologies like "washing, bleaching, dissolving" and the separating of ores in primitive mining, figuring as a kind of "archaism" that "embodies a memory-trace of very ancient production-processes" that are "connected to the origin of techne."[139] Washing, bleaching, and dissolving all suggest chemically transformative processes that may warp, deform, fray, discolor, cleanse, stain, and saturate surfaces and volumes rather than simply inscribing them with a mark. These perspectives on the errancy of water suggest that Flusser's fable could have developed to be more sensitive to the agency of liquid mediations instead of sticking with a terrestrial paradigm of inscription in his understanding of photography. Would liquids and liquid agency constitute, then, examples of noninscrip-tive media and mediation that—at a certain scale—participate in pro-cesses of creating images, information, sound, and other technical events?

The verbs *washing, rinsing,* and *dyeing* all suggest noninscriptive pro-cesses—but what of their products? Is noninscriptive media a stable on-tological category? Although I would like to think that liquids (or even gases) would constitute examples of noninscriptive media, such an em-phasis on media materiality neglects to address the agential role of the observer. Katherine Hayles's definition of inscription technologies (given earlier in this chapter), in which "a device must initiate material changes that can be read as marks," offers a key distinction. In this definition, it is not only the stability of marks on a substrate that matters but also the *presence of a reader*, be they human, animal, or machine. That inscriptions "can be read as marks" necessarily involves both a legible record and a reader (subject) to whom they make sense. In this understanding, inscription has to do with a subject-specific recognition of inscriptions as such, not only the inscription's ontological status as marks on a page or stone. Such a definition raises questions about the ontology of ink, which presumably could be seen as an inscription on paper if it is legible to a reader, despite its materiality as a fluid.

A striking scene in the film *Arrival* (directed by Denis Villeneuve but based on Ted Chiang's short story "Story of Your Life") illustrates this very contradiction at the heart of noninscriptive media. The film imagines a crisis of visitation where octopus-like aliens descend to Earth in crescent-shaped ships, welcoming small groups of humans up and into their cavities. Louise—the protagonist and linguist—faces the challenge of learning to communicate with the "heptapods" (named for their seven appendages, radially symmetric around a bulbous head) across the interface of a glass-like divider, separating the gray, luminous fog of the heptapods' habitat from the theater-like space of the human beings. It is within this gray fog that the heptapods attempt "written" communication, using a starfish-like hand to secrete an inky black calligraphy that magnetically swirls into the desired configuration, like circular brushstrokes that stabilize just long enough to see before dissipating—almost a version of Flusser's ink clouds. In order to respond, Louise and her team photograph, digitize, and analyze the ephemeral writings, separating them into component parts that they can use as an alphabet. Louise composes a response by selecting elements of heptapod writing on a tablet, arranging them in a meaningful circle ("sentence"), and then projecting her final semiogram on a large TV screen. Perhaps what is most striking about the visuality of this scene is that the liquid and the digital are seen as workable substitutions for each other, and manage to facilitate communication despite the difference in materiality between heptapod "ink" and digital image.

The writing system appears to be legible whether it takes place in a liquid medium or a digital medium—echoing Hayles's observation that inscription technologies must initiate material changes that can be *read as marks*. This underlies her distinction between inscription and incorporation in *How We Became Posthuman*.

> In contrast to inscription is incorporation. An incorporating practice such as a good-bye wave cannot be separated from its embodied medium, for it exists as such only when it is instantiated in a particular hand making a particular kind of gesture. It is possible, of course, to abstract a sign from the embodied gesture by representing it in a different medium, for example by drawing on a page the outline of a stylized hand, with wavy lines indicating motion. In this case, however, the gesture is no longer an incorporating practice. Rather, it has been transformed precisely into an inscription that functions as if it were independent of any particular instantiation.[140]

The key word here is "transformation," showing how an embodied gesture (like the wave of a hand, or a secretion of ink) can be so easily captured as "an inscription that functions as if it were independent of any instantiation." If we follow Hayles's point that the reader can abstract anything out of a material instantiation, then "noninscriptive media" could never be a stable ontological category; noninscriptive media would simply be those that have not yet been captured in an inscriptive medium. Think of how people use Snapchat: even if you text me an image designed to disappear after a few seconds, I can always take a screen shot of it for future use.[141] So what is the status of inscription in *Arrival*? Does the ephemeral heptapod writing constitute a form of noninscriptive media, in its liquid/gaseous state that fades over time? Or does the medium not matter, as long as the material changes can be read as marks?

A strictly materialist interpretation might say that the heptapod writing becomes inscriptive media at the moment of digital/photographic capture, transformed into the manipulable pixels on a tablet. However, the most lasting effect, or perhaps residue, of the heptapod writing has to do with Louise's perception of time. Throughout *Arrival*, Louise has a series of flash-forwards that anticipate the birth of her child, who will be terminally ill. What she comes to realize is that the process of learning heptapod writing has shifted the way she orients within time. This seems to be an effect of composing semiographs—a process described in more detail in the original short story by Chiang. Unlike Chinese characters, which stand for either one word or part of a word, heptapod semiographs are each entire sentences or paragraphs. Writing the semiograph requires knowing the entire trajectory of the sentence, since one line might participate in several grammatical components. Thus to get the proportions of the sentence/image/semiograph correct, you have to anticipate what the entire sentence will look like (which Chiang likens to Fermat's principle of least time). Even though the heptapods eventually leave (an irony of the title *Arrival*), Louise is forever changed by this new consciousness in time, peppered by future memories of her child. It would be a mistake to say that learning heptapod writing marks Louise, or reinscribes her subjectivity in some form. It would be more accurate to say that learning heptapod writing reorients her within the stream of time: she no longer sees time as linear but as always already saturated by what will happen. If we take a purely ontological focus on media—fluids versus solids—we miss this important valence of what noninscriptive media or mediation might mean: acquiring orientation in relation to the specificities of one's embodiment. In my interpretation, the real residue of the heptapods is not liquid writing as such but the persistence of a new orientation—or gravitation—within the flow of time. In this sense, noninscriptive media could include the experience of learning gymnastics, swimming (scuba . . .), dance, or sign language—activities through which the body acquires a new set of orientational habits that persist over time. If, as Sara Ahmed has written, gender is a matter of orientation (as I discuss in the introduction), might something like gender also be thought of in terms of noninscriptive mediation?[142]

Chiang's short story "Exhalation" offers yet another way of thinking about noninscriptive media. At the core of the fiction is a machinic being powered by pressurized argon in replaceable lung-tanks, who decides to find out how its brain works through a dangerous experiment in self-dissection. One theory of memory—the inscriptive hypothesis—holds that "all of a person's experiences were engraved on sheets of gold foil."[143] However, the machinic being believes that any theory or memory has to account for the ease of erasure as well as recording—not unlike Freud's mystic writing pad, upon which short-term memory could be cleared while long-term memory might receive more enduring impressions. Using a series of mirrors to examine the back of its head, the being carefully takes apart each mediating layer of its brain until it arrives at the most minute mechanisms, and what it finds is the following:

For many hours I scrutinized the leaves, until I realized that they themselves were playing the role of capillaries; the leaves formed temporary
conduits and valves that existed just long enough to redirect air at
other leaves in turn, and then disappeared as a result. This was an engine undergoing continuous transformation, indeed modifying itself
as part of its operation. The lattice was not so much a machine as it was
a page on which the machine was written, and on which the machine
itself ceaselessly wrote. My consciousness could be said to be encoded
in the position of these tiny leaves, but it would be more accurate to
say that it was encoded in the ever-shifting pattern of air driving these
leaves. . . . Air is in fact the very medium of our thoughts. All that we
are is a pattern of air flow. My memories were inscribed, not as grooves
on foil or even the position of switches, but as persistent currents of
argon [gas].[144]

Memory itself turns out to be a fragile machinic ecology that involves both the agency of air currents and the position of the leaves, sustained and shifting as long as the being has enough pressurized argon
to breathe—where breathing is not a matter of chemical reactions but
of mechanical pressure (especially since argon, a noble gas, is chemically
nonreactive). The patterns of airflow that comprise memory sustain or
change the position of tiny gold leaves, challenging what we think of as
an inscriptive medium (not grooves but currents). Air is a medium with
the agency to orient the gold leaves—a botanical reference that blurs the
natural and the created, the organic and metallic. The central crisis of
the story emerges when the machinic being realizes that in his enclosed
world, the reserves of argon are depleting, and in response he inscribes
his own story on tablets with the hope that some future being will read
his tale. What this story theorizes, then, is a posthuman conception of
memory as pure information pattern, carried not by a series of marks but
by airflow. The brain is not so much a surface that is inscribed but the
fragile positions of gold leaves oriented by currents of argon. By imagining a model of memory that involves the ecology of air and positionality of
leaves, Chiang challenges us to think beyond the paradigm of inscription
and instead to consider the possibility of noninscriptive forms of memory
and information storage. As I have shown with the two stories from Ted
Chiang, ecological situations can facilitate media processes without in-

scription, which favor embodied orientation and patterns of arrangement rather than a strict focus on media objects.

Media Fable

Although *Vampyroteuthis Infernalis* has its own elements of terrestrial bias, Flusser's experimentation with the genre of the "media fable" holds promise as a fictive methodology, particularly for the way that it addresses the epistemological question of how we come to recognize instances of mediation in the first place. *Vampyroteuthis Infernalis* encourages a kind of epistemic humility when we read it as a speculative fiction, by asking us to imagine how media might exist differently from another species' point of view in an environment vastly different from our own (the deep sea). Furthermore, Flusser's and Le Guin's attention to orientational language shows how a terrestrial bias persists in the way we use metaphor in ordinary language, attaching certain sets of values to prepositions like *up* and *down*. These speculative aspects of Flusser's media fable caution that human perspectives (even as they vary across cultures) are not entirely "objective" in the sense of "universally applicable" or "the view from nowhere" (to reference Donna Haraway) but rather emerge from the specificities of embodiment and lived environment. This is Flusser's critique of anthropocentrism at its best.

Yet as a media fable, *Vampyroteuthis Infernalis* also contains a second level of reading, the allegorical. It is at this level that the reader is positioned to have moments of recognition where what is being said about media in the abyss suggests similarities with anthropogenic media (primarily photography, in this fable). As I have shown, Flusser takes the vampire squid as a pretext for talking about posthistorical images and the politics of photography, or how we are transitioning from a society that writes on objects to a society that seeks to inscribe messages on subjects. What the allegorical level adds to the media fable is a certain accountability for why it matters to think about the vampire squid in the first place (since our attention could always be elsewhere). We could say that for Flusser, it is the vampire squid that "flashes up in a moment of danger" (to follow Walter Benjamin), that is, this societal transition to inscription directly on subjects, as if we were already in the liquid milieu of the abyss.

Indeed, what is important is that Flusser's media fable preserves the tension between the speculative and allegorical levels of reading the tale without collapsing them into one grand theory. The fable requires us to split our consciousness somewhat amphibiously between the two levels, reminded with some humility of the limits of human framing, while also keeping a sensibility for what the speculation might teach us through unexpected moments of recognition. This lends a certain politics to the act of speculation and milieu-specific analysis, by remaining self-aware about why we might feel compelled to venture into such a speculation at this historical moment (when we could always be using our time differently). In conclusion, I would like to offer my own fable about inscription that is specific to the milieu of the ocean environment, which flashes up in a moment of danger that we might call the Anthropocene. This other media fable begins with a distant relative of the vampire squid—the Hawaiian bobtail squid.

Euprymna scolopes, or the Hawaiian Bobtail Squid

The Hawaiian bobtail squid is a small and charismatic cephalopod, about the size of a walnut, that lives in warm Pacific waters (figure 2.4). It has a rainbow sheen and, as science writer Ed Yong puts it, the acute problem of being "delicious" to many predators in the ocean.[145] Because the nocturnal Hawaiian bobtail squid dwells in shallow sands of the Hawaiian islands, it contends with very different environmental factors than the vampire squid. The foremost among these is the presence of moonlight, which casts an illuminating shadow across any floating objects, making them visible to creatures living below. Since the Hawaiian bobtail squid prefers to hunt for small shrimp at night, it has developed a symbiotic relationship with the microbe *Vibrio fischeri* in order to perfect a form of camouflage: "Of the thousands of species of microbes in the ocean, only one—Vibrio fischeri— is allowed to enter the squid's body. Once inside, it begins to glow. And that glow, it is said, perfectly matches the moonlight welling down on top of the squid, masking its silhouette from predators looking up from below. The bacteria provide the squid with a kind of luminous invisibility cloak."[146] Yong highlights the significance of this cloaking ability as a form of media in one playful video (where he uses a green screen to make himself disappear and mimic the squid's vanishing act) by saying that the

FIGURE 2.4 Hawaiian bobtail squid. Photo by Chris Frazee and Margaret McFall-Ngai. Wikimedia Commons, March 24, 2014.

Hawaiian bobtail squid "can disappear by glowing."[147] Alternatively, in a YouTube video, Margaret McFall-Ngai compares the Hawaiian bobtail squid to a "Klingon cloaking device" in a whimsical science fiction reference that may remind us of efforts to thwart surveillance technologies in art practice and media theory.[148] McFall-Ngai describes the mechanism for this cloaking device (the light organ containing *V. fischerii* bacteria) as forming a sort of "backwards eye," with an innermost layer of a lens, then a reflector, and finally an ink sac that can expand or contract like an iris, depending on how much the squid needs to dim its light organ to match the intensity of moonlight—not unlike a camera shutter.[149]

In the milieu of shallow moonlit waters, we might say that the Hawaiian bobtail squid inscribes itself into the moonlight through a form of photographic camouflage, modulating its light-producing organ to match its sensation of moonlight from above. However, this is not for the purposes of communication and legibility but for hiding. As Hanna Rose Shell writes, camouflage unfolds in time and space as "an adaptive logic of escape from photographic representation."[150] If the squid desired to create legible "skin paintings" like Flusser's imagined vampire squid, then we might recognize this as a form of inscription analogous to familiar recording media. Yet by inscribing itself so seamlessly into the moonlight of the ocean at night, the Hawaiian bobtail squid enacts a form of ecological media that we find difficult to recognize by analogy to any human inscription technologies (like books) despite its optical sophistication. Perhaps the ocean prompts us to rethink what we mean by inscription, to whom it is legible, and where we look for examples of it. Could we recognize forms of ecological inscription (in the sense of marking into) that do not find analogy in human technologies, or would these be invisible to us? Is counterillumination a form of inscription into an environment, a kind of writing as concealing or camouflage? Or is counterillumination a form of noninscriptive media because it cannot be read as a mark?

How we answer these questions has key implications for conceptualizations of the Anthropocene, which has been (and continues to be) thought of in terms of textuality and inscriptive mediation. As a provisional name for our current epoch, the Anthropocene reorients geology to the future by anticipating a new stratigraphic layer inscribed by human agency, a new chapter in Earth's history. Kathryn Yusoff sees the Anthropocene as a form of "Earth-writing writ large," while Janet Walker envisions it as a form of Earth "re-writing" to emphasize the ongoing material change of the record, through processes like sea level rise.[151] To take Walker's point further, what is striking about Anthropocene narratives is the way they tend to characterize the Earth as a legible text, even though other aspects of anthropogenic climate change are much more turbulent. As I have written previously, we might even consider anticipated mass extinction events, the melting of glacial ice records, ocean acidification leading to the destruction of coral reefs, and more as instances of "negative mediation" that do not fit into the imaginary of strata as text—a point that geologists would be the first to acknowledge.[152] The materiality of these other processes is not so much about sedimentation but about disappearance, saturation, erasure, melting, and other complex chemistries.

If we try to think from the point of view of the Hawaiian bobtail squid, acknowledging (as Flusser does in *Vampyroteuthis Infernalis*) that it is within our human frame and categories that we encounter it, what would inscription look like as a relational and ecological event? Consider how the Hawaiian bobtail squid's cloaking ability involves acquiring the microbe *V. fischerii* from seawater before the squid reaches maturity. Juvenile squid regulate which bacteria (only *V. fischerii*) can enter special ducts in their body, and the bacteria then trigger changes in the development of the light organ. These genetic and developmental changes might be seen as a form of inscription on the body, similar to how Flusser imagines genetic storage when the vampire squid inscribes a memory on another. Yet in the case of *V. fischerii*, such inscription is not meant to store a memory but instead (to borrow a phrase from Bishnupriya Ghosh) results in a form of "multispecies accommodation," enacting genetic changes that make the squid a slightly better home for the bacteria in exchange for light production.[153] Perhaps the Hawaiian bobtail squid and *V. fischerii* model a way of thinking about inscription in terms of Harawavian sympoeisis rather than unidirectional authorship, a relationship that we could only know about from those who wade into moonlit waters with nets and a waiting microscope in their laboratory. What the sympoeisis of the Hawaiian bobtail squid and *V. fischerii* teaches us to look for is not "Earth writing" in the Anthropocene but rather forms of multispecies accommodation whose choreography might be disrupted by the accelerations of global climate change.

However, the Anthropocene prompts another milieu-specific question about the ocean. If the Anthropocene conceives of historical accumulation in terms of strata, can the ocean have history or be history in the same away? Or does the ocean introduce new ways of considering the ontology of the archive that do not follow a terrestrial sense of a hard substrate that bears enduring marks? In the next chapter, I submerge the concept of "database" in the ocean to test the differences between how it has been imagined in computational contexts compared with the ocean as a milieu of storage.

DATABASE / Proteus and the Digital

There is a quiet place under 120 feet of water off the sandy shores of North Carolina where the remains of the submarine *U-352* rest.[1] The U-boat was sunk by the Coast Guard in 1942 and attracts giant clouds of fish, rays, and sand tiger sharks—toothy, but docile. Diving the wreck from a boat requires slowly moving down a yellow descent line, hand over hand, until you arrive at the main hull of the ship. On a normal tank of air, you only have about twenty minutes to spend exploring, since you use air much more quickly on deeper dives. Another yellow rope spans the length of the ship, giving you something to hold onto in case the current is particularly strong. As you glide around the wreck, you may be surprised at both the resilience of the ship's structure and its decay—gaps in the hull that have rusted away and a whole rainbow of life that has colonized its surface in thick fleshy crusts—orange and pink reliefs that you could never chisel off without taking away the remaining metal. It would be easy to think of a shipwreck contained "in" the ocean, as if the ocean were a giant storage vault for the remains of history—a topic to which I return in chapter 4. Yet what I saw all around *U-352* was a demonstration of how the medium of seawater itself actively grows new life-forms on sunken ships, replacing and erasing the traces of what once was. What is the ocean, then—a medium of change, or a storage medium for the preservation of sunken objects?

One literary work that famously dramatizes this tension between the ocean as quiet archive of the past and seawater as a radical force of material transformation is Shakespeare's play *The Tempest*. In Act 1, scene 2, the spirit Ariel famously sings about Ferdinand's drowned father, a result of Prospero's storm. In its description of what happened to the body, the song characterizes seawater as a substance that simultaneously archives and reconfigures:

> *Full fathom five thy father lies;*
> *Of his bones are coral made;*
> *Those are pearls that were his eyes:*
> *Nothing of him that doth fade,*
> *But doth suffer a sea change*
> *Into something rich and strange.*[2]

Like the poetic form of the blazon, Ariel's song attends not the whole body but only parts: eyes and bones, turned to pearls and coral. Yet the song avoids the imagery of corporeal decay and instead imagines the magical transformation—a "sea change"—of the paternal body, stored in the vault of the ocean. As Ian Baucom writes, "Subjectivity, here, endures not a liquidation but a liquefaction. It fades but is not extinguished."[3] Seawater demonstrates its agency as a transformative and creative element that reconfigures sunken bodies, which, for Steven Mentz, "captures the force, physical and metaphoric, of salt-water transfiguring flesh."[4] Ariel's picture of "a sea change" thus embodies the contradiction of seawater as both a storage medium and a transformative force that changes bodies.

This seeming contradiction in the poetic imagination of seawater has, for my purposes, something to teach us about how we think about figurations of databases today.[5] Many theories of media storage assume a default environment of air (for computational storage) and substrate of hard substrates (like tree rings, or geologic strata). Following *Wild Blue Media*'s method of "conceptual displacement," this chapter submerges our conceptions of databases underwater to explore how our expectations of databases change when we assume that their normative environment is the ocean rather than air. Imagining a database in oceanic environmental conditions produces an estrangement effect that makes visible the kind of figurative language that we would normally use to describe media technologies, what

FIGURE 3.1 Microsoft lowers "the cloud" into the Pacific Ocean, 2015.

we value about stable information storage, and what we desire of our media technologies. Once submerged, we might ask: What do databases retain or emulate of the materiality of seawater, and what computational properties might persist in the genetic soup of the ocean? To what extent is the logic of the database compatible with oceanic materiality?

Of course, moments of contact between databases and any liquid (a cup of spilled tea, for example) would usually fry circuits and destroy information. Indeed, the transformative properties of seawater seem antithetical to technical databases and the stable, long-term storage of information. Oceanic immersion of computer databases might be expected, then, to operate on a principle of separation between liquid and digital data, lest seawater damage electronic circuitry. One example that demonstrates this necessary separation of seawater and server is Microsoft's 2016 Project Natick (figure 3.1). Since data centers generate a massive amount of heat, they depend on air-conditioning for their very functionality.[6] Aiming to put the "cloud in [the] ocean for the first time," Microsoft's research team speculated that the ocean could solve the problem of cooling: submersing the container in cold Pacific waters would provide "natural" air-conditioning and, potentially, a source of energy from the movements of waves, tides, or currents. One engineer who had worked in the navy for three years on submarines reflected, "What helped me bridge the gap between datacenters and underwater is that I'd seen how you can put sophisticated electronics under water, and keep it shielded from salt water."[7] The success of the experiment depended on keeping the server hermetically sealed, as seawater would have fried the circuits inside. Although there was certainly a watery "footprint" in the production of the technology (what Joanna Zylinska calls "hydromedia"), Microsoft's submerged cloud does not represent a fusion of information and ocean; the ocean and the database may share a wall, but they must not mix.[8]

Even if the literal submergence of data servers in the ocean requires isolation and protection from seawater, there exists a pattern of figurative language that connects information technologies with water and fluidity. For example, information technologies are frequently described through watery verbs: surfing the web, flows of information, seas of data. The metaphor "information is water" characterizes this assumed equivalency, which saturates contemporary discussions of information technology. The language of fluidity operates as both a verb (information *flows*) and a teleological desire (information technologies should become more fluid). Yet "flow" describes a kind of movement rather than any specific substance. Zygmunt Bauman's diagnosis of an underlying ontological fluidity of technology and modernity shares this sense of abstract fluidity.[9] A more milieu-specific theory would disarticulate abstract "fluidity" from material specificity of "seawater," whose irreducibly biological and chemical composition makes it a powerful agent of transfiguration in life and in the imagination.[10] However, the language of fluidity still has its real-world effects; by setting up water and data to share a natural equivalence or interchangeability, ecological descriptive imagery naturalizes digital technologies and processes.[11]

There has indeed been a persistent trend to characterize databases and oceans in terms of each other. In one view, as described above, computer databases are ocean-like in their ability to present information in nonlinear flows, enabling readers to "surf" content. In another view, the ocean is a natural database that stores the genetic material of microbes and viruses. As I will show, these two views—the ocean as genetic database and the database as an ocean of information—have tended to reinforce a pattern of mutual characterization, of the ocean as always already full of "data" and data/information as always already "fluid." This is similar to a theoretical move in environmental media studies, which has been to view media as environments and environments as forms of media. Both critical approaches utilize simile (through the grammatical structure of "as"), such that one term is seen through another (media as environment, database as ocean, etc.).

My concern is not to prove or disprove how the ocean is or is not like a database but to compare the discursive and material imaginations of databases and oceans, considering moments where watery description and oceanic materiality seem to align and differ. This chapter traces how theories of database aesthetics have drawn on the ocean and the language of fluidity in metaphorical registers to describe digital storage. Focusing on two interactive databases, Google Ocean and ATLAS *in silico*, I show how both works purport to simulate the ocean but actually feature strong terrestrial aesthetics and formal qualities. Through a close analysis of their representational choices and form, I demonstrate how both visualizations push the metaphor of informatic fluidity, a metaphor that encourages us to see the ocean as always already a database and genomic databases as always already fluid. However, both visualizations translate vastly different scales of oceanic materiality: Google Ocean simulates the whole ocean, while ATLAS *in silico* simulates flows of oceanic microbes. Drawing on theories of scale and aesthetics, I argue for the importance of considering a "perceptual aesthetics of scale," sensitive to the scalar properties of seawater. Through this discussion of scale, I show how interactive databases like ATLAS *in silico* and Google Ocean channel only some oceanic properties over others and how matters of scale determine seawater's relation to database logic. The chapter concludes by imagining what it would mean to cultivate a Protean database aesthetic, chemical and transfigurative in the sense of Ariel's song about sea change.

Swimming in Seas of Data: An Aquarium Logic

At its most basic definition, a database is a structured set of data organized to facilitate information retrieval and searches.[12] Analog databases include dictionaries or library catalogs that you can handle and flip through, while digital databases store information on hard drives as ones and zeros. A common misconception is that analog refers to physical storage and digital refers to a kind of immaterial storage. Yet digital databases have physical components as well: the hardware they are stored on, and the electronic polarities that encode ones and zeroes. To describe digital computers, Katherine Hayles offers the metaphor of an Oreo cookie "with an analogue bottom, a frothy digital middle, and an analogue top."[13] Hayles notes that early computers using base ten "were digital not because they used binary code but because they used discrete bit streams"; in contrast, analog computers "represent numbers as a continuously varying voltage."[14] Digital simply means "discrete" (as when a waveform is sampled at set intervals in digital recording), whereas analog means "continuous" (like the ongoing inscription of sound waves on a vinyl record).

Scholars working in the digital humanities often struggle with the relationship between the materiality of their archival objects and the structure of organizing them in a digital database. Regarding the English Broadside Ballad Archive (EBBA), Patricia Fumerton reflects that Broadside Ballads "can be as slippery and multiple in their transformations as Proteus. It takes a team of scholars constantly conferring and passing on their expertise as in an oral tradition of old to tackle and grab hold of ballad ephemera."[15] In Fumerton's characterization of the archive as "protean," the sea god Proteus is—importantly—a single being who changes form. Other cultural imaginations of the *protean* (adj.) rather than *Proteus* (n.) allude to the evolutionary diversity of form among many bodies. For example, Proteus lends his name to the biological kingdom "Protists," which include the radiolaria that nineteenth-century biologist Ernst Haeckel famously studied. In the film *Proteus* (2005), director David Lebrun celebrated Haeckel's thousands of radiolarian illustrations and their diversity of form, specifically through sequences that quickly flashed individual illustrations into an animated sequence, accompanied by a staccato piano/violin duet. The question, then, is whether Proteus refers to a malleable trickster that we (as Menelaus) must wrestle into a stable form, or whether Proteus/the protean stands for a more general multiplicity of potential forms made possible by the ocean environment. The answer depends on the process one wants to describe, and which agent(s) one wishes to highlight—a human intentionally shaping the form of the database, or a plurality of forms emerging independently of human architectural agency. The difference between human agency and seawater agency is thus key to understanding how the ocean environment radicalizes our conception of the database.

One characterization of the database as a kind of "ocean" navigated by a human agent emerges in Grahame Weinbren's article "Ocean, Database, Recut" in *Database Aesthetics*. Weinbren celebrates the "multilinear" structure of databases over the "linear" structure of most print-based narratives and cinema. [16] Using Salman Rushdie's fantastical ocean moon (a literal sea of stories) from the novel *Haroun and the Sea of Stories* as a conceptual example, Weinbren argues that Rushdie's ocean "fulfills two basic criteria of the database: (1) it is composed of smaller elements, the story currents; and (2) it can be traversed in a multiplicity of ways."[17] Here, "the elements of the Ocean database are stories," where, metaphorically, "the swimming user affects the narrative currents and their meaning," much like choose-your-own-adventure narratives.[18] Through the figure of the "swimming user," Weinbren focuses on the structural richness of databases as storytelling structures to be navigated and organized by human shapers. To build on Manovich's earlier arguments about the relation between narrative and database, the role of narrative here appears as a way of "traversing" the database.[19] Such a view linking databases and navigation hearkens back to the etymological roots of cybernetics, which draw from the Greek words for both governance and (in an ocean metaphor) steersmanship.[20]

Yet as distinct material environments, oceans and digital databases structure very different possibilities for agency. For Weinbren, the "swimming user" changes, selects, and extracts the narrative "currents" and stories. In this conception of agency, the human user is the creative force of organization (like Menelaus), selecting data and ordering them (Proteus). However, a milieu-specific consideration of the materiality of seawater shows how Weinbren's model reproduces only some characteristics of the ocean over others, such as its function as a reservoir or storage space. Other properties of seawater like viscosity (degree of fluid "thickness") do not translate as well into his database analogy.[21] The "swimming user" is never imagined to face any resistance or friction from the ambient water or currents; furthermore, the stories in Weinbren's database ocean do not mutate or cross-contaminate—they retain their form. No matter what environmental language or metaphors are used to describe databases, a human user is still imagined to be in control of a stable set of data.[22]

Ariel's song from *The Tempest* suggests a different model of agency, where seawater changes what it touches, rusting, encrusting, and gestating free-floating larvae on any sunken objects or bodies. With the open system of the ocean, objects do not persist in their original state but change over time through their immersion in seawater. If this more gestational sense of the ocean's materiality informed a database aesthetic (beyond fluidity alone), then the user would not be the only force of organization: data would change or even change each other during circulation, before a storyteller or user could draw on them.[23] Beginning with seawater as the creative and organizational agent would mean having us—the interpellated human users—relinquish control over the conditions of storage. This is a point that emerges when thinking milieu specifically with seawater and on which I elaborate in chapter 4.

In addition to fluidity, another point of comparison between databases and aquatic environments has to do with screens and frames. Because digital databases are mediated by the interface of a computer screen—a rectangular frame—the figure of the aquarium is visually appropriate to name databases that aim to catalog and manage the ocean (particularly in Google Ocean and ATLAS *in silico*, which I discuss below). Here I draw inspiration from Gísli Pálsson's discussion of modernist regimes of Icelandic ocean management in terms of "the birth of a gigantic aquarium."[24] Drawing a clear connection with Michel Foucault's *Birth of the Clinic*, Pálsson describes a hierarchy of knowledge that places scientists and their knowledge as outside managers above fishermen, who are positioned "inside, along with whales and fish and other inhabitants of the aquarium."[25] Unlike the vast expanse of the high seas, wild and unpredictable, "aquariums are human constructs, designed and managed for human purposes."[26] An aquarium logic can, then, describe the treatment of the ocean as a finite space of management, subject to prediction and control, by humans who see themselves as outside the aquarium itself. The frame of the computer screen coincides with the rectangular frame of aquaria, providing a visual continuity between practices of collecting aquatic specimens in watery and digital milieu.

The Moorea Biocode project exemplifies such an aquarium logic, where the computer substitutes for oceanic storage of genetic information for the purposes of scientific research and species management. Begun in 2007, the project aims to establish "a library of genetic markers and physical identifiers for every species of plant, animal, and fungi on the island of Moorea," an island in French Polynesia.[27] Referred to in one article as "Moorea's Ark," the endeavor participates in a long tradition of taking the island as an isolated site for both preservation and experimentation.[28] By channeling the biblical imagery of Noah and the Flood, the

Moorea Biocode Project establishes the database itself as a kind of "ark" that could hold genetic data extracted from the unstable database of the fluid ocean. The ark links the Moorea Biocode Project to much earlier histories of curiosity cabinets and species collection, which informed nineteenth-century interest in aquariums.[29] However, abstraction plays a key role in the Moorea Biocode Project, reducing fully fleshed organisms to their DNA. Oceanic microbes and viruses become translated into—or better, remediated by—the database, as a surrogate storage medium for genetic information.

The Moorea Biocode Project raises an important context for why it is important to study oceans in relation to databases today: the issue of biodiversity loss and impending species extinctions. The intensification of anthropogenic and climate change effects—such as ocean warming, ocean acidification, plastic pollution, and overfishing—form the subconscious of many data collection projects. For example, Maya Lin's last memorial, titled *What Is Missing?*, takes the elegiac form of a digital database to draw attention to the problem of decreasing biodiversity.[30] Yet what biodiversity "is" depends on how it is measured and counted. In *Memory Practices in the Sciences*, Jeffrey Bowker complicates the idea that information is simply "out there" in the environment by contrasting two very different types of information collection: ecological diversity and biodiversity. Data collection for ecological studies entails the long-term study of a few sites, whereas data collection for biodiversity studies entails large systemic surveys, or snapshots. These conflicting spatial and temporal parameters have led to problems with standardizing databases since "the data comes in two incompatible flavors, with different scientific approaches."[31] In this way, "strategies for both data collection and habitat management are intimately wrapped up in ontological questions about what kind of thing biodiversity is," yet ironically, "while computer memory is happily outpacing Moore's law, the information-carrying capacity of the earth (in the form of genetic information in species) is diminishing at an inverse exceptional rate."[32]

More public-facing biodiversity databases have focused on photographic images, such as the Census of Marine Life, a ten-year project to survey the ocean's organisms. The Census of Marine Life produced three hardcover books and an interactive website, with a strong reliance on photographic imagery to both capture species and captivate audiences.[33] Stacy Alaimo describes its photographic impulse thus: "Species must be 'captured' in some way before they are lost forever."[34] The website's homepage itself looks like a series of nested aquariums, with differently sized boxes featuring sea creature photographs, or themed links using the icon of a sea creature.

While species databases collect organisms through photographic capture, they might also produce wonder and estrangement. In *Imagining Extinction*, Ursula Heise discusses the potential of endangered species databases like ARKive—a visual database that contains portraits of animals—to highlight the beauty and strangeness of a variety of organisms, and thus create a form of critical distance or defamiliarization. Heise writes, "This goal [of defamiliarization] is quite different from the aims of other databases that seek to convey information and thereby to encourage familiarity rather than the estrangement that ARKive's mission statement implies."[35] The frame of the picture—or frame of an aquarium—might enact a form of species capture but also serve to productively defamiliarize it.

Species databases involve vast transformations of scale and materiality, resizing the ocean into representational models calibrated to human proportions and sensory dispositions. This raises an important question: to what extent does scale matter for thinking with the materiality of seawater? We know that very small organisms like water striders (*Gerridae* family of insects) have microscopic leg hairs that increase local surface tension and enable them to walk on water. In chapter 1, I discussed how James Blish dramatized aquatic surface tension in his science fiction story by the same name, in which microscopic humans living in a puddle cannot pass through the surface tension of water because of nanoscale effects, finally engineering a "supermarine" (rather than submarine) ship to break through. Macroorganisms, of course, have no problem splashing through the surface. Rendering seawater in digital representations involves representational choices about the assumed scale of water, and the scale of the observer. Water's properties change, depending on the relative size of the entity interacting with it. Timothy Clark has called this important difference in material properties across scales of relation "scale effects": "Non-cartographic concepts of scale are not a smooth zooming in and out but involve jumps and discontinuities with sometimes incalculable 'scale effects.'"[36] Clark uses "scale effects" to talk not only about size but also intensity: for example, an activity (like Western levels of consumption) may not make a difference on a small scale, but if every nation consumed resources at the rate of the West, then the climate would warm at an exponentially faster rate. Zooming or jumping between scales too quickly can result in forms of "derangement"—for example, "A poster in many workplaces depicts the whole earth as a giant thermostat dial, with the absurd but intelligible caption 'You control climate change.' A motorist buying a slightly less destructive make of car is now 'saving the planet.'"[37] Despite the illogicity of these examples of derangement, Clark finds "derangement" to be a productive effect when it intentionally highlights the differences *between* scales rather than collapsing everything into one abstract scale. He encourages literary scholars to creatively derange a text "through embedding it in multiple and even contradictory frames at the same time."[38] This formulation positions the critic as a kind of science fiction writer, if we liken "derangement" to Darko Suvin's definition of science fiction as the genre of "cognitive estrangement."[39] What remains to be considered, however, is the environment within which we consider a particular scale. If scale (from *scala*, Latin for "ladder") has to do with levels of analysis, what kind of scale effects might take place in an aquatic environment versus an aerial environment? How smooth or jarring would it be to shift scales between the elements?

The science fictional challenge raised by this chapter is to defamiliarize the database by imagining it in the specificities of an oceanic milieu, and thus to produce moments of estrangement that make us aware of our situated knowledge as terrestrial beings. In what follows, I consider the role of the zoom by attending to materiality, friction, and orientation. Focusing on case studies of two oceanic databases—Google Ocean and ATLAS *in silico*—I consider the kinds of aquatic materialities that are lost in the process of translating (rendering, remediating) the ocean into a digital map, data repository, or articulating it as a medium. Where can we see evidence of terrestrial mapping practices within simulations of oceanic immersion? In what ways do these visualizations assume that oceans are databases, or that databases are oceanic, and how might we trace the abstractions or figurations that make this interchangeability possible?

Google Ocean: The Terrestrial Bias in Database Aesthetics

While at a press conference in Spain in 2006, the renowned ocean scientist and activist Dr. Sylvia Earle (whom I discuss extensively in chapter 1) told the creators of Google Earth that their project was missing something: "I had a chance publicly to say how much I love Google Earth. 'My children,

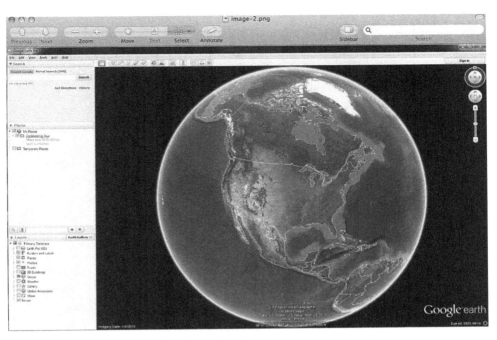

FIGURE 3.2 Screenshot of Google Earth interface, 2014.

my grandchildren think it is great to see their backyard, fly through the Grand Canyon, visit other countries,' I said. 'But, John, when are you going to finish it? You should call Google Earth "Google Dirt." What about the ¾ of the planet that is blue?'"[40] Earle worked with Google's team to add an "explore the ocean layer" to Google Earth, released in 2009, allowing viewers to explore the contours of both mountains and seafloor (figure 3.2). The ocean layer would not only assist with Google Earth's aspirations to become a more complete and totalizing representation of the planet but also remind viewers of just how much of Earth's surface is covered by the seas. As Arthur C. Clarke famously noted, "How inappropriate to call this planet Earth when it is quite clearly Ocean."[41]

Scholars in the field of geography have echoed Earle's sentiments about the underrepresentation of the ocean. Building on Philip Steinberg's *The Social Construction of the Ocean*, Jon Anderson and Kimberly Peters point out that the prefix (geo-) of geography has always exhibited a "sedentary metaphysics" attending to mainly human and terrestrial spaces of habitation. In *Water Worlds: Human Geographies of the Ocean*, they argue that geographers should "develop a new fluid language to understand our water world," moving from a *geography* to a *thalasso*graphy, or "ocean writing."[42] In this aspiration, they join other scholars of literature like Steven Mentz, who also writes about the possibility of thalassography in *At the Bottom of Shakespeare's Ocean* and his academic blog.[43] Through inventing new vocabulary and extending representational practices to seascapes, such scholars hope that the ocean will gain more critical attention both within the humanities and beyond. Yet would this shift in critical vocabulary be enough to address geographic terrestrial bias? If we had the words to describe the ocean, would this solve the problem of underrepresentation?

Part of the problem, in my view, has to do not only with vocabulary but with technologies of perception. As much as I admire and even agree with the sentiment within Earle's ambition to include the ocean in our (abstracted) total view of the planet, the foundation for Google Ocean is a mapping technology originally developed for visualizing land, a structural foundation that predetermines the range of possibilities for oceanic representation.[44] Furthermore, the idea that a new oceanic vocabulary would solve the problem of the ocean's underrepresentation does not take into consideration the fact that databases are constructed for human beings whose bodies and perceptual abilities are attuned to land. In *Imagining Extinction*, Heise notes how one biodiversity database, *The Encyclopedia of Life*, "molds itself after structures of human attention rather than patterns of biological life or ecological crisis alone," by inviting participation from average users that is not possible with more scientifically oriented databases.[45] The necessary anthropocentrism of creating databases and oceanic representations *for human beings* has specific implications for the design of visualizations like Google Ocean, including choice of coloration, the "layer" metaphor, the incorporation of "street view" underwater, and the play of gravity. By analyzing the terrestrial bias encoded within Google Ocean, my goal is not to produce a better vocabulary or visual means of representing the ocean but to be radically self-reflexive and show how a certain terrestrial bias persists within representations of the ocean, even as we willingly suspend disbelief to pretend that the representation is the ocean itself.

Colors train us where to look for details, focusing our attention in a way that predetermines what "matters." The ideological dimensions of such visual choices stand out when contrasted with more mischievous maps, such as Sanna Dullaway's visualization that inverts the colors—the land is a blank shade of blue, and the ocean basins textured with yellow, green, white, and brown—to create a photo "negative" of the norm (plate 5). One could argue that the coloration of the land is simply meant to reflect how most human beings see landscape color, where the sea is blue and the land is green. Yet as Phillip Vannini and Jonathan Taggart point out, Google's colors neglect the "processural qualities" of water as it changes with the seasons: "For Google Maps blue means water, and grey means land. Water, in turn, means lakes, rivers, and seas, whereas grey means earthly dirt." During Canadian winter, "grey and blue are nothing but white here. White everywhere."[46] In Google Ocean, it is convenient to always be summer.

The smooth, blank ocean map has a longer representational history dating back to the seventeenth century. As Steinberg writes in *The Social Construction of the Ocean*, "by the early 17th century, maps featuring sea monsters representing marine nature and ships representing social activity that transpired in the arena of ocean-space began to be replaced by maps portraying a grid over an essentially featureless ocean."[47] Steinberg connects this representational shift to the beginnings of industrial capitalism, precipitating the social construction of the ocean as a blank and empty space to be "traversed by atomistic ships."[48] This loss of sea monsters from maps coincided with the emergence of precise navigational practices enabled by the invention of the sea clock, which—crucially—enabled sailors to pinpoint their longitude.[49] Further, the clock became a key figure with which to interpret hydrographies for early oceanographer Matthew Fontaine Maury. As D. Graham Burnett notes, Maury described the currents as a "clockwork ocean" with regular and reliable inner workings, where the Gulf Stream acted like a "pendulum."[50] To see the ocean in terms of a technical object (the clock) foreshadows how science sees the ocean as a genetic database today; the database is simply a newer technology to enframe the workings of the ocean. The blankness of the sea in Google Ocean remains as an invitation to control, echoing the grid aesthetic that emerged in seventeenth-century mapping practices. However, the fact that each of the "layers" populates the ocean with a number of icons suggests a kind of hybrid form, merging the earlier sea-monster-populated maps and the advent of the grid aesthetic.

While Google Ocean's layers are a simple method of being able to selectively turn on and off content, they also form a sedimentary logic that underlies the entire system. Like geologic strata, the layers are part of

Google's Cartesian rendering of space as a container, able to turn on or off content in a way that does not affect the base map. On the left-hand navigation, users can choose to turn on a layer that makes icons and other content on the map appear. These layers include ARKive: Endangered Ocean Species, Explore the Oceans, Shipwrecks, Census of Marine Life, Cousteau Ocean World, Marine Protected Areas, Dead Zones, Animal Tracking, National Geographic, and Water Sports. The content of each layer might include information, photographs, video, or animations on the map itself. The hypermediacy of the layers—the way they embed a combination of text, images, video, and animation—functions much like the iconography of pre-seventeenth-century maps and their sea monsters, gesturing beyond the screen toward an ocean full of life that cannot be represented in its totality. Of course, icons can also indicate absences, as in the layer "Dead Zones." Oceanic "dead zones" are a common name for hypoxia, which indicates decreased amounts of dissolved oxygen in the water.[51] The "Dead Zones" layer uses icons of dead fish to annotate the larger map, indicating that a particular bay, harbor, or area of the sea lacks the amount of dissolved oxygen necessary to support sea life. Although the icon of the dead fish stands in for a process (deoxygenation), the process is not temporally marked with a start date anywhere, leaving the viewer to wonder what kind of duration the zone has had. Although individual layers like "Dead Zones" refer to more than a terrestrial materiality, the structure of layers operates according to a geologic of strata.

In addition to the aesthetic of layers, we can also locate an element of terrestrial bias in the way Google Ocean renders the experience of gravity and movement for the viewer. Consider Google Ocean's "normative point of view," or the scale and location in which the application opens. You see an image of the planet that fits within your screen frame, positioning you like a satellite, gazing down on North America. The terms *Archimedian standpoint, bomb's-eye view,* or *world target* have given name to this elevated viewpoint, denoting a particular position of power and a way of seeing the whole world as if from the perspective of a projectile bomb or orbiting object.[52] As we zoom into Google's ocean, we meet no resistance but see and hover clearly as if through perfectly clear air, or perhaps outer space. As Stefan Helmreich observes, Google Ocean does not model gravity; the world is rendered weightless and transparent, with "many watery materialities missing," such as the viscosity of seawater.[53] Through the way it facilitates the viewer's movements as if through flight and without friction, Google Ocean appears more like air (or outer space) than ocean.

However, the scalar effect of experiencing gravity changes when moving from satellite view to sea level view in layers like "Animal Tracking" (figure 3.3). In "Animal Tracking," you can see the route that a tagged marine animal swam (such as a great white shark) from a satellite perspective, and then click "play" to see an animation of the animal's route as if from its own perspective. The animation approximates a kind of Crittercam point of view, through what Donna Haraway calls "compounded eyes" (the viewers', the animal's, and the camera's) or the remora's view (an eye stuck to the side of an animal).[54] Yet whereas Crittercam footage tends to offer partial glimpses of the animal's body, in "Animal Tracking" the viewer lacks any representation of the animal's body. The animal itself is invisible, signified only by its movements, taking you along an automated path simulated by the hydrographic contours of Google's map. This automated path—based on GPS data taken from the animal's tracking device—can lead to either a smooth route (as with the fin whale) or a jagged, zig-zag motion (as with the great white shark) that can make the viewer feel disoriented and dizzy, as if on an amusement park ride.[55] In contrast to the frictionless "zoom" between scales in the rest of Google Ocean, the embedded media of "Animal Tracking" anchors the viewer to an embodied sense of motion bordering on nausea. However, the recorded data points in the animal's spatial position are characterized primarily by forward and lateral motion but not the vertical motion that Crittercam footage suggests when accompanying the dives of seals, whales, and turtles—footage that visually implies the experience of gravity (and buoyancy) in saltwater. Like the satellite view we see upon launching Google Ocean, the movement we experience in "Animal Tracking" seems more specific to air rather than water, although the tension between these two views—satellite and sea level—productively gestures toward the partiality of *any* mapping view.

In another example of Google Ocean's terrestrial basis, "Google Street View Oceans" takes a visualization technology developed for *streets* and uses it for the ocean (figure 3.4).[56] Google partnered with the insurance company XL Catlin to form Catlin Seaview Survey, creating underwater views with a technology borrowed from Google Maps for individual streets. Going a step further than the "Animal Tracking" layer (which

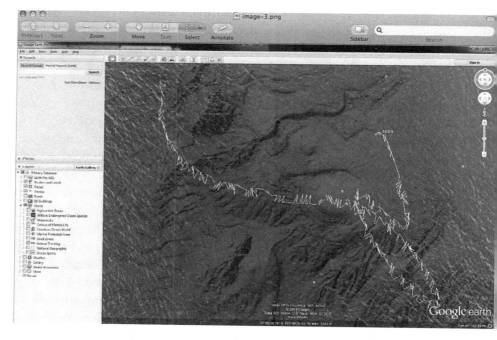

FIGURE 3.3 Screenshot of "Animal Tracking" layer of Google Ocean, featuring the migration data of a great white shark off the coast of California (route shown in white), 2014.

FIGURE 3.4 Screenshot of Google Street View Oceans, 2018.

simulated rather than photographed its linear pathways), Catlin wants to "scientifically record the world's coral reefs and reveal them to all in high-resolution, 360-degree panoramic vision."[57] The project began by surveying thirty-two reefs along the Great Barrier Reef in Australia and has now expanded globally to document a broad range of coral reefs. The documentation of reefs—and translation of the ocean into a navigable, three-dimensional digital space—aims to provide a baseline record of coral reef health in anticipation of future climate changes (such as coral bleaching events triggered by rising ocean temperatures).

Google Street View's gallery of ocean views looks exactly like a composite aquarium, each rectangle a different immersive "swim" adventure for viewers to explore. After selecting a view, you can drag the camera around to look in any direction, a full 360 degrees. However, once you choose to move your base position, you find yourself sliding not in the direction you pointed but along the nearest available (and invisible) street. Unlike in swimming—where one is free to move in any direction—the navigational experience is more like "island hopping" between predetermined points of view. Although Google Street View gives the illusion of being immersed in the ocean with the option to swim in any direction, it is in fact structured and constrained by the linearity of "streets" that cannot be seen but are only indicated by small arrows. Thus, Google Street View exhibits a terrestrial bias not so much in the properties of water it chooses to replicate but in the orientational pattern of "walking on streets" that it submerses into an aquatic context.

In sum, Google Ocean's coloration, simulation of gravity and movement, spatial logic of additive layers, and embedding of Street View demonstrate how very un-ocean-like it is. It is a translation of oceanic space into a digital representation that leaves many of the ocean's material properties behind, such as the friction and gestational qualities of seawater, as a way of streamlining human user interactivity. Although Google Ocean may visually look realistically "blue" to us, its navigational strategies in both satellite view and Street View belie a terrestrial bias, emulating the experience of walking on land, or flying through the air. In its mission to remediate the ocean into an interactive digital map, Google recalibrates its "street" views into a giant, digital, heterotopic aquarium space framed by computer screens. The terrestrial bias in Google Ocean's design is about not only representation but matters of orientation that borrow from terrestrial mapping technologies (Street View) or replicate features of aerial/outer space (frictionless zoom function). Google Ocean is not so much an ocean as it is a digital aquarium.

As a scalar point of contrast, the next section transports these questions about oceanic representation and navigation from the planetary/macroscale of Google Ocean to the nanoscale of microbial DNA in the data visualization ATLAS *in silico*. ATLAS draws on a logic of ocean as genetic database while composing its own scale-dependent choices of representing seawater. As we will see, each scale of representing water has what I call its own "perceptual aesthetics," which also entail shifts in orientational possibilities. This opens the possibility of comparing the milieu-specific possibilities of orientation within the ocean and databases, at different scales of relation.

ATLAS *in Silico*: Digital Oceans and Flows of Information

Sailing around the world aboard the yacht *Sorcerer II*, J. Craig Venter—former lead of the Human Genome Project—had a goal for his Global Ocean Survey: to extract microbial genomes from the ocean into "a rich, distinctive data repository," accessible to scientists from around the world.[58] The Global Ocean Sampling (GOS) project aimed to provide a snapshot of ocean's genome circa 2006. Like all good snapshots, this one would not move: the genomic data extracted from marine microbes would be stable across time, inscribed into its new digital home—a transmutation of living bodies into readable data. Although critiqued by marine microbiologists for "random sampling" at midlatitudes rather than standardizing sampling at specific times, depths, and seasonality, the data collected by Venter's expedition has been made available on two databases: the Community Cyberinfrastructure for Advanced Microbial Ecology Research and Analysis (CAMERA), an online resource for marine metagenomics; and UCSD's division of the California Institute for Telecommunications and Informational Technology (Calit2).[59] As a device for capturing images, CAMERA seems a fitting name. Walter Benjamin famously compared the photographer to the surgeon, cutting into the linear flow of time to isolate a moment.[60] Similarly, the Global Ocean Sampling project's method of shotgun sequencing literally and figuratively "cut" microbial genetic material out of the body of the ocean and into a large soup, later to be iso-

FIGURE 3.5 User interacting with ATLAS *in silico*. Each particle in the stream is a fragment of Global Ocean Survey data, represented by "shape grammar" (middle image) that the user can select, revealing information about where the data was collected. Image courtesy of Ruth West.

lated in a newly crafted database of silicon. As we will see, Venter's CAM-ERA database also performs acts of cutting by isolating microbial genomic data from both the living bodies of microbes and the seawater in which they lived, as a necessary step toward scientific study and manipulation.

The collaborative artwork ATLAS *in silico* draws from Venter's dataset with the aim of making the data more interactive and relatable to the public, specifically through an interface designed to look like the deep sea. Imagine bright blue freeways of data particles streaming across an inked black background of multiple, stacked computer screens (figure 3.5). The dark room creates the feeling of space exploration. Each particle of light stands for "one data record describing a unique protein sequence from the GOS [global ocean survey] data," or one snapshot of microbial genome cut off from the living body.[61] Particles are also referred to as "open-reading frames," the predicted amino acid (protein) sequences of microbial DNA. The reason the sequences are "predicted" is because of Venter's method of "shotgun" sequencing that relies on algorithmically assembling millions of DNA fragments into amino acid sequences. Each particle circulates in a three-dimensional flow, as if highlighting oceanic currents.

ATLAS *in silico* not only shifts the scale of the microbes up to human

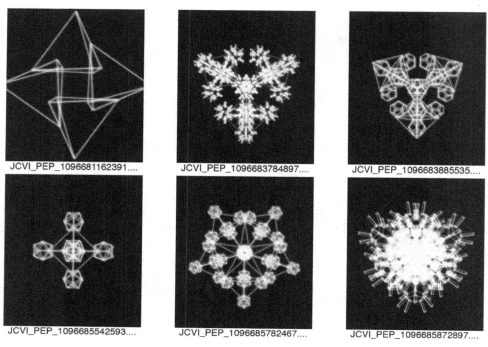

JCVI_PEP_1096681162391....

JCVI_PEP_1096683784897....

JCVI_PEP_1096683885535....

JCVI_PEP_1096685542593....

JCVI_PEP_1096685782467....

JCVI_PEP_1096685872897....

FIGURE 3.6 Examples of the randomly generated "shape grammar" that stand in for unique protein sequences. Image courtesy of Ruth West.

size but also reciprocally shifts the human down to the scale of (predicted) protein sequences. Through both visual and audio feedback (of sounds that relate to viewer position and selected content), ATLAS *in silico* allows for haptic interactivity, putting abstract microbial genomic data in relation to a human scale. Participants can select particles that then enlarge to become "luminous three-dimensional objects that reveal their story in multiple layers of information that intertwine biology, with its social, environmental and metadata contexts," such as salinity and the depth at which they were collected.[62] The "life-size rendering" of the genetic information into a symbolic body ("shape grammar") appears at scale and size that we can view, interpret, and manipulate for the purpose of detecting patterns in the data (figure 3.6).[63] The collaborators write that ATLAS *in silico* allows for "an open-ended auditory data-mining process in hopes of revealing unknown or unpredicted features through the formation of emergent patterns."[64] The artwork not only renders intelligible the mi-

croscopic but speculatively allows human viewers to imagine themselves
immersed in the world of microbes.

It would seem that ATLAS *in silico* presents an innovative and engaged
example of thinking with the materiality of seawater, largely due to its
choice of life-forms (microbes). Microbes can pass on genes to their off-
spring or laterally transfer genes to each other, making them ideal candi-
dates for transcription into an atlas. In *Alien Ocean*, Helmreich describes
the way that marine microbes are often characterized as "living machines."[65] In ATLAS *in silico*, marine microbes are fragmented as informatics particles, manipulable by humans with a variety of research agendas
concerning the origin, evolution, and replication of life. It would be tempt-
ing to say that ATLAS *in silico* represents a way of thinking through the fluidity of microbial genetic information as it is shared in the ocean, as available and constantly circulating within microbe populations themselves.

However, ATLAS *in silico* focuses on a very specific materiality: not the
materiality of seawater as a whole, with its composite chemical and biological properties, or even the full bodies of microbes but the microbial genomic material *extracted* from seawater. Our access to the microbial
genomic data is not direct but transformed across scales, mediums, and
technologies of intelligibility. Indeed, ATLAS *in silico*'s microbes have un-
dergone multiple "transductions" or material conversions from seawater,
to a ship, to shotgun-sequenced DNA fragments, to information in a database, to shape grammar in the final artwork.[66] This practice is not only
a matter of transduction but also a matter of erasure of the bodies of the
microbes, whose genetic data has been liquefied by the process of sequencing. As Stacy Alaimo writes in her analysis of Venter's voyage, which provided the parent data set of ATLAS *in silico*: "Despite the extreme trans-
mogrifications of the microbes, there seems to be no worry that anything
is lost, misread, or radically altered in this transformation from life to
data. . . . The beauty of code, supposedly, is that it floats free of messy materiality, intact and uncompromised."[67] There is no suggestion of a "man-
gling of practice," to use Andrew Pickering's term for the realism of messy
scientific work, and instead only a presumed clean code.[68]

ATLAS *in silico* provides an occasion to consider how the scale of data
matters for thinking materially with water. Because ATLAS *in silico* uses
microbial genetic sequences extracted from seawater and deals with seawater on a microscale, it argues for a conceptual commensurability between the ocean and digital data. This poetics only works through an

analogy at the microscopic level, given that seawater does not demonstrate the same properties as it does on a macroscopic level (encrusting and transfiguring large objects) that we see in *The Tempest*. With microbial DNA fragments, change is conceived of not as transfiguration (*The Tempest*) but as rearrangement. The logic of digitality appears commensurate with seawater only when microbial DNA fragments stand in for seawater. The DNA fragments have been scaled down to units of exchange that cannot be transfigured by seawater in the same way large objects can (like Ferdinand's father in *The Tempest*); instead, participants can interactively recombine them.

Similarly, ATLAS *in silico* considers the ocean as always already a natural database of the genetic material of marine microbes.[69] This biopolitical figuration portrays seawater as a kind of biotechnical soup, first abstracted down to its informatic solute (microbes), and then abstracted again down to only part of the microbes (fragments of protein sequences). ATLAS *in silico*'s materiality also depends on whether we consider the DNA fragments as part of the water or as solute that is suspended in seawater. In the installation itself, fluid dynamics equations animate the movement of the blue dots, and one could argue that they are more the precipitate than the water. What is seawater, what is sediment? Is information atomistic, akin to a stream of sand, or does it belong to its fluid suspension?

On a material level, the element of silicon links microbial bodies with the digital technologies, since silicon is widely present in the internal structures of both diatoms and computer hardware. Viewed in this way, ATLAS *in silico* experiments with the materiality of seawater through its metareflection on the substance of silicon. In his famous "Gaia hypothesis," James Lovelock discusses how the sea is dominated by protista such as diatoms, whose skeletal walls are made of opal, "a special gem-like form of silicon dioxide, usually known as silica, the main constituent of sand and quartz. Silicon is one of the most abundant elements in the Earth's crust; most rocks, from clay to basalt, contain it in combined form. It is not generally considered of importance in biology—there is little silicon in us or in anything we eat—but it is a key element in the life of the sea."[70] The microbes (reduced to genomic data) of ATLAS *in silico* appear reincarnated in new silicon avatars: the array of computers and LCD screens, a journey from silicon to silicon. Yet a crucial difference between the fluidity of microbial genetic information in the wild and in the database is that ATLAS puts the human at the center of the installation. As with Grahame

Weinbren's "swimming user," the user of ATLAS *in silico* selects, organizes, and finds patterns within a database. Unlike actual seawater, the data in the database itself does not autonomously recombine and evolve on its own but constitutes a set of building blocks for future observers to play with; the protean force of seawater is frozen in place. As Lorraine Daston and Peter Galison write, atlases "simultaneously assume the existence of and call into being communities of observers who see the same things in the same ways."[71] Thus, although ATLAS *in silico* uses fluid dynamics equations, this only models a *generic* fluidity; it does not represent a truly protean aesthetic of engaging the chemical force of seawater.

Yet can computers be oceans? The field of Artificial life (A-Life) seems to say yes, aiming not simply to represent life but to simulate the *evolutionary* processes of microscopic life in computers. In Thomas Ray's early simulation *Tierra*, computer scientists "evolved" self-replicating algorithms inside computer memory, involving processes of both growth and rearrangement.[72] A-Life takes the computer as a world in which simplistic, virtual creatures may emerge, compete with each other for resources (memory space for replication), and eventually die out according to a separate series of algorithms, or rules of the virtual world. Separate algorithms constitute the virtual "creatures" that are regarded by some people as mere simulation and by others as an instantiation of real life itself. As Sarah Kember writes, the computer figures as an ocean of life: "The RAM [random access memory] of the virtual computer is referred to as the 'soup' in which the machine codes or 'self-replicating' algorithms 'live' as 'creatures.'"[73] In *Silicon Second Nature*, Helmreich compares the experience of visiting an A-Life conference and moving from one simulation to the next as similar to strolling "from one tank to another at a sea life museum."[74] Here the computer functions as a womb-like ocean, a matrix in both reproductive and computational senses of the term, where silicon substitutes for seawater. However, the same code functions as *both environment and organism*. Put another way, the only "environmental" factors in the A-Life computers are other organisms, continuing to propagate their internal structure. A-Life thus avoids the question of milieu by focusing primarily on the internal generation of organismal form; the "soup" of code is merely metaphorical.

Whereas A-Life incorporates a mechanism for evolution and change, other digital oceans often obfuscate lived ecologies. For example, in Nintendo Wii's Endless Ocean, fish do not age or die. Although the game

renders light underwater in a very convincing way, it does not integrate
principles of change underwater that might modify the landscape, distribution of organisms, or growth of organisms. Although these would be
complicated to render, the game nonetheless promotes the conception of
fish-as-commodities, collectible and domesticated, and underwater landscapes as unthreatened, stable places. As media theorist Alenda Y. Chang
writes, video games have the potential to model more meaningful ecologies: "We need game environments that respond to human agency and yet
seem to possess life independent of player actions: this would constitute a
radical but constructive decentering."[75] What would it look like for Endless Ocean to model an ecologically responsive game environment that
takes into consideration principles of protean change that are vital to seawater's materiality?

One digital artwork that seems to embody a seawater aesthetic of protean change is the Virtual Human Interaction Laboratory's simulation on
ocean acidification at Stanford University.[76] Seeking to educate the public
about the effects of ocean acidification—where the oceans slowly absorb
excess atmospheric carbon dioxide—Jeremy Bailenson and a group of re-
searchers designed a virtual reality simulation that placed the participant
in a Mediterranean coral reef.

> For the next 13 minutes, you become a pink coral among the dark pur-
> ple sea urchins, sea bream and sea snails that swarm around you. But
> by the end of the simulation—which fast-forwards to what the reef will
> look like at the end of this century—those brilliantly varied and col-
> orful species have disappeared and been replaced by slimy green algae
> and the silver Salema Porgy fish—a species that will likely thrive in the
> higher acidity. Eventually, your own coral skeleton disintegrates and
> you disappear. The rocky reef ecosystem has been destroyed. "If ocean
> acidification continues, ecosystems like your rocky reef, a world that
> was once full of biological diversity, will become a world of weeds," the
> narrator says.[77]

Part of the goal of the simulation is to see "how your personal carbon
footprint contributes to ocean acidification," in this case by asking you
to be a coral, and seeing what happens to the reef as acidification intensi-
fies (figure 3.7). In this way, Bailenson's virtual reality simulation seems
to embody a protean aesthetic, having viewers experience what it means
to immerse themselves in the changing nature of seawater over an accel-

FIGURE 3.7 Screenshot of Jeremy Bailenson's virtual reality simulation of how ocean acidification affects a coral reef. Here, arrows point to areas where "sea urchins disappear as the ocean becomes more acidic," 2015.

erated time scale, a speculative future. However, the simulation channels a neoliberal focus on changing the behavior of the individual rather than focusing on systems. The narrative of the simulation has a disciplinary function, couched as an ultimatum: if ocean acidification continues, then a world that was once full of biological diversity will become a world of weeds. Bailenson writes, "We've demonstrated [through other simulations] that either reading about a problem or watching a movie affects peoples' behavior less than having a person actually experience it virtually. More articles about climate change or documentary films—while educational— are unlikely to generate meaningful behavior change on a wide scale."[78] This is a tall claim, neglecting to specify *which* documentary or documentaries were shown and deemed unlikely to change behavior. Furthermore, it assumes that documentary films should be judged by their efficacy as tools for behavioral management rather than as art forms that might provoke reflection without prescribing behavioral solutions.

Although the urgency to address such a possible future is real, I think that the audience Bailenson aims for—the individual—is the wrong target, and an example of what Clark calls "derangements of scale." Rather than focusing on changing the behavior of consumers, Bailenson's simulation would do better to focus on the structural complexity of global carbon emissions. Instead of striving to coerce individuals (with the privilege to experience the 3-D technology) into changing their habits, the simulation could explore possible points of change or vulnerability that could shift the system. For example, it could consider how much of the economy would have to shift to renewable energy, or how much businesses would have to reduce energy consumption, to meaningfully lower carbon emissions. That said, Bailenson's simulation is a thoughtful example of an ocean visualization that actually incorporates the protean agency of seawater into a digital representation of the ocean.

Cultivating a Protean Archive

Each of the digital oceanic visualizations I have discussed here has, by necessity, chosen to emulate certain properties of seawater over others. Google Ocean and ATLAS *in silico* show that scale matters for thinking materially with seawater in ocean representations. On a macroscale, seawater's materiality is a creative and destructive force that sometimes reorganizes, sometimes diffuses, sometimes grows on what it touches, a principle that artists like Ruth Wallen and Jason deCaires Taylor have taken advantage of in their material artwork. Such a principle is missing from Google Ocean: other layers such as Shipwrecks, Census of Marine Life, ARKive, and National Geographic employ a sedimentary logic of accumulation such that you can always return to the objects, marked, at any time of day or after any duration of time—they will still be there. In other words, form does not follow content: while Google Ocean remains a valuable educational tool that may provoke interest and wonder for the public, the materiality of the seawater itself is lost in its digital remediation. The same disjuncture between form and content occurs on the microscale of ATLAS *in silico*, where a mirroring of form and content is made possible through abstractions (for instance, taking microbes out of seawater, and protein fragments out of the microbes). These abstractions enable a picture of an ocean that is compatible with the logic of exchange and digitality. Yet because such abstractions are always negotiated, explored, arranged, and played with by a human user, ATLAS *in silico* shares more with Weinbren's database aesthetics than with the creative autonomy of seawater itself. Part of what I diagnose, then, is the terrestrial bias of the tools and conceptual frameworks that participate in re-creating oceans as digital habitats. Imagining the database underwater pushes at the limits of our conceptions of media, asking us to think *milieu specifically* in terms of scale.[79]

However, thinking about scale in relation to oceanic environments concerns more than just the size of water particles and their realistic representation and/or movement; scale is also about phenomenology and orientation.[80] Scale fundamentally concerns how human observers sense and move within and through the world. As we saw in Google Ocean, a user can zoom into any scalar level regardless of a change in medium (air to water) or temperature (cold to hot). The zoom, then, produces an abstract experience of spatiality. A perceptual aesthetics of scale attends to the differences in how perception occurs for a particular observer.[81] As Joanna Zylinska writes, scale is "part of the phenomena it attempts to measure" rather than a separate metric that can be manipulated from the outside (as in an aquarium logic).[82] Databases not only represent oceanic environments, but are actively part of environments; the energy that it takes to maintain and cool them contributes carbon emissions, intensifying global climate change.

In the context of global climate change and species extinctions, scholars should consider how environmentally responsive databases might create meaningful forms of interaction that facilitate senses of care. At a panel stream I was part of several years ago, scholar-artist Jaime Skye Bianco responded to the polluted state of the Salton Sea in a performative talk combined with video footage, where she circulated a small tray of debris. When the tray passed to me, I looked in, noticing that there were many small barnacles. I was hit by a rotten, sulfurous odor. Guiltily, I quickly passed the tray on, reflecting that the Salton Sea had really made an unignorable effect that was compelling beyond visuals and sound. During the Q&A I asked about recording smell as part of the experience of documenting the Salton Sea, and Bianco replied by saying that by collecting debris from the site, she considered herself to be "cultivating an archive" with all its living bacteria rather than simply collecting or assembling one. In her case, "cultivate" not only was a metaphor but literally entailed misting her objects with water to maintain the odiferous bacterial colonies. I was struck by the potency of cultivation as a way of relating to one's archive that accounts for the way things might endure but also die, and that there must be effort on the part of the curator to continue the liveliness of the archive. Living records need maintenance.

Ruth Wallen's artwork *The Sea as Sculptress* (figure 3.8) perhaps best at-

FIGURE 3.8 Screenshot of Ruth Wallen's website for her 1978 work, *The Sea as Sculptress*, documenting the life-forms seasonally growing on planks of wood immersed in the San Francisco Bay. This macrophotograph portrays a nudibranch, common in May, as indicated by the chart at the bottom of the page.

tests to Bianco's aesthetic of cultivation, bridging seawater and digital materiality. Wallen took her earlier artwork from 1978—the macrophotographic documentation of wooden planks immersed in the San Francisco Bay, and their seasonal changes in life—and resituated these images on a website. This involved two acts of remediation: translating the sea's "sculptures" into photographic slides, from which she gave performative talks; and then more recently "digitizing over a thousand slides and creating an extensive web site as part of the Outdoor Exploratorium."[83] Wallen's work gestures toward the way that the ocean functions as co-artist or even co-scientist in the investigation of seasonal changes of ocean life, adhered to objects. Wallen writes, "As opposed to much of the land art of the time, which took the form of monumental earth works, I wanted to work on a small intimate scale," focusing on changes occurring on tiny areas of the wood.

Spanning art and science, Wallen's work speaks broadly to the way that human communities can work to cultivate an archive of life. Defining water quality expansively as "the flourishing of organisms living in estuary waters" rather than "the absence of pollution," Wallen offers a way of thinking complexly through an aesthetic of seawater and indexicality. The presence of certain organism populations ("indicator species" that serve as an index of health) not only attests to the livability of the bay waters; Wallen's photographs of these organisms also form an indexical relationship to the life they document. This double signification—of organisms signifying the health of waters, and photographs signifying the presence of the organisms—forms the precondition for the work's digital instantiation. Rather than erasing traces of mediation, the digital work involves a nesting of evidence: the digital points to the photographic, which points to the biological, which points to the overall health of the San Francisco Bay in the late 1970s. Even though its final form is not as interactive as ATLAS *in silico* in terms of bodily relation to data, or as exploratory and flexible across scales as the global navigation in Google Earth, *The Sea as Sculptress* incorporates seasonal and biological change, offering one possible way of cultivating a Protean database.

CHAPTER FOUR

UNDERWATER MUSEUMS

For many of us, museums bring to mind the sound of footsteps echoing off cold marble floors, vaulted rooms, and rare cultural objects on pedestals, not to be touched. In this space, lighting, temperature, and humidity are carefully controlled so as not to damage the fragile artworks and archaeological objects. The goal of preservation rules the museum, an archival environment that carefully separates observer from observed yet gathers them together for a shared visual spectacle. Viewers navigate museums bound by gravity, traversing the planar floors of exhibits at a level gaze determined by display choices.

The ocean provides entirely different conditions for thinking about the cultural role, composition, and space of museums. While the chill of the ocean sometimes preserves shipwrecks and cultural artifacts, at other times it seems to be more of an archival limit, washing away and erasing the traces of human lives. The poet Derek Walcott dramatizes this duality of oceanic preservation and reconfiguration in his poem "The Sea Is History," which considers the material traces of the transatlantic slave trade registered by the seafloor. Inviting the reader to "strop on these goggles" to see below the surface, Walcott tells a story of how the "grey vault" of the sea has "locked up" the monuments, martyrs, battles, and tribal memory of struggle—obscured and hidden them away from ter-restrial view at sea, as many Africans were thrown overboard.[1] Dwelling in the depths with these drowned bodies, the poem notes "white cowries clustered like manacles / on the drowned women" and "plucked wires / of sunlight on the sea floor," where multispecies life (cowries as manacles) and the environment (sunlight as wire) evoke the carceral imagery of the slave trade.[2] Through conjuring an amphibious vision mediated by the technology of goggles, Walcott positions the reader to see the history of the transatlantic slave trade at the site of the sea floor. Yet such a view negotiates a tension between the accumulations of material history (bod-ies) in the ocean and their radical reconfiguration in seawater—of "Bone soldered by coral to bone, / mosaics / mantled by the benediction of the shark's shadow."[3] Other poets have drawn attention to the seafloor as a site of middle passage history through experiments in form; for example, M. NourbSe Philip's collection of poems *Zong!* adopts an aqueous disorga-nization in its evocation of the Zong massacre of 1781, with letters on the page swirled into often illegible configurations, reviving the muted voices of the drowned. For both Philip and Walcott, to say "the sea is history" puts in question the materiality of records, for whom they may be legible, and the means of encountering what remains. If the grave of the Atlantic is a museum of sorts, it suggests a different sense of the memorial or mu-seum than those on land—fixed in place, respectfully kept, and garlanded with flowers. How does the environment in which we observe a museum affect how we perceive, move, and contemplate?

In *Wild Blue Media*, I have argued that writers and academics think with and through the environments that they call home, and how we orient to our home environment leaves its impressions and residues in the way that we conceptualize media—what media are, what media should ideally do, and for whom media are legible. I have shown how a tendency to describe media through fluid metaphors can obscure the ways that a terrestrial bias persists in our theorizations of media. At the same time, the low-gravitational environment of the ocean provides cognitively estranging conditions for scholars to gain perspective on normative forms of percep-tion. I compose this chapter on "underwater museums" as a way of bring-ing together the conceptual work of the previous chapters through my own practice of scuba diving. As before, I draw on the method of concep-tual displacement to explore what changes when the museum is under-water, as opposed to on land—but this time, the process involves submerging myself. This chapter develops a comparative media analysis of two different underwater museums, tracing their representations in digital media alongside what I notice from my submerged visitations.

My analysis of the museum underwater draws on the insights from each of the previous chapters on interface, inscription, and database. These three terms, which intentionally echo Friedrich Kittler's definition of media in terms of recording, storage, and processing, provide a matrix through which to consider the submerged museum.[4] Drawing on the practice of scuba diving, I discuss the differences between exploring museums underwater and digitally, and how each mediated environment presents specific interactive possibilities and constraint. My comparative media studies approach attends to the differences in embodied viewing and navigating in Google Street View, online photography portfolios, and the ocean itself. Each mode of encounter presents different interfacial conditions of interaction (through screens or the medium of seawater), different senses of the database (digital or aquatic), and different materialities of inscription and residue (with marine organisms coproducing the sculptural evolution). Understanding the media ecology of underwater museums requires thinking through the combined material processes of interfacing, inscription, and information storage.

The first museum I discuss is Jason deCaires Taylor's *Museo Subacuático del Arte* (*Underwater Museum*) (plate 6). Composed of clusters of human figures placed under thirty feet of seawater, the *Underwater Museum* is home to vibrant communities of sea life, shaped by the materiality of the ocean environment. Encrusted with a rainbow of life-forms, Taylor's spectacular sculptures of human beings that grow and change over time have gleaned international attention. Here, seawater itself—the carrier of coral eggs and other life-forms—figures as an artistic and evolutionary force that transforms the sculptures into colonies of organisms.[5] It is not difficult to see these sculptures as views of a posthuman future, of coevolution between human and other species, and a blurring of boundaries between subject and environment (plates 7 and 8). Yet because the sculptures are primarily of *human* figures underwater they appear somewhat uncanny, with eyes closed and no evidence of breathing—perhaps asleep, resting, or even ghostly. It is no wonder that a popular interpretation of the works assumes that they are a memorial to the Middle Passage, an interpretation that the artist has denied (reductively) in favor of a more strictly

ecological message: coral reefs are in danger, and we are not paying attention. The sculptures signify beyond authorial intention as multispecies
habitats, altering the ways that we normally think about the museum and
processes of mediation.

As a point of contrast, I compare Taylor's *Underwater Museum* with a
nonanthropogenic "museum" in the Yucatán: the "Dos Ojos" (Two Eyes)
cenote (underwater cavern) in Tulum, Mexico. I bring these two museum
environments together for comparison in part because of their geographic
proximity—they are less than one hundred miles apart—and because of
the contrast they offer in thinking about curation (with its human intention) and the multispecies coproduction of history. There are many
cenotes in the Yucatán peninsula because it is largely made from porous
limestone—the residue of past marine life, sedimented into rock.[6] Some
cenotes harbor ancient marine fossils amid striking limestone structures,
and unusually clear freshwater with a visibility range that can exceed two
hundred feet. Whereas sculptures figure as the focus of Taylor's museum,
the walls of the caverns are of most historical interest in the cenotes. As I
explore later in this chapter, these conditions present a very different spatial model—an inverse one, or negative—of Taylor's underwater museum.
The Dos Ojos cenote also challenges normative expectations of the museum through its unique spatiality and conditions of entry and the mir-
rorlike optics of its many surfaces.

These two underwater museum environments present an occasion
for thinking about what we expect out of museums in the first place: a
stable archive of history, static over time, which we slowly explore and
contemplate. Instead, seawater destabilizes this terrestrial expectation
of preservation, with the dynamic role of seawater as a force for change,
and for carrying the larvae of organisms that eventually grow upon the
neutral substrate of the sculptures into a colorful multispecies skin. In
the cenotes, the slow drip of freshwater adds a constructive residue to the
stalactites and stalagmites of cenotes (not unlike the formation of coral
skeletons). By comparing these two sites, I show how seawater participates
in the filtering and formation of history, the residues of human and
multispecies histories at each site, and the interfaces through which one
might experience each of these underwater museums.

Museo Subacuático del Arte

There is an obscure oceanic passage in Book X of Plato's *Republic* that has been overshadowed by the cave allegory and its discussion of ideal forms. In a dialogue between Socrates and the inquisitive character Glaucon, Socrates explains the difficulty of knowing the primary nature of the immortal soul by recourse to the condition of the sea god Glaucus, whose body is constantly changing and modified by existence underwater: "[The soul] is like that of the sea god Glaucus, whose primary nature can't easily be made out by those who catch glimpses of him. Some of the original parts have been broken off, others have been crushed, and his whole body has been maimed by the waves and by the shells, seaweeds, and stones that have attached themselves to him, so that he looks more like a wild animal than his natural self."[7] The sea god Glaucus—whose name gives us the modern term *glaucoma*, referring to the greenish-gray opacity of the ocean—can only be known partially and opaquely, suggesting radically different epistemic conditions than the cave allegory. In the cave allegory, Plato imagines that people see only the shadows of objects cast by a fire, and never the objects themselves. The shadows are untrustworthy because they only represent the real but are not in fact the real itself. Yet in the case of Glaucus, the perceived object is not untrustworthy because it is only a shadow of the real thing; it is untrustworthy because the material thing is in fact changing all the time in seawater. As Gaston Bachelard put it much later (and in reference to freshwater rather than saltwater), "a being dedicated to water is a being in flux. He dies every minute; something of his substance is constantly falling away."[8]

Glaucus's body, too, is in flux: sculpted, maimed, and reworked by seawater, and decorated by various animal and plant attachments. This poses an ontological problem for Plato, who speculates that we would know Glaucus's "primary nature" if only we could lift him "out of the sea in which it now dwells, and if the many stones and shells (those which have grown all over it in a wild, earthy, and stony profusion . . .) were hammered off it. Then we'd see what its true nature is and be able to determine whether it has many parts or just one and whether or in what manner it is put together."[9] This assumption—that to know something's primary nature is to isolate it by extracting it out of its constitutive and sustaining element of habitation—reflects a terrestrial bias and the Cartesian assumption that space is an empty container for objects rather than as the sustaining precondition for their emergence.[10] Oceanic conditions prevent us from so easily thinking the object in isolation from its environment, especially with gelatinous organisms whose entire structure is buoyed by the surrounding milieu of water.

The subaquatic human figures in Jason deCaires Taylor's *Underwater Museum* offer a strong visual connection to Plato's description of Glaucus. Located in Isla Mujeres, Mexico, the *Museo Subacuático del Arte* is one of several world-wide locations where Taylor has installed his coral-friendly sculptures, uniquely conducive to fostering marine life (plates 6–8).[11] Photo documentation from Taylor's website reveals whole colonies of colorful organisms that have occluded what were once human forms. These multispecies colonies—including spiny urchins, bright pink tunicates, purple sea fans, fire coral, schools of striped fish, and algae—suggest something entirely other and posthuman, distorting anthropomorphic forms. This fantastical growth is made possible, of course, by the seawater that surrounds them. Biologist Helen Scales notes that the sculptures were made to be "as appealing to reef life as possible" through their composition in pH-neutral marine-grade cement, free of other substances like metals. The installation of the sculptures was even timed to coincide with coral spawning events, so that coral larvae rather than algae larvae would be likely to adhere.[12] Some areas of each sculpture were left intentionally rough to provide traction for young larvae; one man's "pitted and textured skin [was] ideal to promote coral growth."[13] Looking at the sculptures, it is difficult to tell where human form ends and marine form begins—the very erasure of original form that Plato laments. Instead, we end up with more of a Giovanni Arcimboldi painting—a barely recognizable human face made up of so many component sea creatures.

In terms of his intention for the works, Taylor both embraces and resists the way that seawater preserves and changes submerged objects. In an artist's statement, he writes that the works serve both as art and as "artificial reefs, attracting marine life, while offering the viewer privileged temporal encounters, as the shifting sand of the ocean floor, and the works change from moment to moment."[14] Art meets artifice to provide new habitats, drawing attention to the deteriorating condition of reefs worldwide as a result of human activity, hurricane damage, and climate change. Taylor proposes seeing the works as alternative scuba sites, meant to alleviate pressure from natural reefs closer to Isla Mujeres. Whereas "clumsy scuba divers and snorkelers accidentally whack and break corals," "artificial reefs, in various guises, are deployed to help divert the flow of diving traffic away from natural reefs."[15] Although it could be argued that the *Underwater Museum* also serves to bring in extra tourism to those very sites, the sculptures certainly contribute to a greater awareness of ocean health and marine environments. The film *Angel Azul* documents the unwanted proliferation of algae on the sculptures, most likely caused by "the influx of nutrient pollutants from land and the overfishing of grazers like parrot fish."[16] Taylor expresses the desire for certain organisms to colonize the sculptures but not others, according to human aesthetic taste as well as a sense of what constitutes ecological balance.

Despite the fact that the figures are designed to change over time, Taylor advertises the experience of commissioning a sculpture of yourself as an "immortalization process," one that was, he adds, "described by a previous volunteer as the only way to 'live for ever.'"[17] Similarly, Taylor intends for the works as a whole to "immortalize" a message about climate change. When the organization Mission Blue profiled Taylor's works, he described the sculptures in this way:

> We have a countdown on our natural reefs at the moment. Scientists are predicting that in 50 years we would have lost almost 70% of our natural reefs, which is quite a heavy statistic. I kind of want to set in stone how we knew this was going to happen so that in 50 years time, when people look back and say "They knew! Why did they not do anything? Why did they not take action?" I want it to be immortalized there in stone that we knew this was going to happen and we were responsible.[18]

The irony is that Taylor frames his works as an *immortalization* of human awareness of climate change through underwater sculptures designed to *change* over time.[19] This approach (and goal) of immortalizing our awareness of climate change channels the more terrestrial goal of long-term preservation; by contrast, the underwater sculptures are celebrated because of their capacity for cultivating multispecies colonies of colorful life. If the sculptures immortalize anything, it would seem to be change itself.

The question of whether the sculptures are more geared toward ephemerality or permanence is complicated by the fact that they exist across several different media in addition to seawater: high-quality photographs on the internet and magazines, Google Street View as 360-degree panoramas, and a terrestrial gallery in Kukulcan Mall. Each medium involves different conditions of engagement and different processes of mediation. My first encounter with the sculptures was as digital photographs, curated on Taylor's website; I was enchanted and impressed by the images of human faces transformed and colonized by rainbows of marine life. Taylor's photos constituted so many surreal portraits, often highlighting the replacement of a human feature by another organism. For example, a purple sea urchin takes the place of a woman's hair bun; fire coral takes the place of a beard; an outgrowth of tunicates forms a strange proboscis. Yet there are also mutations. Carpets of something yellow take the place of one person's skin; something with fronds pours out of another sculpture's eye socket, curving around its neck. As Elizabeth Deloughrey writes, "It's this uncanniness, the engagements with human forms that appear distorted, larger, closer, and essentially 'matter out of place,' to borrow from Mary Douglas (*Purity and Danger*, 36), that makes [the sculptures] *unheimlich*, both familiar and radically defamiliarizing."[20]

It was not until I dove the *Underwater Museum* in person that I began to consider the formal qualities of Taylor's photographs—their frontality and clarity—as terrestrial conventions. The orientation of nearly all his photos is upright, aligned with the same gravitational conditions as we experience on land. As I would find out in person, this was not always an easy position to achieve. During a research trip in 2014, I joined a dive charter for US$80—fairly standard for diving prices but prohibitively expensive for most locals—and headed out on a small boat. We first swam by several natural reefs that impressed me with their profusion of large purple sea fans and density of life. Every inch of rock surface had been colonized by something, and clouds of fish hovered close by. Following the divemaster, our group headed onward into the cloudier distance. All of a sudden we came upon the first sculpture—a gate with a circular opening—and paused to take pictures. Without being able to see too far ahead, we kept swimming. Gradually, out of the haze, I recognized the large installation "Silent Evolution," comprised of around one hundred life-sized sculpture casts of people. They were assembled to stand in concrete hexagons, forming a meandering crowd on the seafloor. I could not help but wonder where all the colorful life I had seen in the photographs was, since they were now overrun by algae (figure 4.1). Unlike Glaucus, these sculptures could somewhat return to their "original forms," with large die-offs of organisms revealing concrete faces underneath.

FIGURE 4.1 Jason deCaires Taylor's "Silent Evolution." Photo by author, July 2014.

As a result of the poor visibility, my photographic documentation of "Silent Evolution" appeared rather murky, since the haze of seawater changed the quality of light. By contrast, Taylor's photographs were taken on particularly clear days, with the sculptures appearing so distinctly that they almost could have been photographed in the air; his photographs sampled a slice in time with maximum growth, with many colors of organisms thriving. However, the clarity of the water in Taylor's photographs obscures what is in fact most novel about the sculptures: their immersion in the substance of seawater that shapes, builds, and erodes. In Taylor's photographs seawater is invisible, allowing the viewer to forget the element responsible for growing on and sculpting objects. There is thus a gap between how the underwater museum exists in Taylor's photographic documentation (invisible) and how one encounters the museum underwater (cloudy). To a diver, the medium of the seawater that sustains the sculptures is much more obvious than to a spectator of the photographs alone.

The opacity of seawater suggests other reorientations to concepts in media. As in chapter 2, I argued that the term *inscription* does not seem adequate to describe the processes of mediation at work in forming the sculptures. Whereas the term *inscription* (as a form of recording) has to do with making a mark or cut on some kind of surface, the ambient environment of the ocean leaves other residual forms on the sculptures themselves. As Astrida Neimanis has written, water can be viewed as a "gestational" substance because of its role in sustaining life, "owed to full aqueous immersion."[21] In this sense, the seawater itself—full of all kinds of larvae and plankton—is the carrier of life and the environment for life. Once immersed underwater, the ocean as co-artist takes over the agency of sculptural evolution, leaving crusts of aquatic life clinging to the accommodating surfaces of the works. The works are not so much inscribed by seawater as they are coated with the fleshy residues of tunicates, bryozoans, anemones, corals, and other organisms that adhere with their own gluey substances.

It also matters whether the *Underwater Museum* is experienced through the interfaces of computer screens or through diving the sculptures in the ocean environment. Chapter 1 discussed the difference between theorizations of the interface in media theory and how they compare to the distributed interface of the lungs in scuba diving. But what was also significant about the oceanic interface that mediated my visitation of the sculpture was the possibilities and constraints that it placed on movement. One of the difficulties in photographing the works in "Silent Evolution" was the presence of a robust current; if I wanted to pause and study a face more closely, I had to swim against the current and find the stability for the camera to focus. Visiting the sculptures meant navigating the experience of drift, where the current itself put a limitation on how long one could view and swim around the sculptures. In addition, I constantly negotiated my proximity to the works through controlling my buoyancy so as not to sink and hit the sculptures—especially when swimming "overhead."

This entire dimension of the physical body's relations with the sculptures—of constant movement and negotiation—was missing from the digital and photographic forms of the underwater museum. Absent as well was the pleasure of "flying" over, upside-down, and around the sculptures as I desired, free to see what kinds of colorful life lay in the tiniest of corners—like carpets of tunicates and the tips of new corals, slowly growing by laying residues of calcium carbonate on skeletal foundations. Although most of Taylor's photographs are portraits of individuals viewed from the front, I found that it was easiest to hover over the sculptures since they were packed too tightly for a diver to swim in between (plate

7). My normal encounter with the sculptures was from this bird's eye (fish-eye?) perspective, less of a face-to-face than an appreciation of tops of heads. It took effort to swim against the current and switch to a vertical position to look them in the face—the position that in portraiture would be called "frontality." Viewing the sculptures overhead had the effect of encountering them as a crowd rather than as individuals, one giant organism—or a forest for fish. I was surprised to recognize that one of my favorite sculptures from Taylor's photographs, on the right edge of one cluster, was not a large woman but a short man with a suitcase (plates 6, 8). He seemed much more alone in the ocean than when I had seen him in the photograph, and his body seemed to have changed upon this closer look: instead of bright pink tunicates, a swath of green algae now coated most of his figure.

Diving through the underwater museum calls attention to seawater as a connective fluid, and it made me realize that the very fluid supporting my efforts bore the dissolved material traces of the objects I had come to "visit" in the first place. Rather than a roving eye wandering the museum, I found myself more like an immersed, bubble-breathing disturbance whose presence ever so slightly altered the flows around the historical objects. Whereas Deloughrey concluded that Taylor's sculptures participate in "figuring maritime space as a multispecies and embodied place in which the oceanic contours of the planet, including its submarine creatures, are no longer outside of the history of the human," I was more struck by what the museum required of me as a visitor: constant movement and negotiation, an awareness of finding myself in the same world as the sculptures, sharing a sense of the vulnerability and fragility with the submerged figures—perhaps an ethic of proximity.[22]

The dynamics of movement in Google Street View's interface for viewing the *Underwater Museum* were entirely different than those I experienced in the ocean. As I discussed in chapter 3, Google Street View is a terrestrial mapping technology that that has now been applied to the oceans to educate the public and document a baseline image of reef health, through Google's partnership with Catlin Seaview Survey. There are now a collection of underwater "streets" to traverse, simulating the experience of a dive (figure 4.2). Even though the simulation is supposedly underwater, the "streets" in Google Street View remain the guiding navigational aesthetic, invisible but indicated by arrows that appear when you move your cursor. This provides the illusion of free movement, despite

FIGURE 4.2 Screenshot of Google Street View of the *Underwater Museum*, 2014.

the fact that your movement is in fact constrained by the pathways swum by the diver with the recording camera (although you can pivot in place). In choosing a direction, you cannot tell whether the arrows correspond to "streets" that lead up and over the sculptures or down into their midst. Diving with Google Street View, you do not have to worry about buoyancy, navigation, sinking, or running into any objects—Google's translation of the ocean into digital space simulates the ocean's visual qualities rather than its viscous, buoyant, or chemical properties. To quote diving ethnographer Stephanie Merchant, there are a "plethora of possible lines of action afforded by the wreck . . . counter to that traditionally expected in a land-based heritage site" that could involve flying up and around a site, sideways or even upside down.[23] Instead, Google Street View confines the viewer's movement to the structure of lines and its viewing positions to nodes—resembling the structure of a network. Thus, a major difference between Google Street View and diving the sculptures in person has to do with what constraints exist on the orientation of the body and its movement, as well as the navigator's potential effects of witnessing on the environment itself (for example, the diver's potential intrusiveness and ripples of disturbance if they bump into the works).

Because of its Caribbean location, the *Underwater Museum* also upwells the history of the transatlantic slave trade. The sculptures have provoked many viewers to interpret the works as being *memorials* to the Middle Passage, especially because some of the sculptures were cast from people of African descent, evoking the very image of the drowned slave, especially in the Grenada site. Connecting the seafloor with Middle Passage history has precedents in the poetic work of Walcott and Kamau Brathwaite, as well as is the Detroit music group Drexciya. Drexciya's "sonic science fiction" imagines a world where the unborn babies of mothers thrown overboard during the Middle Passage survived, transitioning from breathing in the watery womb to breathing in water, creating their own bubble metropolis—inspiring a recent song by the hip-hop group clipping.[24] The surprise of survival and transhuman adaptation call attention to the ocean as a site of utopian possibility, vehicle for remembrance, and space from which to launch critique.

Although Taylor has avoided such possibilities and strongly denied any connection between his works and the Middle Passage, he has said that he is "very encouraged how it has resonated differently within various communities and feel[s] it is working as an art piece by questioning our identity, history and stimulating debate."[25] Although Taylor sees the sculptures as simply speaking to issues of ecology and coral reef health, the sculptures possess a signifying power beyond his intentions. One telling reaction to Taylor's disavowal, on the website of America's Black Holocaust Museum, was to leave the original text describing the sculptures crossed-out, identified as a misreading (figure 4.3).

> It remembers the captive Africans who died on slave ships during the Middle Passage, the crossing from Africa to the Americas. About a third of captives died from the horrible conditions on board. Their bodies were thrown into the Atlantic. Others, particularly women with children, who were often allowed to move about unshackled on deck, threw themselves over. Many believed in reincarnation and hoped to escape slavery and be reborn to a life of freedom.[26]

The fact that the Black Holocaust Museum left the text crossed out rather than simply deleting it serves as an expression of resistance to the authorial intention of the works, leaving the viewer to negotiate between "correct" reading and the compelling force of the "misreading." The image of the drowned slave thus haunts Taylor's work both visually and typographically in the exact sense of the phrase "under erasure," as Derrida would have it, in danger of disappearing but still partially visible. To me, this typographic strategy evokes the very aesthetic of sea change that the

Vicissitudes: NOT Sculptural Homage to Victims of the Middle Passage

Posted May 23 2012

From the website www.underwatersculpture.com of Jason DeCaire Taylor

Jason DeCaire Taylor, a British sculptor, creates beautiful and haunting life-size sculptures underwater in the oceans. These evolve to become reefs, many in places where the original reefs have suffered environmental degradation. His exhibits can be seen either by diving or glass-bottom boats, all over the world.

"Vicissitudes" is a large circle of figures shackled together and holding hands, off the coast of Grenada in the Caribbean.

It remembers the captive Africans who died on slave ships during the Middle Passage, the crossing from Africa to the Americas. About a third of captives died from the horrible conditions on board. Their bodies were thrown into the Atlantic. Others, particularly women with children, who were often allowed to move about unshackled on deck, threw themselves over. Many believed in reincarnation and hoped to escape slavery and be reborn to a life of freedom.

The paragraph above, posted here on 5/23/12, is erroneous. It perpetuates a myth circulating around the web. We apologize to our visitors and to the artist for our error – and thank the visitors who left comments on the exhibit bringing this to our attention. Please go to the Vicissitudes exhibit and read the artist's statement describing this work.

Vicissitudes by Jason deCaire Taylor

FIGURE 4.3 Screenshot from the website of America's Black Holocaust Museum, 2014.

sculptures embody, of the human figure "crossed" by new organisms but still partially discernable (plate 8). Furthermore, the event of the *Zong* massacre—that insurance money could be collected if slaves were thrown overboard—draws a disturbing resonance with Ariel's song in *The Tempest* about the sea-changed body turned into pearls and coral, in that both the slaves and the coral/pearls were worth something. Surely the environmental message about coral reef degradation would only be enlivened rather than obscured by these resonances with Middle Passage history, unless this history was seen as a detriment to the role of the sculptures as a tourist attraction?

When I first viewed the sculptures on the artist's website in 2014, the photographs were arranged by the name of each sculptural work ("Silent Evolution," "Vicissitudes," "Anthropocene," etc.). As I write in 2019, the website has changed to divide the photographs into several categories: "recent," "submerged," "terrestrial," "nocturnal." Additionally, viewers can sort by "uncolonised," "colonised," and "corals"—an unusual taxonomy.[27] The words *colonized* and *uncolonized* evoke very different things for ecologists compared with scholars who study Caribbean history or postcolonial theory. For a marine ecologist, "colonized" might connote a certain density of life attached to an underwater surface. For humanities scholars thinking about the Caribbean, "colonized" would immediately evoke the violence and exploitation of Africans and indigenous peoples by Western countries. Consider Henri Bergson's famous description of memory: "There is no perception which is not full of memories. With the immediate present data of our senses we mingle a thousand details of our past experience."[28] The "perception" of the *Underwater Museum* would depend on whether one is talking to someone whose first thought on hearing the word *colonized* has to do with marine life or someone whose first thought is of deep historical injustice.

To return to the taxonomic categories of the website—uncolonized, colonized, and corals—I wondered what it would mean to consider "corals" as a third term. In Taylor's schema, uncolonized meant the raw sculpture as he had made it, and colonized referred to sculptures on which a variety of marine organisms had grown—some wanted (like purple fans), others (like algae) not. Coral is separated out as other: colorful, productive, a collective full of individual polyps (a "colonial organism"). Coral is both an organism and a habitat, filtering ocean water and providing shelter to young fish and multispecies larvae. However, one might read the difference between "colonized" and "coral" not only in terms of species difference but also in terms of levels of precarity. Because they are sensitive to temperature changes, coral reefs are in danger of bleaching during ocean warming events (2016 being a notably bad year), an effect of anthropogenic climate change.

As I floated in the ocean, gazing at the *Underwater Museum*, I experienced a moment of reversal. Perhaps it was backward to think that I was diving into the ocean to observe the artificial habitat of the *Underwater Museum*; perhaps it was the ocean that was bathing in my carbon exhalations and carbon footprint. Was I its habitat?

Dos Ojos and Dreamgate Cenotes

As I researched additional diving sites that were near Jason deCaires Taylor's *Underwater Museum*, I became curious about the Yucatán cenotes. Nestled in the coastal forest, cenotes naturally occur when water courses underground through limestone; cavern openings form when the roof col-

FIGURE 4.4 The entrance to the "Dreamgate" cenote. Photo by author, July 2014.

lapses in, enabling diving access (figure 4.4). The limestone structures inside these freshwater caverns slowly change over time, offering natural museum-like conditions of visitation and sometimes the preservation of human cultural material. As one scholar writes, the natural conditions of cenotes "make for good conservation of palaeontological and cultural material" because of the cool water temperature (~ 25° C), a form of natural air-conditioning. Furthermore, cenotes can be quite dark: "A young cenote with little incidence of light is naturally even better for conservation as it inhibits the development of micro-organisms."[29] Cenotes played a significant role in Mayan mythology, as "portals and means of communication with the region where the gods of rain and fertility dwelt."[30] Browsing a few photographs online had me hooked: the clarity of the freshwater cenotes was stunning, filtering down and refracting crystal-blue light from what looked like occasional openings above the caverns. What I would discover is that these conditions afford a variety of optical effects, although media in the caverns would not be what I was expecting.[31]

To get to Dos Ojos, my diving guide Rigo drove me and three others down a long highway that parallels the coast between Playa del Carmen and Tulum, where there were many turnoff signs pointing to the locations of different cenotes. After making our exit, we drove down a long, bumpy dirt road before arriving at a larger parking lot with large cement tables available for helping assemble and put on dive gear. Rigo spent a good twenty minutes going over safety procedures, from flashlight protocol, to how to alert him to a problem, to the safe distance to keep between oneself and the other divers/floor/ceiling, to how to enter the water from the entrance platform, and how to kick properly. [32] Cavern diving is considered "technical diving" because it requires much more precise buoyancy control and a special fin-kick that slowly propels you forward, without kicking up sediment. This is extremely important for both the safety and the pleasure of the dive, because reduced visibility can obscure your ability to navigate. [33] When not obscured, the natural clarity of cenotes like Dos Ojos is in the range of two hundred to three hundred feet, which visually is like looking through air or very clear glass. [34]

After our briefing, we each picked up our thirty pounds of gear and walked down a very long, very steep staircase to the cavern entrance—an open blue maw, somewhere between a mouth and an eye, or an azure looking glass. Half of the pool was open to the air, and the side facing us was covered by a steep overhanging hillside. When I finally jumped in with my hot, heavy gear on—it was July in the Caribbean—I opened my eyes to pleasantly cold conditions, and a few small fish approached my mask in the blue tinted water, clear as air. Rigo gathered us at one end of the pool, gesturing to the cavern entrance below our feet. *Oh boy*, I thought, *here we go*. As we slowly sank, deflating our vests and adjusting to neutral buoyancy, we headed toward a small, dark tunnel that opened up into the base of a sloped, giant room of water with light streaming down from the high ceiling. While hanging suspended at the dark bottom, gazing up to boulders and cathedral-like light, I realized with some surprise that I was not afraid.

What I immediately liked about diving the caverns—which began to feel like journeying back in time—were the entry requirements of visitation. To enter the caverns, you needed to become temporarily transhuman, bringing your own prosthetics of air supply, wet suit, technology, flashlight. From this cyborgian condition, you gained temporary passport to the cenote, aware of just how easy it would be for your very presence to affect the surrounding limestone. Unlike diving in the open ocean, diving Dos Ojos required much more control over your buoyancy, demanding constant attention so as not to disturb or hit any sediment, limestone structures, or other divers. With boat diving, the emphasis is usually on a quick descent from ship to seafloor, and a casual pace of swimming. Because the floor and depth of water usually do not change too much during an ocean dive, you only need to adjust your buoyancy control device (BCD) a few times. Yet in the cenotes, you had to slow down your swimming speed so as not to run into a group ahead, or the limestone walls and ceiling. The terrain also changed, sometimes as deep as forty feet and sometimes as shallow as ten feet. This required making small adjustments to your buoyancy (through inflating or deflating your vest) throughout the dive, careful to not drift out of control either upward or downward. Just like in outer space, movements underwater are amplified—one of the reasons that NASA'S NEEMO program trains astronauts at an underwater base.[35]

Diving Dos Ojos seemed, at times, like an obstacle course or video game because of the way you needed to constantly negotiate, in slow motion, the changing terrain and depths without hitting anything. My instructor Rigo even mentioned that the "Temple of Doom" cenote was named after the video game Doom, not the Indiana Jones movie, because that is what exploring it felt like: a video game where you were the avatar, dodging delicate cavern structures. This need for constant attention and self-monitoring of the body greatly distinguished the experience of diving Dos Ojos from open water diving, to the point where diving in the ocean felt almost reckless and imprecise by contrast. The stakes of good buoyancy control in the cenotes had to do with respect for the environment and other divers: we did not want to damage any of the limestone structures on the ceiling or floor, nor stir up sediment through an unplanned landing and cloud the visibility. Yet buoyancy control also marked the inexperienced divers (fluctuating, out of control) from the experienced divers (calm and precise in their movement), the less from the more fish-like.[36] I reflected that perhaps buoyancy control itself offers a kind of ethics, as a mindful negotiation of oneself and a practice of care, with the aspiration of being as minimally disruptive as possible.

Between the coolness of the water and the prohibition on touching the surrounding limestone, the cenote felt distinctly like a museum. The fossils that we encountered—a snail, perhaps the fanned bodies of crinoids—hinted at past coral reefs from before the last ice age. Although the cavern was freshwater, the sea was very much present. As we swam, guided by a thin rope line marking the path, I noticed that part of the limestone formations along our path were dull, likely hit by the air tanks of careless divers. Fortunately, the limestone columns that adorned the surrounding open caverns were untouched, thousands of years in the making. Stalactites and stalagmites had slowly dripped into existence, sustained by the surrounding water, a kind of calcified residue of past ages. While it almost felt like the cavern was a snapshot, it was in fact very much alive, the limestone structures still growing among a few small fish. As an archive of the past, the cenotes require us to consider a watery vocabulary of mediation beyond inscriptive paradigms, accounting for mineral growth and the dripped formations of limestone.

Indeed the concept of inscription seemed, to me, to be inadequate to describe not only the limestone structures but also what was happening with our bubbles. Along the tighter passages we swam in with low ceilings, you could see small pockets of air that had pooled together. It took me a while to realize that these small pools of air were not "natural" but were, in fact, the exhalations of past divers collecting at the roof.[37] These bodily exteriorizations of air produced a variety of optical phenomena: sometimes they looked like liquid mercury, sometimes like solid rock, sometimes like a mirror, sometimes transparent. During our dive, I would occasionally hear a thunderous "boom" that sounded like a large truck was driving overhead. When I asked Rigo about this later, he said that the boom was actually the effect of bubbles pooling together and flowing to the surface—"raining up" rather than down. Divers had left an amorphous residue of bubbles on the cavern ceiling, a form of noninscriptive media that nonetheless signified past presence. My air bubbles pooling at the ceiling constituted an ephemeral residue that, upon reaching a critical mass, would "pop" and overflow to the sky, producing a booming sound effect that future divers would hear—an affective delay.[38]

The second cenote that I dove, "Dreamgate," was famous for having even more impressive limestone structures, and for being much darker and narrower. Yet the reason I was interested in this specific cenote was because it featured a halocline, or a border between freshwater and saltwater. Most cenotes in the Yucatán are freshwater, but a few connect to the ocean and thus have a layer of heavier saltwater at the bottom. Some haloclines can be quite dramatic—a sulfurous yellow border at the base of a pit, sometimes with a fallen tree surreally sticking up out of the abyss into the clear upper water. Dreamgate's halocline was more subtle. When I shined my flashlight on it, the border of halocline shimmered, looking paradoxically like an underwater river—a moving surface within the depths of the underwater cavern.[39] I thought of what poet Kamau Brathwaite once wrote, "the unity is submarine," a sort of literal condition in the caverns, whose saltwater is evidence of a subterranean connection to the sea.[40]

During lunch in between dives, Rigo surprised me with a question: "If you were James Cameron, how would you film the halocline?" Our conversation had turned to science fiction films and deep sea exploration, and Rigo—who leads dives to cenotes probably four or five times per week—responded, "I think I would film the halocline in a film about traveling to other dimensions." What struck me about this comment was not just that it proposed a compelling idea for a new novel or movie, or provided yet another link between the alien ocean and science fiction. Rather, instead of opposing land and ocean, Rigo's comment compared *two kinds of water.* Not only does cenote diving feel like a descent into another dimension; within the caverns, one can still pass into yet more dimensions through encountering new bodies of water.

It struck me that the spatiality of the halocline—of an interface between two types of water, or of a surface *underwater*—diverges from the normative spatiality assumed in ongoing conversations in literary theory about surface reading versus depth reading.[41] As I discussed in chapter 1, this debate assumes a human observer looking at/from the surface, "down" into the depths. With the shimmer of the halocline in mind, one might imagine the possibility of beginning observations from the depths—or multiple surfaces within the depths.[42] What would "surface" reading be like if the interpreter/observer was imagined to be floating in the middle of a column of water? Yet the halocline was not the only striking surface. As I looked up to the sky from the entrance of the Dreamgate cenote, through surface waters swirled with jungle dust and pollen (figure 4.5), I thought about how clear the waters around me were compared to the distant surface and its magnifying effects. From my submerged point of view, the surface appeared as a distant site of optical distortion rather than that which is "obvious" or superficial, as Sharon Marcus and Steven Best envision it in their influential issue of *Representations.*[43] If literary criticism has taken surface observation as its normative point of view, then underwater perspectives offer fundamentally different possibilities for figuring interpretation in spatial terms. A literary hermeneutics from within the water column, gazing at the sky, would require an entirely dif-

FIGURE 4.5 Looking at the sky from under the surface in the "Dreamgate" cenote. Photo by author, July 2014.

ferent formulation of the surface and the depths that accounted for the experience of optics underwater (such as the magnification I mentioned above), as well as factors of embodied observation for the critic buoyed by seawater.

As I have shown, the cenotes and Taylor's *Underwater Museum* are very different kinds of aquatic "museums." The cenotes were freshwater, whereas the *Underwater Museum* inhabited saltwater. In the cenotes, ancient geological structures surround the diver as they move through water. The diver feels enveloped by the surrounding caverns, almost womb-like in their dark passage, where the environment itself was the museum. In the *Underwater Museum*, however, the sculptures were the main attraction (instead of walls). The diver was free to move speedily around them, within the vast expanse of the ocean. In this way, the cenotes and *Underwater Museum* are inversions of each other—one made of objects, the other composed of walls. Yet because of the spatial constraints of the cenotes, I felt that they were more museum-like than the *Underwater Museum*. Not only were they natural repositories of ancient geological formations but, as a diver, one had to exercise a higher degree of skill not to accidentally drift into the formations or hit them.

Displacing the museum from land to seawater asks us to rethink what we expect museums to be. Instead of a quiet archive of historic objects we see in terrestrial museums, meant to be preserved as intact as possible, locating a museum underwater (manmade or nonanthropogenic) sets up objects to continually change, bearing the residues (rather than inscriptions) of organisms and mineral-rich waters over time. One's sense of an interface also changes underwater. In the ocean or in a cavern, there is no Plexiglas boundary between the visitor and the historic object or formation, and the visitor is responsible for negotiating their own body movement so as not to crash into them. As a result, the visitation involves not only visual spectacle but also the embodied experience of moving around the sculptures in a fluid medium, making it difficult to contemplate from one stationary spot. Underwater, I felt caught up and surrounded by currents carrying the very substances and organisms responsible for making the sculptures and cavern formations that I had come to observe. Aquatic environments disrupt the ways that we conventionally think of a "museum" in the first place—not as a static collection of things to be preserved but perhaps as an ephemeral and shifting flow.

Diving as Humanist Method

Wild Blue Media has explored the potential of diving—both imaginatively and literally—as a strategy for shaking up the conditions of interpretation in literary and media studies, displacing readers from familiar routines and into new environments. When thinking through seawater, the interface is more than a surface, the archive or database may be mobile and transient, and processes of inscription and recording give way to watery processes of mediation involving residues and saturation. In all their ecological and spatial diversity, the oceans prompt a fundamental reexamination of the underlying environmental poetics and metaphorics of our concepts and theoretical positions.

Although scuba diving is more conventionally associated with scientific research or maritime industries, I see diving as a method of cognitive estrangement that makes visible the terrestrial biases that have calcified in the way that we figuratively speak about the world. On a basic level, diving provided access to underwater archives that I could not otherwise have reached. By visiting such archives in person, I observed phenomenological details that would not have been apparent by studying someone else's two-dimensional images from afar. In my analysis of Taylor's sculptures in this chapter, there were details that I would not have noticed had

I not visited the underwater museum in person—particularly concerning the environmental conditions of mediation through which a viewer approaches the artworks. These conditions include clarity of air/ocean, the difficulty of access, the normal viewpoint (hovering overhead vs. frontality), and the duration of interactions. Because it provides access to human cultural objects, diving can function as a kind of ethnographic or media archaeological practice—although the term *archaeological* tends to suggest that which can be dug up out of the earth.[44] In another sense, humanists and artists can use scuba diving as a form of witnessing environmental change like coral bleaching, historical sites of interest, or hidden infrastructure. Artist Trevor Paglen recently documented fiber-optic cables off the coast of Miami in a project called "Deep Web Dive," as a way of witnessing the infrastructure that carries not only the internet but also National Security Agency (NSA) mass surveillance. Diving enables the study of media underwater, a site-specific technique of visitation.[45]

Diving can also change our techniques of reading and our assumptions about the spatiality of interpretation. Diving was the precondition for my close reading of Jacques Cousteau's autobiographical nonfiction *The Silent World* in chapter 1. Without going through diving certification, I would not have had the experience and literacy to understand the physiological dimensions of Cousteau's diving experimentation or been in a position to theorize the whole volume of the body as an interface through which one might sense and interpret surroundings. Through PADI's dive training, I was under no illusion that diving enables you to become a free amphibian able to shuttle between surface and depth easily and at will. Divers are always attentive to the duration and depth of their dive, because these factors determine the length of the decompression stop needed—a pause that one takes hovering at fifteen feet below the surface in order to exhale the excess gas absorbed during the dive. As a diver, you become alienated from the land in the very process of becoming able to breathe comfortably deep underwater and have to spend time reversing that process to go safely back to sea level elevation. Had I not had this understanding from experience, I may have taken Cousteau at his word that he and his comrades were amphibious "menfish" free to swim wherever they pleased. Instead, I was able to consider the gradual process of terrestrial excommunication that happens in diving, and how you cannot rush to the surface immediately when you have been underwater for too long or too deep. This temporary excommunication was part of my theorization of the interface in diving, of the whole body as a distributed interface that is open to risk an pain. In these ways, diving helped me to develop a more nuanced concept of the interface specific to the human body underwater.

Although the experience of being literally in the water has informed the development of this book, I am quite aware that this privilege was contingent on my own health and physical condition. I reinjured an anterior cruciate ligament (ACL) during the writing of this book, and spent a summer rehabilitating before I could explore local California waters. Yet the situation is not as simple as saying that the able-bodied can dive, and the disabled cannot. In fact, diving can give people the experience of movement even if they have sustained a prior injury; for example, the dive shop I frequented in Honolulu would occasionally take injured veterans, many with amputations, visiting the nearby military base. In addition, several dive shops around the world are run by people who are hearing-impaired, but fluent in sign language.[46] Through sign language they retain their full range of gestural communication, whereas the hearing only have the few basic signs they pick up from dive classes.

Beyond literal submersion, there is more than one way to go diving. *Wild Blue Media* has also approached diving as an imaginative process, often facilitated by technical media. Media play a vital role in extending our sensorium, channeling forms of oceanic estrangement. For example, disorienting films like the fishing documentary *Leviathan* awaken us to particular habits of movement and sensation, and indeed, even make us feel seasick. Filmed on GoPro cameras that were sometimes submerged alongside the ship, sometimes buried in piles of fish, sometimes tilted toward blinding ship lights, *Leviathan* challenges the viewer to identify the position from which they are looking. The soundscape of *Leviathan* is equally estranging, amplifying the intense rumble of the engine alongside the crash of the waves and echoes of fish hitting the deck. Through its tilts and screeches, *Leviathan* makes us perhaps a bit nauseous, disrupting the balance of our inner ear. Ocean media not only represent the seas but have the potential to disrupt habitual and normative forms of sensation. Of course, part of the challenge of analyzing ocean media is negotiating the relationship between the materiality of the ocean's representation and the materiality of the ocean itself. In chapter 3, I discussed how the frictionless medium of movement in Google Ocean and ATLAS *in silico* was unlike the ocean and more like air or outer space. My analysis depended on navigating both visualizations as three-dimensional environments, and comparing these to the experience of diving in the ocean. This comparative approach led me to think about aesthetics of friction and scale, and choices of how to render water at different scales. Media play a role not only in representing the ocean but also through characterizing how we expect to move within it (the way movies about outer space condition how we expect to move in zero gravity, even though the majority of us will never travel there).

Diving can also be a form of literary speculation. Chapter 2 asked the reader to join Flusser in imaginatively "diving into Vampyroteuthis"—not to see it from a distance but to consider the abyssal environment as if from its point of view. Flusser considered how many of the ways we speak about the world would not make sense to cephalopods—whose name means "head-foot"—because they have an entirely different body plan. Thus diving into *Vampyroteuthis Infernalis* entailed not only imaginative submersion in the abyss (and considering what media would work there) but also teasing out the implications of theorizing media from a cephalopod body rather than a human body as the "norm." Flusser's fable results in a qualified notion of objectivity—an objectivity that must own up to the conditions of its own possibility, emerging from a culturally conditioned embodied observer, in a particular environment, sometimes with technical prostheses. "Diving into Vampyroteuthis" is a strategy that leads to a literary form of comparative media studies—a promising model for future inquiry.

I have written this book at a time of extreme environmental change, when it often feels inadequate to be slowly composing a work of theory rather than advocating for immediate policy changes in carbon emissions, fishing, and pollutants. However, the slow and careful work of academic writing can have a pre-activist role, by taking time to consider how visual media and narratives work to challenge what we take for granted (if we produce them to create a broader public consciousness). Working with a radically situated knowledge specific to the ocean environment—or displacing the familiar into the ocean—is ultimately about examining how we tell stories and create media environments, and questioning the values and perspectives built into each. *Wild Blue Media* hopes to have left the reader somewhat at sea but with new tentacles with which to spin yarns.

NOTES

Preface

1 Beebe, "Descent into Perpetual Night," 475.
2 Beebe, "Descent into Perpetual Night," 478.
3 "Homer used two adjectives to describe aspects of the colour blue: *kuaneos*, to denote a dark shade of blue merging into black; and *glaukos*, to describe a sort of 'blue-grey,' notably used in Athena's epithet *glaukopis*, her 'grey-gleaming eyes.' He describes the sky as big, starry, or of iron or bronze (because of its solid fixity). The tints of a rough sea range from 'whitish' (*polios*) and 'blue-grey' (*glaukos*) to deep blue and almost black (*kuaneos, melas*). The sea in its calm expanse is said to be 'pansy-like' (*ioeides*), 'wine-like' (*oinops*), or purple (*porphureos*). But whether sea or sky, it is never just 'blue.' In fact, within the entirety of Ancient Greek literature you cannot find a single pure blue sea or sky." Sassi, "Sea Was Never Blue."
4 See, for example, Mentz, *At the Bottom of Shakespeare's Ocean*; *PMLA* 125, no. 3 (May 2010), special section on "ocean studies"; Gillis, "Blue Humanities," in the magazine of the National Endowment for the Humanities.
5 Cronon, "Trouble with Wilderness," 89.
6 Halberstam, "Wildness, Loss, Death," 147.

Introduction

1 A full set of diving gear includes mask, snorkel, fins, weights, wet suit, tanks, buoyancy control device (BCD, or vest), regulator, backup regulator, BCD inflation hose, and submersible pressure gauge. If you dive in cold water, you will need a hood, gloves, insulated booties, and either a 7mm wet suit or a dry suit.

2 Burnett, "Looking at the Surface."

3 Seminar title advertised by the Divers Alert Network, accessed May 19, 2014, http://www.diversalertnetwork.org/training/seminars/breathing/.

4 As Stephanie Merchant notes in "Deep Ethnography: Witnessing the Ghosts of SS *Thistlegorm*," PADI programs promote the horizontal glide, with arms folded across the chest, as a streamlined, normative posture. Initially, I preferred to have my hands out in front of me but have since conformed.

5 Anthropologist Marcel Mauss's discussion of what he calls "techniques of the body" proceeds from an example about swimming and the ways that teaching children how to swim have changed over time. Rather than teaching them to swim, dive, and then open their eyes underwater, Mauss writes how a newer method starts by getting children comfortable in the water, including opening their eyes. Thus, "even before they can swim, particular care is taken to get the children to control their dangerous but instinctive ocular reflexes, before all else they are familiarized with the water, their fears are suppressed and a certain confidence is created, suspensions and movements are selected." Mauss, "Techniques of the Body," 71.

6 Cousteau, *Silent World*, 3.

7 Of course, many people become extremely adept at adapting to new milieu (consider gymnast Simone Biles's talent for orienting in the air). Yet just because one can learn to swim well, or parachute well, or throw aerials does not necessarily mean that the way one speaks about movement and orientation will suddenly change; language is a collective practice.

8 In her discussion of the amphibious lifeworlds of the nomadic Bajau people living in the Coral Triangle, Annet Pauwelussen writes that amphibiousness refers to "the capacity to move in both marine and terrestrial environments" and "the capacity to move in and between worlds that relate and partly intermingle, yet are not reducible to one another." Pauwelussen, "Amphibious Anthropology," 3. In chapter 1, "Interface: Breathing Underwater," I discuss a conditional version of amphibiousness in scuba diving as excommunication from the surface world as the price for spending time below.

9 Wittgenstein, *Philosophical Investigations*. Of course, coastal and seafaring cultures also offer their own vocabularies for the ocean. For example, in *Waves of Knowing*, Karin Amamoto Ingersoll discusses indigenous forms of ecological knowledge in Hawai'i that formed through the practice of traditional surfing and its vocabularies for types of water, weather, and movement.

10 Godfrey-Smith, *Other Minds*; Balcombe, *What a Fish Knows*.

11 Helmreich, *Sounding the Limits of Life*; Shiga, "Sonar."

12 Felt, *Soundings*. Rebecca Rutstein has produced a series of stunning sculptures and paintings inspired by Marie Tharp's work. For a description of her exhibition *Fault Lines*, see http://www.formandconcept.center/rebecca-rutstein-fault-lines-exhibition/, accessed June 1, 2019. More of the artist's work can be seen at http://rebeccarutstein.com/, accessed June 1, 2019.

13 Helmreich, *Alien Ocean*.

14 Gabrys, *Program Earth*; see chapter 2, "From Moss Cam to Spill Cam," and chapter 7, "Sensing Oceans and Geospeculating with a Garbage Patch."

15 Carson, "Undersea," 4.

16 Carson, "Undersea," 4–11.

17 Gabrys, "From Moss Cam to Spillcam" in *Program Earth*, 57–80.

18 Schuppli, "Slick Images."

19 Starosielski and Walker, *Sustainable Media*.

20 Merchant, "Negotiating Underwater Space," 230.

21 Alaimo, "Foreword" to *Disability Studies and the Environmental Humanities*, xi.

22 Burnett, "Looking at the Surface."

23 Ahmed, "Orientations Matter," 274. By inquiring about the background of the tables themselves, Ahmed reminds us that tables appear in Marxist and feminist conversations about labor and privilege. The feminist table is a "disorientation device" to the extent that it poses the question: who has time to sit quietly at tables, or better, who has a clear table, ready for writing?

24 Ahmed, "Orientations Matter," 253. The feminist implication of the argument, then, points to the "political necessity of clearing spaces in order that some bodies can work at the table."

25 Ingold, "Earth, Sky, Wind, and Weather," S29.

26 Rozwadowski, *Fathoming the Ocean*.

27 This image of the human sitting at an underwater desk was playfully but seriously brought into realization by former Maldives president Mohammad Nasheed's "Underwater Cabinet Meeting" from 2009 (see plate 3).

28 For more on the role of metaphor in science studies, see, for example, Beer, *Darwin's Plots*; Lakoff and Johnson, *Metaphors We Live By*.

29 Dick, "My Definition of Science Fiction," 100.

30 Suvin, *Metamorphoses of Science Fiction*, 15–27. To develop his theory of estrangement, Suvin drew on the early twentieth-century Marxist playwright Bertold Brecht's term *Verfremdungseffekt* (estrangement/alienation effect), a theatrical technique that makes the audience self-aware of themselves as observers rather than immersed in the drama that enfolds them. I share this Brechtian goal of terminal defamiliarization, provoking a new unsettled state in the reader/observer.

31 Jue, "Intimate Objectivity."

32 BBC, *Blue Planet*, "The Deep," September 19, 2001.

33 Yaszek, "Science, Fiction and American Public Policy"; Thomas, "Forms of Duration."

34 Haraway, "Situated Knowledges," 196.
35 Haraway, "Situated Knowledges," 187.
36 D. Smith, "Women's Perspective as a Radical Critique of Sociology"; Harding, "Rethinking Standpoint Epistemology: What is 'Strong Objectivity'?"; Collins, "Learning from the Outsider Within."
37 D. Smith, "Women's Perspective as a Radical Critique of Sociology," 7.
38 Haraway, Modest_Witness@Second_Millennium, 37.
39 Abram, Spell of the Sensuous, 24.
40 Abram, Spell of the Sensuous, 42.
41 Abram, Spell of the Sensuous, 42.
42 Bourdieu, Logic of Practice, 56.
43 Bourdieu, Logic of Practice, 54, 53.
44 Bourdieu, Logic of Practice, 54.
45 Luce Irigaray's Marine Lover of Friedrich Nietzsche exemplifies such a project.
46 Canguilhem, "Living in Its Milieu."
47 McLuhan, Understanding Media, 8.
48 McLuhan, Understanding Media, 8.
49 Guillory, "Genesis of the Media Concept," 321.
50 "It quickly emerged that the unique and proper area of competence of each art coincided with all that was unique to the nature of its medium. The task of self-criticism became to eliminate from the effects of each art any and every effect that might conceivably be borrowed from or by the medium of any other art." Greenberg, "Modernist Painting," 775.
51 Hayles, Writing Machines.
52 For a critique of the geologic paradigm, see Simonetti, "Stratification of Time."
53 J. J. Cohen, Prismatic Ecology.
54 Feld, "Acoustemology"; Lopez, Arctic Dreams; Valentine, "Gravity Fixes."
55 Brathwaite, ConVERSations with Nathaniel Mackey; Deloughrey, Routes and Roots; Glissant, Poetics of Relation; Hessler, Tidalectics.
56 Ingold, "Earth, Sky, Wind, and Weather," S32.
57 For more on the aspiration of purification, see Latour, Pasteurization of France.
58 Nixon, Slow Violence and the Environmentalism of the Poor.
59 Nixon, Slow Violence and the Environmentalism of the Poor, 9.
60 See, for example, the special section on "ocean studies" in PMLA 125, no. 3 (May 2010); Gillis, "Blue Humanities"; Mentz, At the Bottom of Shakespeare's Ocean; Brayton, Shakespeare's Ocean.
61 Early work in the ocean humanities called for a study of the circulation of bodies, texts, and commodities across oceans rather than continents. Paul Gilroy's pathbreaking text, The Black Atlantic: Modernity and Double Consciousness, showed that a version of area studies based around continents (North American studies, European studies, African studies) was inadequate for an analysis of the Middle Passage and its legacies because the slave trade took place across oceans. Gilroy argued that cultural

historians might instead "take the Atlantic as one single, complex unit of analysis" and use it to produce transnational and intercultural perspectives, a necessary reconceptualization for studying the Middle Passage and African diaspora. Gilroy, *Black Atlantic*, 15. As a consequence of Gilroy's intervention, the field of literary studies has explored configuring around ocean basins rather than continents. The primal scene of the slave trade has since appeared in a number of oceanic literary studies, which have approached the ocean as a space where bodies disappear and transform, where property is lost, and where ships traverse currents to the new world—a submarine imaginary I discuss in chapter 4, on underwater museums. See Baucom, *Spectres of the Atlantic*; Allewaert, *Ariel's Ecology*; Wardi, *Water and African American Memory*; Deloughrey, *Routes and Roots*; Sharpe, *In the Wake*.

62 Helmreich, *Sounding the Limits of Life*, 186.

63 M. Cohen, *Novel at Sea*; Casarino, *Modernity at Sea*; Mentz, *At the Bottom of Shakespeare's Ocean*; Mentz, *Shipwreck Modernity*; Brayton, *Shakespeare's Ocean*.

64 Best and Marcus, "Surface Reading."

65 The field of geography has advanced its own critique of a terrestrial bias in ocean space, a topic I take up in more detail in chapter 3 in a discussion of Google Street View. For example, Philip Steinberg's key text *The Social Construction of the Ocean* and the collection *Water Worlds: Human Geographies of the Ocean*, coedited by Jon Anderson and Kimberly Peters, move beyond geography's focus on the terrestrial and fixed senses of space. They aim to develop an ocean specificity adequate to its fluid and mobile properties, moving from the geographic to the hydrographic. Other ocean humanities scholars have explored the traditional navigational practices of non-Western seafaring peoples and their implications for spatial theory. Each of these studies foregrounds the ways that contact with the ocean shapes one's ways of orientating and navigating within the world as a knowing subject. Edwin Hutchins's study *Cognition in the Wild* contrasts Western paradigms of navigation (where the landscape is fixed, and you move around it) to Micronesian navigating practices (where you are still, and the environment moves around you), focusing on theories of cognition. Deloughrey's *Routes and Roots* takes the concept of "tidalectics"—or "tidal dialectics," borrowed from Brathwaite—as a starting point for thinking through transoceanic imaginaries in indigenous and diasporic literary studies.

66 Baucom, "Hydrographies," 308.

67 Kroll, *America's Ocean Wilderness*.

68 Brayton, *Shakespeare's Ocean*.

69 Steinberg and Peters, "Wet Ontologies, Fluid Spaces."

70 For example, in *We Are the Ocean*, anthropologist Epeli Hau'ofa contrasts the notion of islands isolated "in" the sea with an understanding of a more networked "sea of islands" connected by water and the seafaring practices of peoples in Oceania. Similarly, Teresa Shewry's *Hope at Sea: Possible Ecologies in Oceanic Literature* works through oceanic interconnection rather than isolation as a precondition for the formation of hope: "A shark, a river, a forest, a community, a memory, or an imaginary are all

agents that may allow people an awareness of future openness and promise." Shewry, *Hope at Sea*, 3. In *Waves of Knowing: A Seascape Epistemology*, Karen Ingersoll shows how indigenous practices of surfing in Hawai'i become a way of navigating in the world and producing ecological knowledge.

71 Bachelard, *Water and Dreams*, 6.

72 Other work on seawater specifically (as opposed to fresh or "sweet" water) has been potent in imagining specifically feminine alterity. Luce Irigaray's *The Sex Which Is Not One* explores fluid mechanics as a figuration for understanding feminine forms of power and being that are of another order entirely from those of patriarchy. Yet in their chapter "Water and Gestationality" in *Thinking with Water*, Mielle Chandler and Astrida Neimanis eschew any hard-and-fast groundings of water in any particular gender, offering the term *gestationality* to identify how water may help us rethink agency. For Chandler and Neimanis, "gestationality defies the either/or structure of activity and passivity; it is neither active nor passive, and yet both active and passive." Chandler and Neimanis, "Water and Gestationality," 62. See also Alaimo, "States of Suspension."

73 Alaimo, "States of Suspension," 476.

74 Alaimo, "States of Suspension," 477–78.

75 Posthuman subjectivity has also been taken up in the context of water and race. Monique Allewaert's *Ariel's Ecology* argues that eighteenth-century American plantations gave rise to particular ecologies and labor practices that blurred the boundaries between persons and environment, offering a genealogy of posthuman subject formation squarely anchored in the transatlantic slave trade. Christina Sharpe's *In the Wake: On Blackness and Being* traces the ways that the slave ship marks and haunts contemporary black life as a specter of containment, situating white supremacy as a kind of weather or climate that produces premature black death. Her analytic of "wake-work" conjures the wake of the ship, the wake of the funeral, and the sense of consciousness of being awake in order to imagine ways to live and survive in the wake of slavery and "the afterlife of property." Sharpe, *In the Wake*, 18. Eva Hayward argues that race and racial thinking have shaped how we understand oceans and marine life, as registered by artist Ellen Gallagher's *Watery Ecstatic*, Sigmund Freud's "Oceanic Feeling," and the Detroit music group Drexciya and its mythologization of slaves who survived the Middle Passage to create their own undersea bubble metropolis. Hayward, "Wail Bones."

76 Sculptor Jason deCaires Taylor has recently dedicated work to this theme. Taylor's *Raft of Lampedusa* features a sunken sculpture of human figures adrift on a small raft, made out of his signature concrete that encourages coral growth. Yet because the sculpture is already underwater, it appears as a kind of memorial to those North Africans already lost in the Mediterranean crossing.

77 Carson, *Sea around Us*, 15.

78 Rozwadowski, *Machine in Neptune's Garden*.

79 In the last decade, several key studies have emerged that concern infrastructure and

methods of remote sensing in the ocean. Nicole Starosielski's *The Undersea Network* patiently outlines the history of undersea cables across ocean basins that constitute vital communication networks—including telegraphs—and today's fiber-optic network that channels the majority of global internet traffic. John Shiga's work on the history of sonar technologies in "Sonar" and "Ping and the Material Meaning of Ocean Sound" looks at the intersection of the military industrial complex and the characterization of the ocean as a transmission medium. Helen Rozwadowski's historical research on the history of marine technologies and oceanographic voyages in *Fathoming the Ocean* outlines older modes of oceanic measurement, from dredging to find seafloor animals to measuring ocean depth by sounding (dropping a length of weighted rope). In many of these studies, remote-sensing technologies necessarily translate signals into (usually visual) formats that are calibrated to the human sensorium. Taking interest in acoustic technologies that transduce sound into visual formats for human interpreters, in *Alien Ocean* Helmreich draws an analogy between signal transformation and the work of anthropology to develop the idea of a "transductive ethnography." How we come to know about the ocean as a medium depends on the particularities of the technical instruments that scientists use to study the "information" in the seafloor sediment, and how these instruments transduce or transform what they detect into forms that are (visually) legible for human observers. Channeling a Latourian sensibility for tracing chains of mediation, Helmreich's transductive ethnography is a reminder to consider all the mediating apparatuses, fluids, and signal translations that contribute to making features of (oceanic) environments tangible to scientists and nonscientists alike.

80 Kittler, *Draculas Vermächtnis*, 8.

81 Huhtamo and Parikka, *Media Archaeology*, 3.

82 Fuller, *Media Ecologies*, 3.

83 Postman, "Humanism of Media Ecology," 11.

84 Recent studies about the environmental impact of media technologies include Maxwell and Miller, *Greening the Media*; Gabrys, *Digital Rubbish*; Maxwell, Raundalen, and Vestberg, *Media and the Ecological Crisis*; Parks and Starosielski, *Signal Traffic*; J. Smith, *Eco-Sonic Media*; Rust, Monani, and Cubitt, *Ecomedia*; Parikka, *Medianatures*; Hu, *Prehistory of the Cloud*.

85 Starosielski and Walker, *Sustainable Media*, 3. In a later chapter in this edited volume, Minori Ishida compellingly demonstrates the necessity of looking for feedback loops, showing how radiation from the Fukushima Daiichi nuclear meltdown corrupted photographic documentation of the event itself. See Ishida, "Lack of Media," 125–27. Jussi Parikka also charts a series of feedback loops between how geology produces media, and how media frame how we see and understand and investigate geology, envisioning a version of media theory "irreducible to the enthusiasm for software." Parikka, *Geology of Media*, 28.

86 Starosielski and Walker, *Sustainable Media*, 3.

87 Peters, *Marvelous Clouds*, 4.

88 Helmreich, *Sounding the Limits of Life*; Shiga, "Ping and the Material Meanings of Ocean Sound"; Peters, *Marvelous Clouds*; Eidsheim, *Sensing Sound*.

89 Kember and Zylinska, *Life after New Media*, xv.

90 Kember and Zylinska, *Life after New Media*, xiii.

91 Horn, "There Are No Media," 8.

92 Horn, "There Are No Media," 8.

93 Nixon, *Slow Violence and the Environmentalism of the Poor*.

94 Jue, "Anthropocene's Negative Media."

95 Peters, *Marvelous Clouds*, 55.

96 Peters, *Marvelous Clouds*, 55–56.

97 Peters, *Marvelous Clouds*, 112.

98 Hayles, *How We Think*, 17.

99 Flusser, *Writings*, 184.

100 Von Uexküll, *Foray into the Worlds of Animals and Humans*, 44–52.

101 Hayward, "Fingery-Eyes"; see also Hayward, "Enfolded Vision"; Hayward, "Sensational Jellyfish"; Hayward, "More Lessons from a Starfish."

102 Kittler, *Draculas Vermächtnis*, 8. Norm Friesen also identifies transmission, storage, and processing as Kittler's key terms for defining media functions. Friesen, *Media Transatlantic*, 103.

103 Bakhtin, *Dialogic Imagination*.

104 See Katherine Hayles's critique of object-oriented ontologies in "Speculative Aesthetics and Object-Oriented Inquiry."

105 Benjamin, "Theses on a Philosophy of History," 255.

One. Interface

1 Hookway, *Interface*, 59–60.

2 Throughout *World without Sun*, the fantastical imagery of advanced underwater technologies is tempered by Cousteau's voice-over, full of domestic analogies. Not only does the submarine dock in a "garage" but the men "sunbathe" in the underwater habitat Conshelf II (replete with sunglasses and a leisure book), and they even bring a pet parrot.

3 Drucker, "Reading Interface," 213.

4 Breathing pressurized air in a decompression chamber and breathing pressurized air underwater produce different physiological responses. According to an article in *Alert Diver* magazine, immersion in water does matter because of the temperature change. Thermal stress from colder temperatures results in changes in blood circulation and the urge to urinate: "Many people do not fully appreciate the physiological impact of being immersed in water. An immediate response to the hydrostatic pressure is that

a substantial amount of blood normally remaining in the capacitance vessels (veins) of the legs is pushed to the central volume (in the chest). A well-known study of this effect found that an average of 700 mL of blood is pushed to the heart during the resting phase of the cardiac cycle. The heart is stretched by the increased blood volume and responds immediately by contracting harder and then, over a short period, by suppressing certain hormones to promote increased fluid elimination through the kidneys. This is a healthy response to the physiological perception of the presence of excess fluid volume. Practically, this is why people have to urinate even after fairly short periods of immersion." Nochetto, "Air vs. Nitrox."

5 The exception, here, would be to think about elevation changes in mountain climbing. High-altitude climbers sometimes bring oxygen with them as well—not just divers!

6 Other biologically centered ocean science fictions include Samuel Delany's "Driftglass"; Joan Slonczewski's *Door into Ocean*; Frank Schatzing's *Swarm*; Peter Watts's *Starfish*; Jack Vance's *Blue World*; Vonda McIntyre's *Superliminal*; Michael Crichton's *Sphere*; M. M. Buckner's *Watermind*; China Miéville's *Kraken*; and the manga series *Children of the Sea* by Daisuke Igarashi.

7 Paksy Plackis-Cheng, "Hero of the Planet, Sylvia Earle, on the Earth's Blue Lungs," accessed June 1, 2019, http://www.impactmania.com/article/sylvia-earle/.

8 Lev Manovich, "Cinema as Cultural Interface," accessed May 18, 2019, http://manovich.net/index.php/projects/cinema-as-a-cultural-interface.

9 Drucker, "Reading Interface," 213; Galloway, *Interface Effect*, vii.

10 Hoffman, "Interface Theory of Perception," 1.

11 Hoffman, "Interface Theory of Perception," 8–9.

12 Drucker, "Reading Interface," 219.

13 Drucker, "Reading Interface," 213.

14 Galloway, *Interface Effect*, 31.

15 Galloway, *Interface Effect*, 44.

16 Galloway, *Interface Effect*, 92.

17 Cited in Hookway, *Interface*, 59.

18 Fuller and Cramer, "Interface," 149.

19 Hookway, *Interface*, 59.

20 The interface would "define and separate areas of unequal energy distribution within a fluid in motion, whether this difference is given in terms of velocity, viscosity, directionality of flow, kinetic form, pressure, density, temperature, or any combination of these. From difference the interface would produce fluidity." Hookway, *Interface*, 59.

21 It is surprising that Hookway does not cite many female scholars, given the long cultural and intellectual history involving women and water. At bare minimum, Luce Irigaray and Katherine Hayles deserve a mention, since Irigaray extensively worked with fluid mechanics to think through feminism and Hayles has written extensively on the history of both cybernetics and chaos theory that Hookway discusses at length.

22 Blish, "Surface Tension," 408. See also Milburn, *Nanovision*, chapter 2.

23 M. Cohen, "Chronotopes of the Sea," 647–48.

24 Blish, "Surface Tension," 416.

25 Although Blish hints that the microscopic humans retain an echo of the genetic do-
    nor's personality pattern and possibly a Jungian notion of ancestral memory, any his-
    torical writing and storage would have to be able to survive the corrosive effects of
    water.

26 Blish, "Surface Tension," 398. As I explain in chapter 3, which considers this question
    at length, Vilém Flusser concludes that genetic information would be the most reli-
    able form of information storage in an aquatic environment.

27 Blish, "Surface Tension," 401.

28 As my biochemist dad was fond of saying: as soon as you have water, you have chemistry.

29 Blish, "Surface Tension," 401.

30 Blish, "Surface Tension," 401.

31 Blish, "Surface Tension," 397.

32 Although Cousteau's first film, *Le monde du silence*, contained controversial footage
    of killing a gray whale and dynamiting a coral reef, he later became an advocate for
    ocean conservation and marine protection.

33 Cousteau, *Silent World*, 12.

34 Gagnan suggested using a demand valve that had previously been used to feed cooking
    gas automatically into the motors of automobiles. Using two demand valves—one to
    modulate the pressure of air from 150 atm to 6 atm in the valve, and then a second to
    change the 6 atm to ambient pressure—Gagnan designed the prototype of the "Aqua-
    Lung," or what was to become modern scuba.

35 Cousteau, *Silent World*, 3.

36 Cousteau, *Silent World*, 19.

37 Cousteau, *Silent World*, 3.

38 Alaimo, "States of Suspension."

39 Neimanis, *Bodies of Water*.

40 Cousteau, *Silent World*, 152.

41 Cousteau, *Silent World*, 20.

42 In contemporary diving courses, the metaphor of the "soda can" is used to illustrate
    the parallels between rising slowly and slowly opening a soda can, or rising quickly
    and having the soda can froth over. In cases of either prolonged diving and/or deep
    diving, one must do a "safety stop" for three to five minutes at fifteen feet below in
    order to allow the extra gas to exit (precipitate out of) the body.

43 Cousteau, *Silent World*, 10–11.

44 "Proprioception," accessed August 19, 2018, https://www.medilexicon.com/dictionary
    /72809.

45 Hansen, *Bodies in Code*, 123.

46 Hansen, *Bodies in Code*, 112.

47 Dyson, *Sounding New Media*, 129.

48 Osmosis is the term from chemistry denoting how molecules move across a semiper-
    meable membrane from a more concentrated solution to a less concentrated one.
49 "Nitrogen Narcosis," https://medical-dictionary.thefreedictionary.com/nitrogen+narcosis,
    accessed May 18, 2019.
50 *Oxford English Dictionary*, s.v. "nitrogen narcosis," www.oed.com, accessed August 24,
    2014.
51 Cousteau, *Silent World*, 22.
52 Cousteau, *Silent World*, 23.
53 Cousteau, *Silent World*, 23.
54 Cousteau, *Silent World*, 88.
55 Cousteau, *Silent World*, 89.
56 Cousteau, *Silent World*, 89.
57 Cousteau, *Silent World*, 89.
58 *Oxford English Dictionary*, s.v. "Saturation," www.oed.com, accessed August 24, 2014.
59 Jue and Ruiz, introduction to *Saturation*.
60 Cousteau, *Silent World*, 18–19.
61 Cousteau, *Silent World*, 137.
62 Parts of this analysis appear in Jue, "Churning up the Depths," though not specifically
    in relation to interfaces.
63 Egan, "Oceanic," 4.
64 Freud, *Civilization and Its Discontents*, 7–18.
65 Egan, "Oceanic," 8.
66 *Oxford English Dictionary*, s.v. "rapture," www.oed.com, accessed August 24, 2014.
67 Egan, "Oceanic," 28.
68 Egan, "Oceanic," 28–29.
69 Egan, "Oceanic," 30.
70 Best and Marcus, "Surface Reading," 9.
71 M. Cohen, "Narratology in the Archive of Literature," 66.
72 Cheng, "Skins, Tattoos, and Susceptibility," 101.
73 Delbourgo, "Divers Things," 161–164, 174–176. Delbourgo connects the practice of
    free diving with colonialism, noting that in the Caribbean, divers were typically na-
    tives employed to dive for sponges or valuable items that had fallen from ships into
    the ocean. Yet routinely exposing the body to seawater through free diving resulted in
    certain amphibious changes: for example, tougher skin, effects on the eyes, expanded
    lung capacity, and sometimes the crippling that comes with the bends. Amphibious-
    ness in this historical context is not a posthuman condition of empowerment or the
    transcendence of environmental constraints but rather the effect of labor in service
    of colonial power.
74 Hammond, "Menfish and the Great Hydrosphere," 696.
75 Earle, *Sea Change*, 27.
76 "Divers in Japan and Korea—mostly women, known as *ama*—have honed breath-hold
    diving techniques to perfection, passing traditions from mother to daughter through

generations." Earle, *Sea Change*, 16. Although the diving culture she inhabited was masculinist, Earle was mentored by the renowned scientist and 1950s TV personality Eugenie Clark, nicknamed the "Shark Lady"—a guide in navigating the seas of patriarchy.

77 Earle, *Sea Change*, 106.

78 Earle, *Sea Change*, 100.

79 Earle, *Sea Change*, 101.

80 Earle, *Sea Change*, 110.

81 Earle, *Sea Change*, 100.

82 In Open Water Dive training, I learned that the dive charts for calculating safe dive times were based on male two-hundred-pound bodies, since they were developed by the military.

83 "Tektite" is the name for a small meteorite that falls to rest on the ocean floor.

84 Earle, *Sea Change*, 68, 76, 122.

85 Earle, *Sea Change*, 69. The inversion shows, of course, that men can expect to be referred to without reference to gender or marital status.

86 Earle, *Sea Change*, 66.

87 Earle, *Sea Change*, 66.

88 Earle, *Sea Change*, 70, 62, 91.

89 Earle, *Sea Change*, 75.

90 Earle, *Sea Change*, 59.

91 Galloway, Thacker, and Wark, *Excommunication*, 11.

92 Ten Bos, "Towards an Amphibious Anthropology"; Gagné and Rasmussen, "Introduction"; Krause, "Towards an Amphibious Anthropology of Delta Life"; Pauwelussen, "Amphibious Anthropology."

93 Earle, *Sea Change*, 43.

94 Earle, *Sea Change*, 24–25.

95 Earle, *Sea Change*, 122.

96 Earle, *Sea Change*, 47.

97 Earle, *Sea Change*, 5–6.

98 Earle, *Sea Change*, 6–7.

99 Earle, *Sea Change*, 6–7, 31.

100 Carson, *Edge of the Sea*, 5–6.

101 By "science fictional alienation," I allude to the productive kind of estrangement effect (*Verfremdungseffekt*) that Darko Suvin describes in *Metamorphoses of Science Fiction*, an aesthetic effect that shocks a reader or spectator into a form of self-consciousness.

102 Earle, *Sea Change*, 16.

103 Kember and Zylinska, *Life after New Media*.

104 Starosielski, "Materiality of Media Heat"; Starosielski, "Thermocultures of Geologic Media."

105 For an extended discussion of historicity and breathing relations, see J. O. Taylor, "Auras and Ice Cores"; Choy, "Air's Substantiations"; Menely, "Anthropocene Air."

106 Interview with Kristina Gjerde, *IUCN Marine News* 12 (November 2015): 16.

107 Jue, "Performative Science Fiction."

108 Alaimo, *Exposed*, 155.

109 See, for example, Alaimo, *Exposed*; Neimanis, *Bodies of Water*; Barad, *Meeting the Universe Halfway*.

110 Alaimo, *Exposed*, 167, 168.

Two. Inscription

1 Kittler, *Discourse Networks 1800/1900*, 356.

2 Taibbi, "Great American Bubble Machine."

3 The blog *Vulgar Army: Octoprop to Octopop* presents a collection of images from Europe, America, and Japan dating back to the 1830s that show octopi, vampire squid, kraken, and other tentacular creatures. The blog exhibits these cartoons in order to "identify and criticise themes in the use of the octopus as a polemic metaphor, for example, its use as signifying 'action at a distance' or in dehumanising a group." "About," *Vulgar Army: Octoprop to Octopop*, accessed May 24, 2014, http://octoprop.wordpress.com/.

4 Vampire squid are a genus of the class *Cephalopoda* (the name means "head-foot"), which includes octopi, squid, cuttlefish, and the nautilus.

5 This also translates as "eight arrival pass" or "go everywhere pass." See Hong Kong's MTR website, accessed May 24, 2014, http://www.octopus.com.hk/home/en/index.html.

6 *Dream of the Fisherman's Wife* is an example of the Japanese erotic art *shunga*.

7 Hsu, "Put an Octopus on It!"

8 According to NRO spokesperson Karen Ferguson, "NROL-39 is represented by the octopus [in its logo], a versatile, adaptable, and highly intelligent creature. Emblematically, enemies of the United States can be reached no matter where they choose to hide. 'Nothing is beyond our reach' defines this mission and the value it brings to our nation." Szoldra, "US Spy Agency Boasts 'Nothing Is beyond Our Reach' with New Logo."

9 Haraway, *Staying with the Trouble*.

10 *Vampyroteuthis Infernalis* was originally published in German in 1987, but I refer to the 2011 English translation by Rodrigo Maltez Novaes.

11 Kirksey, *Multispecies Salon*.

12 Flusser, *Vampyroteuthis Infernalis*, 27–28.

13 As outlined in the introduction, I propose "milieu specificity" as an evolution from "media specificity" as theorized (in different circumstances) by Katherine Hayles (*Writing Machines*) and Clement Greenberg ("Modernist Painting," 755).

14 Letter to Milton Vargas, 1981, reprinted in Flusser, *Vampyroteuthis Infernalis*, 142.

15 Flusser, *Vampyroteuthis Infernalis*, 142, 146.

16 Flusser, *Vampyroteuthis Infernalis*, 28.

17 Flusser, *Vampyroteuthis Infernalis*, 126.

18 Suvin, *Metamorphoses of Science Fiction*, 5.

19 There is a similarity here with how Eric Kluitenberg defines "imaginary media"—inclusive of such things as *Star Trek* universal translators, spiritual mediums, and divine clockwork—as things that often get left out of materialist media history. Kluitenberg writes that "imaginary media can therefore be read as an ironic allegorical comment on the impossible desires that the imagining subject projects onto its surroundings, desires that estrange it further from its own illusion of selfhood." Kluitenberg, "On the Archaeology of Imaginary Media," 66.

20 Flusser, *Vampyroteuthis Infernalis*, 115.

21 Flusser, *Writings*, 46.

22 For a more detailed biography, see Finger, Guldin, and Bernardo, *Vilém Flusser*.

23 Flusser, *Freedom of the Migrant*, 25.

24 Flusser imagines modifications of television as something like a proto-internet: if only television viewers could also send messages (or images) to one another. Of course, this is early media theory. As Alexander Galloway and Eugene Thacker convincingly argue, interconnection is not an automatic guarantor of freedom because it makes both networked entities vulnerable. Galloway and Thacker discuss communication-as-vulnerability in terms of technology, but the same logic could be analogized to agricultural monoculture, which enables single diseases to wipe out entire crops. As Deleuze wrote, "the quest for 'universals of communication' ought to make us shudder." Quoted in Galloway and Thacker, *Exploit*, 23.

25 Hayles, *Writing Machines*, 24. Under Hayles's definition of inscription, ink that has dried on paper would count (like calligraphy), but ink that flowed into the ocean (say, an octopus's glandular ink cloud) would be of more uncertain ontological status. Even though the medium of ink might be the same, the environment plays an important factor in the stability and legibility of media.

26 *Oxford English Dictionary*, s.v. "Inscription," www.oed.com, accessed May 21, 2019.

27 Blish, "Surface Tension."

28 Flusser, *Vampyroteuthis Infernalis*, 73.

29 Flusser, *Vampyroteuthis Infernalis*, 66.

30 Flusser, *Vampyroteuthis Infernalis*, 71.

31 Flusser, *Vampyroteuthis Infernalis*, 73–74.

32 Flusser, *Vampyroteuthis Infernalis*, 73.

33 Tuan, *Space and Place*, 34–50.

34 Flusser, *Vampyroteuthis Infernalis*, 43.

35 Flusser, *Vampyroteuthis Infernalis*, 78.

36 Flusser, *Vampyroteuthis Infernalis*, 40, 42.

37 Flusser, *Vampyroteuthis Infernalis*, 78.

38 Flusser, *Vampyroteuthis Infernalis*, 79.

39 Flusser, *Vampyroteuthis Infernalis*, 78.

40 The "spiral" figure of the vampire squid presents a way for thinking the nonlinearity

of posthistory related to a variety of phenomena, including the camera apparatus and the temporality of genetic engineering.

41 Flusser, *Vampyroteuthis Infernalis*, 77.

42 Even in textbooks such as *Invertebrate Zoology* (edited by Ruppert, Fox, and Barnes), the physiological axes have to be flipped for cephalopods. For example, what for vertebrates is the dorsal side becomes the "back" of the squid; what is ventral becomes the "front."

43 Artist David Zink Yi's squid sculpture was inspired by the otherness of Flusser's squid and its liquid media. Douglas, "Fish Tale."

44 De Castro, "Exchanging Perspectives," 465.

45 De Castro, "Exchanging Perspectives," 471.

46 De Castro, "Exchanging Perspectives," 474–75.

47 Le Guin, "Author of Acacia Seeds," 616. Le Guin uses the Latin prefix "thero-" for wild beasts.

48 Le Guin, "Author of Acacia Seeds," 619.

49 There is, of course, also the question of indigenous forms of orienting to the world through language, discussed (for example) in studies like Julie Cruikshank's *Do Glaciers Listen?*, a vital and necessary field of study beyond the scope of my immediate project.

50 Lakoff and Johnson are quick to point out that although there is a "systematic character of metaphorically defined concepts," metaphors often logically contradict each other (for example, "time is money" vs. "time is a moving object").

51 Lakoff and Johnson, *Metaphors We Live By*, 235.

52 Lakoff and Johnson also discuss ontological metaphors and structural metaphors as two other major categories.

53 Lakoff and Johnson, *Metaphors We Live By*, 14.

54 Lakoff and Johnson, *Metaphors We Live By*, 181.

55 Lakoff and Johnson, *Metaphors We Live By*, 57.

56 Ricoeur, *Rule of Metaphor*.

57 Suvin, *Metamorphoses of Science Fiction*, 361.

58 Suvin, *Metamorphoses of Science Fiction*, 347–48, 351.

59 Suvin, *Metamorphoses of Science Fiction*, 351.

60 Suvin, *Metamorphoses of Science Fiction*, 357.

61 Suvin, *Metamorphoses of Science Fiction*, 367.

62 Suvin, *Metamorphoses of Science Fiction*, 369.

63 De Man, "Epistemology of Metaphor," 17.

64 Ricoeur, *Rule of Metaphor*, 144.

65 De Man, "Epistemology of Metaphor," 23.

66 De Certeau, *Practice of Everyday Life*, 115.

67 In "Lives We Metaphor By," Stefan Helmreich aptly criticizes one of Lakoff and Johnson's favorite examples, "argument is war," for the way it assumes a precultural body. Argument can also be understood as "a connected series of statements to establish a

definite proposition," notably absent of any war terminology. By turning "metaphor" into a verb in his title "Lives We Metaphor By," Helmreich stresses metaphorical formation as a living activity rather than a reified cultural code.

68 See Nagel, "What Is It Like to Be a Bat?," 435–50.

69 In *A Foray into the Worlds of Animals and Humans*, Uexküll writes, for example, that the tick is really only sensitive to three "perception marks": warmth, light, and the scent of butyric acid, a chemical present in animal sweat. The tick's perceptual world is defined by the presence or absence of these three things, whereas another animal would notice a different range of sensations.

70 Uexküll, *Foray into the Worlds of Animals and Humans*, 70.

71 Flusser, *Vampyroteuthis Infernalis*, 53, 63.

72 Flusser, *Vampyroteuthis Infernalis*, 126.

73 Flusser, *Vampyroteuthis Infernalis*, 127.

74 Flusser, *Vampyroteuthis Infernalis*, 127.

75 Flusser, *Vampyroteuthis Infernalis*, 129.

76 Flusser, *Vampyroteuthis Infernalis*, 129.

77 Flusser, *Vampyroteuthis Infernalis*, 130.

78 Derrida, *Archive Fever*, 36.

79 Flusser, *Vampyroteuthis Infernalis*, 141–42.

80 Flusser, *Vampyroteuthis Infernalis*, 136.

81 Flusser, *Writings*, 84.

82 Flusser, *Vampyroteuthis Infernalis*, 23.

83 Flusser, *Writings*, 26.

84 One artistic work that illustrates this is Natalie Jeremijenko's project *One Tree*, in which one thousand fruitless walnut trees were cloned from one tree's tissue, then planted in pairs around the San Francisco Bay Area, each pair developing in response to its microclimate and locale. See Natalie Jeremijenko, "One Tree(s)," *Inspiration Green*, accessed May 22, 2019, http://www.medienkunstnetz.de/works/one-trees.

85 Flusser, *Vampyroteuthis Infernalis*, 46.

86 Hayward, "Enfolded Vision."

87 Flusser, *Writings*, 49.

88 Flusser was researching and writing about the vampire squid two years before the publication of *Towards a Philosophy of Photography*, as evidenced by letters he wrote to Milton Vargas in 1981. Flusser, *Vampyroteuthis Infernalis*, 129–42.

89 Peters, *Marvelous Clouds*, 52.

90 Many thanks to Whitney Trettien for this colorful observation, which she offered in response to my presentation "Vampire Squid Media" at a November 2013 graduate colloquium sponsored by the Duke University Program in Literature.

91 Flusser, *Vampyroteuthis Infernalis*, 105. This question of how an underwater species would develop means of preserving history is not only science fictional but figures into many nature documentaries. "Aliens of the Deep Sea," for example, laments the fact that octopus mothers die before their young hatch, preventing members of an

otherwise highly intelligent species from passing down the knowledge gained during their lifetimes. See *Nature of Things*, season 49, episode 28, "Aliens of the Deep Sea," directed by Jérôme Julienne and John Jackson, 2010, http://www.cbc.ca/natureofthings /episodes/aliens-of-the-deep-sea.

92 Filmmaker David Gatten literalized a kind of water writing in his work *What the Sea Said*, where he submerged 16 mm film for two weeks, taking the ocean as a co-artist in the production of celluloid inscriptions.

93 Serres, *Hermes*, 29–38.

94 Flusser, *Towards a Philosophy of Photography*, 45–46.

95 Flusser, *Vampyroteuthis Infernalis*, 109.

96 Flusser, *Towards a Philosophy of Photography*, 38.

97 Flusser, *Vampyroteuthis Infernalis*, 115.

98 This fascination with squid ink may also remind us of China Miéville's novel *Kraken* and its fictional religion based around squid, with holy texts written in teuthic ink.

99 J. Cohen, "Seeing without Eyes."

100 Kripke et al., "Visualizing Biological Complexity in Cephalopod Skin," 486–87.

101 Godfrey-Smith, *Other Minds*, 112.

102 Monterey Bay Aquarium, "Tentacles," accessed June 3, 2019, https://www.montereybay aquarium.org/animals-and-exhibits/exhibits/tentacles.

103 Lanier, "What Cephalopods Can Teach Us about Language."

104 In characterizing *Vampyroteuthis infernalis*, Flusser likely drew from knowledge of other cannibalistic cephalopods, such as the Humboldt squid (*Dosidicus gigas*), which swim in schools and have a reputation for being extremely violent.

105 Flusser, *Vampyroteuthis Infernalis*, 23; Ellis, "Introducing *Vampyroteuthis infernalis*, the Vampire Squid from Hell."

106 Johnson, "*Vampyroteuthis Infernalis*."

107 Flusser, *Vampyroteuthis Infernalis*, 109, 105.

108 Flusser, *Vampyroteuthis Infernalis*, 110–11. While this characterization of *Vampyroteuthis infernalis* may seem hyperbolic and fantastical, recent studies have shown that coleoid cephalopods can edit their RNA (responsible for making proteins), with impacts on the formation of nerve cells. See Yong, "Octopuses Do Something Really Strange to Their Genes."

109 Meerloo, *Rape of the Mind*; Flusser, *Vampyroteuthis Infernalis*, 91–92.

110 Flusser, *Vampyroteuthis Infernalis*, 109.

111 Connecting photographic and sexual reproduction, Joel Snyder provocatively alludes to the womb-like dark of the camera's interior as a matrix for creating photographs agentially directed by both the photographer and something else. Snyder, "What Happens by Itself in Photography?," 364. However, my concern with Flusser's discussion of photography and sexuality has more to do with the rapist and totalitarian connotations of the vampire squid transmitting memories on others through sex.

112 Barthes, *Camera Lucida*, 27.

113 Flusser, *Towards a Philosophy of Photography*, 33.

114 Mulvey, "Visual Pleasure in Narrative Cinema."

115 Sontag, *On Photography*, 13–15; Haraway, *Primate Visions*, 26–58.

116 A similar process is involved in Man Ray's "Rayographs," where, in his darkroom, he arranged objects on undeveloped photo paper and then turned on the lights, sometimes with multiple exposures.

117 Drawing on work in science, technology, and society, Charis Thompson develops the notion of "ontological choreography" as "the dynamic coordination of technical, scientific, kinship, gender, emotional, legal, political, and financial aspects of [assisted reproductive technology] clinics." Thompson, *Making Parents*, 8.

118 Flusser, *Vampyroteuthis Infernalis*, 113.

119 Flusser, *Vampyroteuthis Infernalis*, 114.

120 Flusser, *Vampyroteuthis Infernalis*, 111.

121 Flusser, *Vampyroteuthis Infernalis*, 145.

122 Flusser, *Vampyroteuthis Infernalis*, 146. Ursula Le Guin would probably agree.

123 "I will argue for an understanding of SF as the literature of cognitive estrangement." Suvin, *Metamorphoses of Science Fiction*, 4.

124 Flusser, *Writings*, 68.

125 Wall, "Photography and Liquid Intelligence," 109.

126 Wall, "Photography and Liquid Intelligence," 109.

127 Not all fluids are the same. Consider Helmreich's call for a form of theory specific to seawater ("Nature/Culture/Seawater"), or Bachelard's discussion of different kinds of fluids (blood, milk, sweet or fresh water) in poetry (*Water and Dreams*).

128 Wall, "Photography and Liquid Intelligence," 109.

129 Wall, "Photography and Liquid Intelligence," 109.

130 Wall, "Photography and Liquid Intelligence," 109.

131 Wall, "Photography and Liquid Intelligence," 110. Water is involved in all the major ways that we produce energy; for example, it cools nuclear reactors, powers dams, and is required for hydraulic fracturing. An exception to the general treatment of water in science fiction films is Andrei Tarkovsky's film adaptation of Stanisław Lem's novel *Solaris*, which takes place on a space station orbiting the (sentient) ocean planet Solaris, a looming presence outside the window portals.

132 Zylinska, "Hydromedia."

133 Zylinska, "Hydromedia."

134 Flusser, *Writings*, 128.

135 Flusser, *Vampyroteuthis Infernalis*, 109.

136 Flusser, *Vampyroteuthis Infernalis*, 110.

137 Derrida, *Dissemination*, 7.

138 Milburn, *Nanovision*, 120. Here, Milburn describes the disseminative science fiction horror of the world reduced to gray goo by nanotechnological accident.

139 Wall, "Photography and Liquid Intelligence," 109.

140 Hayles, *How We Became Posthuman*, 198–99.

141 Thanks to Negar Mottahedeh for this observation.

142 Sara Ahmed, "Orientations Matter."

143 Chiang, "Exhalation," 745.

144 Chiang, "Exhalation," 750.

145 Yong, "Nature's Cutest Symbiosis.".

146 Yong, "Lovely Tale of an Adorable Squid and Its Glowing Partner."

147 Yong, "Nature's Cutest Symbiosis."

148 Of course, the desire not to be seen has emerged as a central concern for a variety of contemporary artworks that engage the politics of technical surveillance and biometrics: for example, Zach Blas's *Facial Weaponization Suite* (2011–14), Hito Steyerl's *How Not to Be Seen: A Fucking Didactic Educational .MOV File* (2013), and Adam Harvey's *CV Dazzle* (2010). These artworks take invisibility as an aspiration, showing the pervasiveness of how identity capture and biometric recognition operate today. As Zach Blas and Jacob Gaboury write, "One of the greatest challenges to contemporary queer and feminist scholarship is to reconcile the historical project of identity politics with neoliberalism's co-optation of identity as a means to enact power through new structures of control, such as digital media and computational technologies." Blas and Gaboury, "Biometrics and Opacity," 155. Perhaps the Hawaiian bobtail squid flashes up in a moment of danger that is the surveillance state but only with the help of its symbiotic bioluminescent bacteria, a chthonic partner.

149 iBiology, "Hawaiian Bobtail Squid."

150 Shell, *Hide and Seek*, 18.

151 Yusoff, "Excess, Catastrophe, and Climate Change," 1010; Walker, "Projecting Sea Level Rise."

152 Jue, "Anthropocene's Negative Media."

153 Ghosh, "Becoming Undetectable in the Chthulucene."

Three. Database

1 Olympus Diving, "Shipwreck U-352," accessed June 2, 2019, https://www.olympusdiving .com/en/u-352. I dove the wreck in person in June 2015.

2 Shakespeare, *Tempest*, I.2.396–401. In the play, Ferdinand's father is still alive, and Ariel only sings the song at Prospero's bidding to mislead Ferdinand.

3 Baucom, "Hydrographies," 302.

4 Mentz, *At the Bottom of Shakespeare's Ocean*, 8.

5 Neimanis helpfully outlines an even more nuanced description of seawater's agency beyond the duality of storage and erasure, naming its "gestational" and "archival" properties, as well as the "capacity to dissolve" and "differentiate." Neimanis, "Feminist Subjectivity, Watered," 30–31.

6 Hu, *Prehistory of the Cloud*; Hogan, "Water Woes and Data Flows."

7   Chansanchai, "Microsoft Research Project Puts Cloud in Ocean for the First Time."

8   Zylinska, "Hydromedia."

9   Bauman, *Liquid Modernity.*

10 Nicole Starosielski persuasively argues that underwater environments do not exist as purely natural spaces, apart from histories of race and nation. Studies of underwater cinema would do well to move "beyond fluidity" by considering the ocean as a social space, "a territory over which inequality continues to circulate." Starosielski, "Beyond Fluidity," 165.

11 MacLeod, "Water and the Material Imagination."

12 "In computer science database is defined as a structured collection of data. The data stored in a database is organized for fast search and retrieval by a computer and therefore it is anything but a simple collection of items. Different types of databases—hierarchical, network, relational and object-oriented—use different models to organize data." Manovich, "Database as a Symbolic Form."

13 Hayles, "Print Is Flat, Code Is Deep," 75.

14 Hayles, "Print Is flat, Code Is Deep," 75–76.

15 The EBBA team abandoned cataloging standards like rhyme schemes and stanzas, which proved inconsistent across ballads and were sometimes impossible to determine due to cramped printing; these challenges made the sea god Proteus a useful figure for the ballad archive. Fumerton, "Digitizing Ephemera and Its Discontents," 56.

16 Weinbren, "Ocean, Database, Recut," 64.

17 Weinbren, "Ocean, Database, Recut," 66.

18 Weinbren, "Ocean, Database, Recut," 69.

19 Manovich, "Database as a Symbolic Form."

20 Wiener, *Cybernetics*, 11.

21 Feminist scholars like Luce Irigaray (*The Sex Which Is Not One*) have found viscosity to be a potent material metaphor as an intermediary between fluid and solid that retains some internal form; Nancy Tuana theorizes "viscous porosity" as a way of imagining beings necessarily constituted out of relationality. French writer Jules Michelet attributes viscosity to the biological component of seawater: "Chemical analyses do not explain this characteristic [of viscosity]. In it [seawater], there is an organic substance which these analyses reach only by destroying it, by taking away from it its special properties and by reducing it violently to the general elements," like salt and H_2O. Michelet, *Sea*, 52–53.

22 This notion goes at least as far back as the acronym ACID (atomicity, consistency, isolation, durability) popularized in the 1970s, which named a desired set of properties for database transactions. This more rigid programming framework has recently given way to another clever acronym, BASE (basic availability, soft-state, eventual consistency), to account for conditions when one is searching for something while new data is still flowing into the database that has yet to settle on a stable structure. This accounting for newness seems to suggest that modern computing demands emulate more of a *fluid* state than a rigid state, although it is uncertain if the two

philosophies would (to pursue the chemical analogy) neutralize each other. Yet if we step back and think about the metaphorical use of "fluid" in BASE, "fluid" describes the *structure* of the data organization, not the materiality of the data entries or their capacity to become protean, to change. Both ACID and BASE acronyms do not describe individual data entries; they describe the *structure* of search queries, again showing how "fluidity" as a general description of movement differs from the ontological specificity of seawater as an agential material. See Roe, "ACID vs. BASE."

23 Chandler and Neimanis, "Water and Gestationality," 62.
24 Pálsson, "Birth of the Aquarium," 209.
25 Pálsson, "Birth of the Aquarium," 211.
26 Pálsson, "Birth of the Aquarium," 223.
27 Moorea Biocode Project, accessed June 2, 2012, http://mooreabiocode.org/about/biocode -objectives.
28 Deloughrey, "Myth of Isolates"; Michael Shapiro, "Moorea's Ark."
29 Brunner, *Ocean at Home.*
30 Maya Lin, "What Is Missing?" accessed May 22, 2019, http://whatismissing.net/home.
31 Bowker, *Memory Practices in the Sciences*, 186.
32 Bowker, *Memory Practices in the Sciences*, 185.
33 Census of Marine Life, accessed July 5, 2018, http://www.coml.org/.
34 Alaimo, "Feminist Science Studies and Ecocriticism," 196.
35 Heise, *Imagining Extinction*, 84.
36 Clark, "Derangements of Scale," 149.
37 Clark, "Derangements of Scale," 151.
38 Clark, "Derangements of Scale," 163.
39 Suvin, *Metamorphoses of Science Fiction.*
40 Quoted in Earle, "Deep Dive into the Ocean in Google Earth."
41 As Helmreich notes in *Alien Ocean*, no one has yet successfully traced the origin of this quote, despite its popularity and frequent citation.
42 Anderson and Peters, *Water Worlds*, 10.
43 Steven Mentz, *The Bookfish* (blog), http://stevementz.com/.
44 Even visualizations of the land can be misleading; because Google Earth is composed of many satellite photographs taken over time, any moving objects such as ships or cars are seen dotted across Google's Earth.
45 Heise, *Imagining Extinction*, 64.
46 Vannini and Taggart, "Day We Drove on the Ocean," 91.
47 Steinberg, *Social Construction of the Ocean*, 105.
48 Steinberg, *Social Construction of the Ocean*, 105.
49 Sobel, *Longitude.*
50 Burnett, "Mapping Time," 13.
51 National Ocean Service, "What Is a Dead Zone?," accessed September 2, 2013, http://oceanservice.noaa.gov/facts/deadzone.html.
52 Arendt, *Human Condition*; Virilio, *Speed and Politics*; Chow, *Age of the World Target.*

53 Helmreich, "From Spaceship Earth to Google Ocean," 1225.

54 Haraway, *When Species Meet*, 250.

55 For these tracks to be meaningful, one would need to combine a study of the animal's movements along with a clear understanding of the tracking technology itself, of when it was possible to broadcast locational data, in addition to other contexts involving seasons, currents, and the movements of food sources.

56 Google Street View Oceans, accessed June 24, 2015, https://www.google.com.au/maps /streetview/#oceans.

57 Catlin Seaview Survey, accessed September 1, 2017, http://catlinseaviewsurvey.com /about/about.

58 This quotation is from a page on the Venter Institute's website that is now extinct, but the language of the original is preserved in Sun et al. "Community Cyberinfrastructure," D546.

59 "Analysis and comparison of complex metagenomic data is driving the development of a new class of bioinformatics and visualization software. CAMERA will integrate these tools with its database, couple them with large-scale compute resources, and make them widely available to the research community," Seshadri et al., "CAMERA: A Community Resource for Metagenomics," 395.

60 Benjamin, "The Work of Art in the Age of Mechanical Reproduction," in *Illuminations*, 248.

61 ATLAS *in silico*, accessed September 2, 2013, http://www.atlasinsilico.net/#about.

62 ATLAS *in silico*, accessed September 2, 2013, http://www.atlasinsilico.net/about.html.

63 West, "Algorithmic Object as Natural Specimen"; West, "Sensate Abstraction."

64 Goßmann et al., "Scalable Auditory Data Signatures for Discovery Oriented Browsing in an Expressive Context," 1.

65 Helmreich, *Alien Ocean*, 27.

66 Transduction describes the transformation of a signal from one medium to another, such as sonar data into a visual readout. Drawing an analogy between signal transformation and the work of anthropology in *Alien Ocean*, Helmreich develops the idea of a "transductive ethnography" most clearly in a chapter on descending in the *Alvin* submarine, thinking through the similarities between cyborg and ethnographic presence underwater in the mediating bubble of the submersible.

67 Alaimo, "Feminist Science Studies and Ecocriticism," 195.

68 Pickering, *Mangle of Practice*.

69 Helmreich rather poetically notes the equation of database and microbial genomic data: "If the sea was once a chaotic and cosmic amnion, an archive of life primeval and life to come, those pasts and futures nowadays read more like a mix-and-match database than a straightforward, stratigraphic archaeological record." Helmreich, *Alien Ocean*, 99.

70 Lovelock, *Gaia*, 88.

71 Daston and Galison, *Objectivity*, 27.

72 For a more detailed discussion of *Tierra*, see chapter 9 in Hayles, *How We Became Post-human*; Christa Sommerer and Laurent Mignonneau, "Art as a Living Process."

73 Kember, *Cyberfeminism and Artificial Life*, 518.

74 Helmreich, *Silicon Second Nature*, 107.

75 Chang, "Back to the Virtual Farm," 15.

76 Bailenson, "Virtual Reality Could Make a Real Difference in the Environment."

77 Bailenson, "Virtual Reality Could Make a Real Difference in the Environment."

78 Bailenson, "Virtual Reality Could Make a Real Difference in the Environment."

79 Hayles, *Writing Machines*.

80 Jue, "From the Goddess Ganga to a Teacup."

81 Jue, "From the Goddess Ganga to a Teacup."

82 Zylinska, *Minimal Ethics for the Anthropocene*, 29.

83 Wallen, "Sea as Sculptress."

Four. Underwater Museums

1 Walcott, "Sea Is History," 365, 364.

2 Walcott, "Sea Is History," 365, 364.

3 Walcott, "Sea Is History," 364.

4 Kittler, *Draculas Vermächtnis*, 8.

5 Tracing the long history of the term "life form," Stefan Helmreich and Sophia Roosth write that, "life form has moved from its origins as a term referring to abstract, ideal-ized, aesthetic possibilities through reference to biogeographic and evolutionary pos-sibilities to, today, conjectural and future possibilities." Helmreich and Roosth, "Life Forms," 27.

6 Inspired by Banu Subramaniam's book *Ghost Stories for Darwin* (2014), Stefan Helmreich offers a fascinating reading in "Ghost Lineages, Ghost Acres, and Darwin's 'Diagram of Divergence of Taxa'" of Darwin's diagram of evolution, tracing likeness to branching coral with atoll formation, colonial histories, and the materiality of limestone.

7 Plato, *Republic*, 282.

8 Bachelard, *Water and Dreams*, 6.

9 Plato, *Republic*, 283.

10 Neimanis, "Feminist Subjectivity, Watered."

11 Taylor has installed underwater sculptures in Grenada, Mexico, Lanzarote, London, the Maldives, Norway, the Bahamas, and Indonesia. See "Projects," https://www.underwater sculpture.com/projects/, accessed May 27, 2019.

12 McCormick, Scales, and Taylor, *Underwater Museum*, 25.

13 McCormick, Scales, and Taylor, *Underwater Museum*, 111.

14 Taylor, Underwater Sculpture, author's website, accessed August 1, 2014, http://www .underwatersculpture.com/.

15 McCormick, Scales, and Taylor, *Underwater Museum*, 26.

16 McCormick, Scales, and Taylor, *Underwater Museum*, 28.

17 Jason deCaires Taylor, email to author, December 2, 2014. You can apply to have a sculpture created in your likeness by submitting four photographs of yourself and paying €500 for materials.

18 Mattison, "Ocean Art Documentary Highlights Humanity's Ties to Coral Reef."

19 Of course, there exists more evidence that we knew climate change was going to happen than the sculptures! And who is the future we that would dive down to witness them?

20 Deloughrey, "Submarine Futures of the Anthropocene," 37.

21 Neimanis, "Feminist Subjectivity, Watered," 30.

22 Deloughrey, "Submarine Futures of the Anthropocene," 42.

23 Merchant, "Deep Ethnography," 127.

24 The radio show *This American Life* commissioned a new song from clipping., called "The Deep," based on the Drexciya mythology. See "We Are in the Future," *This American Life*, August 18, 2017, https://www.thisamericanlife.org/623/we-are-in-the-future.

25 Noted in a comment in an article posted by America's Black Holocaust Museum, "Vicissitudes: NOT Sculptural Homage to Victims of the Middle Passage," May 5, 2012, https://abhmuseum.org/vicissitudes-sculptural-homage-to-victims-of-the-middle-passage/.

26 America's Black Holocaust Museum, "Vicissitudes: NOT Sculptural Homage to Victims of the Middle Passage," May 5, 2012, https://abhmuseum.org/vicissitudes-sculptural-homage-to-victims-of-the-middle-passage/

27 See Taylor, Underwater Sculpture, http://underwatersculpture.com.

28 Bergson, *Matter and Memory*, 24.

29 Lopez, "Underwater Archaeological Exploration of the Mayan Cenotes," 102.

30 Lopez, "Underwater Archaeological Exploration of the Mayan Cenotes," 106.

31 I did have some apprehension about diving into a giant hole until I realized that we would be driving to it rather than taking a boat, so I would not have to take any motion sickness medication. Instead I could enjoy the dive with full alertness!

32 Reflecting on this later, especially my initial fear of diving in the dark, I realized that for me it is far easier to fear something from looking at a picture and guessing than actually trying it out in person. In person you can measure your body, technology, and mobility against the real situation and conditions of immersion, gaining confidence from the fact that your gear works and that you have triple checked your tanks, regulator, and gauges. I felt that my body was a measure, the test against which I knew if I was safe or if something was wrong.

33 I have an example of the fin kick used in cavern diving on my professional website, http://www.melodyjue.info/new-page-2 in the video "Diving the Mayan Riviera" around minute 16:30, as demonstrated by my instructor, Rigo.

34 In contrast, diving off the coast of Cancun had visibility around thirty-five feet, which is considered decent for the ocean, although deeper ocean waters can have visibility exceeding one hundred feet.

35 NASA Extreme Environment Mission Operations (NEEMO) sends astronauts and scientists to live in the underwater research station Aquarius. See NASA, "About NEEMO," accessed September 2, 2017, https://www.nasa.gov/mission_pages/NEEMO/about_neemo .html.

36 By the end of the second day, Rigo said he would give my buoyancy control an A-. Not bad.

37 In her diving ethnography of the SS *Thistlegorm*, Merchant also noticed the presence of accumulated bubbles along the ceiling: "I raised my hand and it passed through the mirror into air, the exhalation of those who had been there before me." Merchant, "Deep Ethnography," 129.

38 Peter Sloterdjik has extensively philosophized about bubbles in his *Sphären* trilogy, which moves from self (bubble) to world (globe) to plurality (foam). If the crisis of modernity is its "shellessness," then "an inquiry into our location is more productive than ever, as it examines the place that humans create in order to have somewhere they can appear as those who they are. Here, following a venerable tradition, this place bears the name 'sphere.' The sphere is the interior, disclosed, shared real inhabited by humans—in so far as they succeed in becoming humans." Sloterdjik, *Bubbles*, 28.

39 I was extremely disappointed that I had not made time to dive Angelita, a cenote further away that had an even more dramatic and sulfurous yellow halocline that in photographs appeared like fog, obscuring parts of trees and divers.

40 Brathwaite, "Caribbean Man in Space and Time," 1.

41 Best and Marcus, "Surface Reading."

42 I discuss this debate at length in Jue, "Churning Up the Depths."

43 Best and Marcus, "Surface Reading."

44 For an example of diving as ethnographic practice, see Merchant, "Deep Ethnography."

45 Diving (or swimming) can also be a way to get to know a place. Artist Vanessa Daws calls this *psychoswimography*, a version of Guy Debord's "psychogeography," or a way of studying the psychic effects of a particular milieu. Daws writes, "My art practice uses swimming as a starting point. I work in a range of art forms including video, sound, animation, drawing and publications. Through journey, encounter, conversation and swimming, my work investigates where this drive to immerse oneself in water comes from. Is it the sheer thrill of the unknown? Or the desire to feel the water on our skin, the cold on our head, adapt our breathing and feel we exist?" Daws, "Psychoswimography." See also Shapton, *Swimming Studies*.

46 Thomas Koch at Aqua Hands Diving runs one such shop: https://www.aquahands.com /about.

BIBLIOGRAPHY

Abram, David. *The Spell of the Sensuous: Perception and Language in a More-Than-Human World*. New York: Pantheon, 1996.

Ahmed, Sara. "Orientations Matter." In *New Materialisms: Ontology, Agency, and Politics*, edited by Diana H. Coole and Samantha Frost, 234–57. Durham, NC: Duke University Press, 2010.

Alaimo, Stacy. *Exposed: Environmental Politics and Pleasures in Posthuman Times*. Minneapolis: University of Minnesota Press, 2016.

Alaimo, Stacy. "Feminist Science Studies and Ecocriticism." In *The Oxford Handbook of Ecocriticism*, edited by Greg Gerrard, 188–204. Oxford: Oxford University Press, 2014.

Alaimo, Stacy. Foreword to *Disability Studies and the Environmental Humanities: Toward an Eco-Crip Theory*, ix–xvi. Omaha: University of Nebraska Press, 2017.

Alaimo, Stacy. "States of Suspension: Trans-corporeality at Sea." *Interdisciplinary Studies in Literature and the Environment* 19, no. 3 (2012): 476–93.

Allewaert, Monique. *Ariel's Ecology: Plantations, Personhood, and Colonialism in the American Tropics*. Minneapolis: University of Minnesota Press, 2013.

Anderson, Jon, and Kimberley Peters, eds. *Water Worlds: Human Geographies of the Ocean*. New York: Routledge, 2014.

Arendt, Hannah. *The Human Condition*. 1958. Chicago: University of Chicago Press, 1958.

Bachelard, Gaston. *Water and Dreams: An Essay on the Imagination of Matter*. Translated by Edith R. Farrell. 1983. Dallas: Dallas Institute of Humanities and Culture, 2006.

Bailenson, Jeremy. "Virtual Reality Could Make a Real Difference in the Environment." SFGATE, August 15, 2014. http://www.sfgate.com/opinion/article/Virtual-reality -could-make-real-difference-in-5691610.php.

Bakhtin, Mikhail. *The Dialogic Imagination.* Translated by Caryl Emerson and Michael Holoquist. 1981. Austin: University of Texas Press, 1983.

Balcombe, Jonathan. *What a Fish Knows: The Inner Lives of Our Underwater Cousins.* New York: Farrar, Straus and Giroux, 2016.

Barad, Karen. *Meeting the Universe Halfway: Quantum Physics and the Entanglement of Matter and Meaning.* Durham, NC: Duke University Press, 2007.

Barthes, Roland. *Camera Lucida.* Translated by Richard Howard. New York: Hill and Wang, 2010.

Baucom, Ian. "Hydrographies." *Geographical Review* 89, no. 2 (1999): 301–13.

Baucom, Ian. *Specters of the Atlantic: Finance Capital, Slavery, and the Philosophy of History.* Durham, NC: Duke University Press, 2005.

Bauman, Zygmunt. *Liquid Modernity.* Malden, MA: Blackwell, 2000.

Beebe, William. "A Descent into Perpetual Night." In *American Sea Writing: A Literary Anthology,* edited by Peter Neill and Nathanial Philbrick, 475–86. New York: Library of America, 2000.

Beer, Gillean. *Darwin's Plots: Evolutionary Narrative in Darwin, George Eliot and Nineteenth-Century Fiction.* Cambridge: Cambridge University Press, 1983.

Benjamin, Walter. *Illuminations: Essays and Reflections.* 1955. New York: Schocken, 2007.

Bergson, Henri. *Matter and Memory.* Translated by Nancy Margaret Paul and W. Scott Palmer. 1912. Mineola, NY: Dover, 2004.

Best, Stephen, and Sharon Marcus. "Surface Reading: An Introduction." *Representations* 108, no. 1 (2009): 1–21.

Blas, Zach, and Jacob Gaboury. "Biometrics and Opacity: A Conversation." *Camera Obscura* 31, no. 2 (2016): 155–65.

Blish, James. "Surface Tension." In *The Science Fiction Hall of Fame,* edited by Robert Silverberg, 1:394–425. New York: Orb, 1998.

Bourdieu, Pierre. *The Logic of Practice.* Stanford, CA: Stanford University Press, 1980.

Bowker, Geoffrey. *Memory Practices in the Sciences.* Cambridge, MA: MIT Press, 2008.

Braithwaite, Kamau. *Caribbean Man in Space and Time: A Bibliographical and Conceptual Approach.* Mona, Jamaica: Savacou, 1974.

Brathwaite, Kamau. *ConVERSations with Nathaniel Mackey.* Rhinebeck, NY: WePress, 1999.

Brayton, Dan. *Shakespeare's Ocean: An Ecocritical Exploration.* Charlottesville: University of Virginia Press, 2012.

British Broadcasting Corporation. *Blue Planet.* DVD. September 19, 2001.

British Broadcasting Corporation. *Blue Planet II.* DVD. October 29, 2017.

Brunner, Bernd. *The Ocean at Home: An Illustrated History of the Aquarium.* Princeton, NJ: Princeton Architectural Press, 2005.

Buckner, M. M. *Watermind.* New York: Tor, 2008.

Burnett, D. Graham. "Looking at the Surface." In *Isola and Norzi: Liquid Door*, edited by Andria Hickey and Paola Nicolin, 32–37. New York: Art in General, 2010.

Burnett, D. Graham. "Mapping Time: Chronometry on Top of the World." *Daedalus* 132, no. 2 (Spring 2003): 5–19.

Canguilhem, Georges. "The Living and Its Milieu." *Grey Room* 3 (Spring 2010): 6–31.

Carson, Rachel. *The Edge of the Sea*. 1955. New York: Mariner, 1998.

Carson, Rachel. *The Sea around Us*. 1950. Oxford: Oxford University Press, 1991.

Carson, Rachel. "Undersea." In *Lost Woods: The Discovered Writing of Rachel Carson*, edited by Linda Lear, 3–11. Boston: Beacon, 1999.

Casarino, Caesar. *Modernity at Sea: Melville, Marx, Conrad in Crisis*. Minneapolis: University of Minnesota Press, 2002.

Chandler, Mielle, and Astrida Neimanis. "Water and Gestationality: What Flows beneath Ethics." In *Thinking with Water*, edited by Cecilia Chen, Janine MacLeod, and Astrida Neimanis, 61–83. Montreal: McGill-Queen's University Press, 2013.

Chang, Alenda Y. "Back to the Virtual Farm: Gleaning the Agriculture-Management Game." *Interdisciplinary Studies in Literature and the Environment* 19, no. 2 (2012): 1–16.

Chansanchai, Athima. "Microsoft Research Project Puts Cloud in Ocean for the First Time." Microsoft, February 2, 2016. https://news.microsoft.com/features /microsoft-research-project-puts-cloud-in-ocean-for-the-first-time/.

Cheng, Ann. "Skins, Tattoos, and Susceptibility." *Representations* 108, no. 1 (Fall 2009): 98–119.

Chiang, Ted. "Exhalation." In *Wesleyan Anthology of Science Fiction*, edited by Arthur B. Evans, 742–56. Middletown, CT: Wesleyan University Press, 2010.

Chiang, Ted. "Story of Your Life." In *Stories of Your Life and Others*, 91-146. 2002. Reprint, New York: Vintage, 2016.

Chow, Rey. *Age of the World Target: Self-Referentiality in War, Theory, and Comparative Work*. Durham, NC: Duke University Press, 2006.

Choy, Timothy. "Air's Substantiations." In *Lively Capital*, edited by Kaushik Sunder Rajan, 121–54. Durham, NC: Duke University Press, 2012.

Chun, Wendy. "The Enduring Ephemeral, or the Future Is a Memory." *Critical Inquiry* 35, no. 1 (Autumn 2008): 148–71.

Clark, Timothy. "Derangements of Scale." In *Telemorphosis: Theory in the Era of Climate Change*, edited by Tim Cohen, 1:148–66. Ann Arbor, MI: Open Humanities Press, 2012.

Cohen, Jeffrey Jerome, ed. *Prismatic Ecology: Ecotheory beyond Green*. Minneapolis: Minnesota University Press, 2013.

Cohen, Julie. "Seeing without Eyes." *The Current*, May 20, 2015. http://www.news.ucsb .edu/2015/015408/seeing-without-eyes.

Cohen, Margaret. *The Novel at Sea*. Princeton, NJ: Princeton University Press, 2012.

Cohen, Margaret. "Chronotopes of the Sea." In *The Novel*, edited by Franco Moretti, 2:646–66. Princeton, NJ: Princeton University Press, 2006.

Cohen, Margaret. "Narratology in the Archive of Literature." *Representations* 108, no. 1 (2009): 51–75.

Collins, Patricia Hill. "Learning from the Outsider Within: The Sociological Significance of Black Feminist Thought." *Social Problems* 33, no. 6 (1986): S14–S32.

Cousteau, Jacques-Yves. *The Silent World*. With Frédéric Dumas. 1953. Washington, DC: National Geographic Adventure Classics, 2004.

Cousteau, Jacques-Yves. *World without Sun*. Film. Los Angeles: Columbia Pictures, 1964.

Crichton, Michael. *Sphere*. 1987. New York: HarperCollins, 2011.

Cronon, William. "The Trouble with Wilderness; or, Getting Back to the Wrong Nature." In *Uncommon Ground: Rethinking the Human Place in Nature*, 69–90. New York: Norton, 1996.

Cruikshank, Julie. *Do Glaciers Listen? Local Knowledge, Colonial Encounters, and Social Imagination*. Vancouver: University of British Columbia Press, 2010.

Daston, Lorraine, and Peter Galison. *Objectivity*. New York: Zone, 2010.

Daws, Vanessa. "Psychoswimography: Santa Barbara." *Visual Artist's News Sheet*, March–April 2015. http://vanessadaws.com/wp-content/uploads/2012/11/Psychoswimography-Santa-Barbara.pdf.

de Castro, Eduardo Batalha Viveiros. "Exchanging Perspectives: The Transformation of Objects into Subjects in Amerindian Ontologies." *Common Knowledge* 10, no. 3 (Fall 2004): 463–84.

de Certeau, Michel. *The Practice of Everyday Life*. Berkeley: University of California Press, 2002.

Delany, Samuel R. "Driftglass." In *Aye, and Gomorrah: And Other Stories*, 102–21. New York: Vintage, 2003.

Delbourgo, James. "Divers Things: Collecting the World under Water." *History of Science* 49, no. 2 (June 2011): 149–85.

Deloughrey, Elizabeth. "The Myth of Isolates: Ecosystem Ecologies in the Nuclear Pacific." *Cultural Geographies* 20, no. 2 (2013): 167–84.

Deloughrey, Elizabeth. *Routes and Roots: Navigating Caribbean and Pacific Island Literatures*. Honolulu: University of Hawai'i Press, 2009.

Deloughrey, Elizabeth. "Submarine Futures of the Anthropocene." *Comparative Literature* 69, no. 1 (2017): 32–44.

de Man, Paul. "The Epistemology of Metaphor." In *On Metaphor*, edited by Sheldon Sacks, 11–28. Chicago: University of Chicago Press, 1977.

Derrida, Jacques. *Archive Fever: A Freudian Impression*. Translated by Eric Prenowitz. Chicago: University of Chicago Press, 1998.

Derrida, Jacques. *Dissemination*. Translated by Barbara Johnson. London: Bloomsbury, 2004.

Dick, Philip K. "My Definition of Science Fiction." In *The Shifting Realities of Philip K. Dick: Selected Literary and Philosophical Writings*, edited by Lawrence Sutin, 99–100. New York: Vintage, 1995.

Douglas, Sarah. "Fish Tale: An Artist Tested the Limits of Ceramic." *Observer*, July 20, 2011. http://observer.com/2011/07/fish-tale-an-artist-tested-the-limits-of-ceramic/.

Drucker, Johanna. "Reading Interface." *PMLA* 128, no. 1 (2013): 213–20.

Dyson, Frances. *Sounding New Media: Immersion and Embodiment in the Arts and Culture.* Berkeley: University of California Press, 2009.

Earle, Sylvia. "A Deep Dive into the Ocean in Google Earth." Google Maps blog, February 2, 2009. http://google-latlong.blogspot.com/2009/02/deep-dive-into -ocean-in-google-earth.html.

Earle, Sylvia. *Sea Change: A Message from the Oceans.* 1995. New York: Ballantine, 1996.

Earle, Sylvia. *The World Is Blue: How Our Fate and the Ocean's Are One.* Washington, DC: National Geographic, 2009.

Egan, Greg. "Oceanic." In *The Year's Best Science Fiction: 16th Annual Collection*, edited by Gardner Dozois, 1–36. New York: St. Martin's, 1999.

Eidsheim, Nina. *Sensing Sound: Singing and Listening as Vibrational Practice.* Durham, NC: Duke University Press, 2015.

Ellis, Richard. "Introducing *Vampyroteuthis infernalis*, the Vampire Squid from Hell." The Cephalopod Page. Accessed August 10, 2014. http://www.thecephalopod page.org/vsfh.php.

Feld, Steven. "Acoustemology." In *Keywords in Sound*, edited by David Novak and Matt Sakakeeny, 12–21. Durham, NC: Duke University Press, 2015.

Felt, Hali. *Soundings: The Story of the Remarkable Woman Who Mapped the Ocean Floor.* New York: Picador, 2013.

Finger, Anke, Rainer Guldin, and Gustavo Bernardo. *Vilém Flusser: An Introduction.* Minneapolis: University of Minnesota Press, 2011.

Flusser, Vilém. *Freedom of the Migrant: Objections to Nationalism.* Translated by Anke K. Finger and Kenneth Kronenberg. Urbana: University of Illinois Press, 2013.

Flusser, Vilém. *Towards a Philosophy of Photography.* Translated by Antony Mathews. London: Reaktion, 2000.

Flusser, Vilém. *Vampyroteuthis Infernalis.* Translated by Rodrigo Maltez Novaes. New York: Atropos, 2011.

Flusser, Vilém. *Writings.* Edited by Andreas Ströhl. Translated by Erik Eisel. Minne-apolis: University of Minnesota Press, 2002.

Freud, Sigmund. *Civilization and Its Discontents.* Translated by James Strachey. 1930. New York: Norton, 2010.

Friesen, Norm. *Media Transatlantic: Developments in Media and Communication Studies be-tween North American and German-speaking Europe.* New York: Springer, 2016.

Fuller, Matthew. *Media Ecologies: Materialist Energies in Art and Technoculture.* Cam-bridge, MA: MIT Press, 2007.

Fuller, Matthew, and Florian Cramer. "Interface." In *Software Studies*, edited by Mat-thew Fuller, 149–53. Cambridge, MA: MIT Press, 2008.

Fumerton, Patricia. "Digitizing Ephemera and Its Discontents: EBBA's Quest to Capture the Protean Broadside Ballad." In *Studies in Ephemera: Text and Image in*

Eighteenth-Century Print, edited by Kevin Murphy and Sally O'Driscoll, 55–98. Lewisburg, PA: Bucknell University Press, 2013.

Gabrys, Jennifer. *Digital Rubbish: A Natural History of Electronics*. Ann Arbor: University of Michigan Press, 2011.

Gabrys, Jennifer. *Program Earth: Environmental Sensing Technology and the Making of a Computational Planet*. Minneapolis: University of Minnesota Press, 2016.

Gagné, Karina, and Matthias Borg Rasmussen. "Introduction—An Amphibious Anthropology: The Production of Place at the Confluence of Land and Water." *Anthropologica* 58, no. 2 (2016): 135–49.

Galloway, Alexander R. *The Interface Effect*. Cambridge, UK: Polity, 2013.

Galloway, Alexander R., and Eugene Thacker. *The Exploit: A Theory of Networks*. Minneapolis: University of Minnesota Press, 2007.

Galloway, Alexander R., Eugene Thacker, and McKenzie Wark. *Excommunication: Three Inquiries in Media and Mediation*. Chicago: University of Chicago Press, 2014.

Ghosh, Bishnupriya. "Becoming Undetectable in the Chthulucene." In *Saturation: An Elemental Politics*, edited by Melody Jue and Rafico Ruiz. Durham, NC: Duke University Press, forthcoming.

Gillis, John R. "The Blue Humanities." *Humanities* 34, no. 3 (May–June 2013). https://www.neh.gov/humanities/2013/mayjune/feature/the-blue-humanities.

Gilroy, Paul. *The Black Atlantic: Modernity and Double Consciousness*. Cambridge, MA: Harvard University Press, 1993.

Glissant, Édouard. *Poetics of Relation*. Translated by Betsy Wing. Ann Arbor: University of Michigan Press, 1997.

Godfrey-Smith, Peter. *Other Minds: The Octopus, the Sea, and the Deep Origins of Consciousness*. New York: Farrar, Straus and Giroux, 2016.

Goßmann, Joachim, Ben Hackbarth, and Ruth West, with Todd Margolis, J. P. Lewis, and Iman Mostafavi. "Scalable Auditory Data Signatures for Discovery Oriented Browsing in an Expressive Context." *Proceedings of the 14th International Conference on Auditory Display, Paris, France* (June 24–27, 2008): 1–6.

Greenberg, Clement. "Modernist Painting." In *Art in Theory, 1900–2000: An Anthology of Changing Ideas*, edited by Charles Harrison and Paul J. Wood, 754–59. Malden, MA: Blackwell, 2003.

Guillory, John. "The Genesis of the Media Concept." *Critical Inquiry* 36, no. 2 (Winter 2010): 321–61.

Halberstam, Jack. "Wildness, Loss, Death." *Social Text* 32, no. 4 (Winter 2014): 137–48.

Hammond, Lorne. "Menfish and the Great Hydrosphere." *Environmental History* 10, no. 4 (October 2005): 695–97.

Hansen, Mark B. N. *Bodies in Code: Interfaces with Digital Media*. New York: Routledge, 2006.

Haraway, Donna. *Modest_Witness@Second_Millenium. FemaleMan_Meets_OncoMouse: Feminism and Technoscience*. New York: Routledge, 1997.

Haraway, Donna. *Primate Visions*. New York: Routledge, 1989.

Haraway, Donna. "Situated Knowledges: The Science Question in Feminism and the Privilege of Partial Perspective." In *Simians, Cyborgs, and Women*, 183–202. New York: Routledge, 1991.

Haraway, Donna. *Staying with the Trouble: Making Kin in the Chthulucene.* Durham, NC: Duke University Press, 2016.

Haraway, Donna. *When Species Meet.* Minneapolis: University of Minnesota Press, 2007.

Harding, Sandra. "Rethinking Standpoint Epistemology: What Is 'Strong Objectivity'?" In *Feminist Epistemologies*, edited by Linda Alcoff and Elizabeth Potter, 49–82. New York: Routledge, 1993.

Hau'ofa, Epeli. *We Are the Ocean: Selected Works.* Honolulu: University of Hawai'i Press, 2008.

Hayles, N. Katherine. *How We Became Posthuman: Virtual Bodies in Cybernetics, Literature, and Informatics.* Chicago: University of Chicago Press, 1999.

Hayles, N. Katherine. *How We Think: Digital Media and Contemporary Technogenesis.* Chicago: University of Chicago Press, 2012.

Hayles, N. Katherine. "Print Is Flat, Code Is Deep: The Importance of Media-Specific Analysis." *Poetics Today* 25, no. 1 (2004): 67–90.

Hayles, N. Katherine. "Speculative Aesthetics and Object-Oriented Inquiry." *Speculations: A Journal of Speculative Realism* 5 (2014): 158–79.

Hayles, N. Katherine. *Writing Machines.* Cambridge, MA: MIT Press, 2002.

Hayward, Eva. "Enfolded Vision: Refracting the Love Life of the Octopus." *Octopus: A Journal of Visual Studies* 1 (2005): 29–44.

Hayward, Eva. "Fingery-Eyes: Impressions of Cup Corals." *Cultural Anthropology* 25, no. 4 (2010): 577–99.

Hayward, Eva. "More Lessons from a Starfish: Prefixial Flesh and Transspeciated Selves." *Women's Studies Quarterly* 36, nos. 3–4 (2008): 64–85.

Hayward, Eva. "Sensational Jellyfish: Aquarium Affects and the Matter of Immersion." *Differences* 23, no. 3 (2012): 161–96.

Hayward, Eva. "Wail Bones: Ellen Gallagher and the Black Atlantic." Paper presented at New York University, November 11, 2016.

Heise, Ursula. *Imagining Extinction: The Cultural Meanings of Endangered Species.* Chicago: University of Chicago Press, 2017.

Helmreich, Stefan. *Alien Ocean: Anthropological Voyages in Microbial Seas.* Berkeley: University of California Press, 2009.

Helmreich, Stefan. "From Spaceship Earth to Google Ocean: Planetary Icons, Indexes, and Infrastructures." *Social Research* 78, no. 4 (2011): 1211–42.

Helmreich, Stefan. "Ghost Lineages, Ghost Acres, and Darwin's 'Diagram of Divergence of Taxa.'" *Catalyst: Feminism, Theory, Technoscience* 4, no. 2 (2018): 1–17.

Helmreich, Stefan. "Lives We Metaphor By." Presented at "Connections: Ethnographic Explorations—A Celebration of Professor James Howe's Years of Service to MIT." MIT Anthropology, Cambridge, MA, June 4, 2012.

Helmreich, Stefan. "Nature/Culture/Seawater." *American Anthropologist* 113, no. 1 (2010): 132–44.

Helmreich, Stefan. *Silicon Second Nature: Culturing Artificial Life in a Digital World.* Berkeley: University of California Press, 2000.

Helmreich, Stefan. *Sounding the Limits of Life.* Princeton, NJ: Princeton University Press, 2015.

Helmreich, Stefan, and Sophia Roosth. "Life Forms: A Keyword Entry." *Representations* 112, no. 1 (2010): 27–53.

Herzog, Werner. *The Wild Blue Yonder.* Film. Munich: Werner Herzog Filmproduktion, 2005.

Hessler, Stephanie, ed. *Tidalectics: Imagining an Oceanic Worldview through Art and Science.* Cambridge, MA: MIT Press, 2018.

Hoffman, Donald. "The Interface Theory of Perception: Natural Selection Drives True Perception to Swift Extinction." In *Object Categorization: Computer and Human Vision Perspectives*, edited by Sven J. Dickinson, Aleš Leonardis, Bernt Schiele, and Michael J. Tarr, 148–65. Cambridge: Cambridge University Press, 2009.

Hogan, Mél. "Water Woes and Data Flows: The Utah Data Center." *Big Data and Society* 2, no. 2 (2015): 1–12.

Hookway, Branden. *Interface: A Genealogy of Mediation and Control.* Cambridge, MA: MIT Press, 2014.

Horn, Eva. "There Are No Media." *Grey Room* 29 (Winter 2008): 6–13.

Hsu, Hsuan. "Put an Octopus on It!" *Salon*, July 5, 2012. http://www.salon.com/2012/07/05/put_an_octopus_on_it/.

Hu, Tung-hui. *A Prehistory of the Cloud.* Cambridge, MA: MIT Press, 2015.

Huhtamo, Erkki, and Jussi Parikka, eds. *Media Archeology: Approaches, Applications, Implications.* Berkeley: University of California Press, 2011.

Hutchins, Edwin. *Cognition in the Wild.* Cambridge, MA: MIT Press, 1995.

iBiology. "The Hawaiian Bobtail Squid—Vibrio Fischeri Association." YouTube, December 7, 2016. https://www.youtube.com/watch?v=O4gx-iBe-Hg.

Igarashi, Daisuke. *Children of the Sea.* 5 vols. San Francisco: VIZ Media, 2009–13.

Ingersoll, Karin Amamoto. *Waves of Knowing: A Seascape Epistemology.* Durham, NC: Duke University Press, 2016.

Ingold, Tim. "Earth, Sky, Wind, and Weather." *Journal of the Royal Anthropological Institute* 13, s1 (April 2007): S19–S38.

Irigaray, Luce. *Marine Lover of Friedrich Nietzsche.* New York: Columbia University Press, 1991.

Irigaray, Luce. *The Sex Which Is Not One.* Translated by Catherine Porter with Carolyn Burke. Ithaca, NY: Cornell University Press, 1985.

Ishida, Minori. "The Lack of Media: The Invisible Domain Post 3.11." In *Sustainable Media: Critical Approaches to Media and the Environment*, edited by Nicole Starosielski and Janet Walker, 113–27. New York: Routledge, 2016.

Johnson, Brad. *"Vampyroteuthis Infernalis."* Animal Diversity Web, 2000. Accessed August 10, 2014. http://animaldiversity.ummz.umich.edu/accounts /Vampyroteuthis_infernalis/.

Jue, Melody. "The Anthropocene's Negative Media." *Humanities Circle* 3, no. 2 (2016): 83–100.

Jue, Melody. "Churning Up the Depths: Nonhuman Ecologies of Metaphor in *Solaris* and 'Oceanic.'" In *Green Planets: Ecology and Science Fiction*, edited by Gerry Canavan and Kim Stanley Robinson, 226–42. Middletown, CT: Wesleyan University Press, 2014.

Jue, Melody. "From the Goddess Ganga to a Teacup: On Amitav Ghosh's novel *The Hungry Tide*." In *Scale in Literature and Culture*, edited by Michael Tavel Clarke and David Wittenberg, 203–24. New York: Palgrave, 2017.

Jue, Melody. "Intimate Objectivity: On Nnedi Okorofor's Afrofuturism." *Women's Studies Quarterly* 45, nos. 1–2 (2017): 171–88.

Jue, Melody. "Performative Science Fiction." *Science Fiction Studies* 45 (2018): 423–24.

Jue, Melody, and Rafico Ruiz, eds. *Saturation: An Elemental Politics*. Forthcoming.

Kember, Sarah. *Cyberfeminism and Artificial Life*. New York: Routledge, 2003.

Kember, Sarah, and Joanna Zylinska. *Life after New Media: Mediation as Vital Process*. Cambridge, MA: MIT Press, 2012.

Kirksey, Eben S., ed. *The Multispecies Salon*. Durham, NC: Duke University Press, 2014.

Kittler, Friedrich. *Discourse Networks 1800/1900*. Translated by Michael Metteer. Stanford, CA: Stanford University Press, 1992.

Kittler, Friedrich. *Draculas Vermächtnis: Technische Schriften*. Leipzig: Reclam, 1993.

Kluitenberg, Eric. "On the Archaeology of Imaginary Media." In *Media Archaeology: Approaches, Applications, and Implications*, edited by Erkki Huhtamo and Jussi Parikka, 48–69. Berkeley: University of California Press, 2011.

Kohn, Eduardo. *How Forests Think: Toward an Anthropology beyond the Human*. Berkeley: University of California Press, 2013.

Krause, Franz. "Towards an Amphibious Anthropology of Delta Life." *Human Ecology* 45, no. 3 (2017): 403–8.

Kripke, Elizabeth, Stephen Senft, Dmitry Mozzherin, and Roger Hanlon. "Visualizing Biological Complexity in Cephalopod Skin: A Synergy of Art and Science Technologies." *Leonardo* 48, no. 5 (2015): 486–87.

Kroll, Gary. *America's Ocean Wilderness: A Cultural History of Twentieth-Century Exploration*. Lawrence: University Press of Kansas, 2008.

Lakoff, George, and Mark Johnson. *Metaphors We Live By*. 1980. Chicago: University of Chicago Press, 2003.

Lanier, Jaron. "What Cephalopods Can Teach Us about Language." *Discover* magazine, April 2, 2006.

Latour, Bruno. *The Pasteurization of France*. Cambridge, MA: Harvard University Press, 1988.

Le Guin, Ursula. "The Author of Acacia Seeds." In *The Real and the Unreal*, 617–26. New York: Saga, 2012.

Lem, Stanisław. *Solaris*. 1961. New York: Mariner, 2002.

Lin, Maya. "What Is Missing?" http://whatismissing.net/home.

Lopez, Barry. *Arctic Dreams*. New York: Vintage, 2001.

López, Luis Alberto Martos. "Underwater Archaeological Exploration of the Mayan Cenotes." *Museum International* 60, no. 4 (2008): 100–110.

Lovelock, James. *Gaia: A New Look at Life on Earth*. 1977. Oxford: Oxford University Press, 2006.

MacLeod, Janine. "Water and the Material Imagination: The Sea of Memory against the Flows of Capital." In *Thinking with Water*, edited by Cecilia Chen, Janine MacLeod, and Astrida Neimanis, 40–60. Montreal: McGill-Queen's University Press, 2013.

Manovich, Lev. "Database as a Symbolic Form." *Millennium Film Journal*, no. 34 (Fall 1999). http://www.mfj-online.org/journalPages/MFJ34/Manovich_Database _FrameSet.html.

Mattison, Courtney. "Ocean Art Documentary Highlights Humanity's Ties to Coral Reef." Mission Blue, May 24, 2014. http://mission-blue.org/2014/05/ocean-art -documentary-highlights-humanitys-ties-to-coral-reefs/.

Mauss, Marcel. "Techniques of the Body." *Economy and Society* 2, no. 1 (1973): 70–87.

Maxwell, Richard, and Toby Miller. *Greening the Media*. Oxford: Oxford University Press, 2012.

Maxwell, Richard, Jon Raundalen, and Nina Lager Vestberg. *Media and the Ecological Crisis*. New York: Routledge, 2012.

McCormick, Carlo, Helen Scales, and Jason deCaires Taylor. *The Underwater Museum: The Submerged Sculptures of Jason deCaires Taylor*. San Francisco: Chronicle Books, 2014.

McIntyre, Vonda. *Superluminal*. Los Angeles: New English Library, 1986.

McLuhan, Marshall. *Understanding Media: The Extensions of Man*. 1964. Cambridge, MA: MIT Press, 1994.

Meerloo, Joost. *The Rape of the Mind: The Psychology of Thought Control, Menticide, and Brainwashing*. Ann Arbor: World, 1956.

Menely, Tobias. "Anthropocene Air." *Minnesota Review* 83 (2014): 93–101.

Mentz, Steven. *At the Bottom of Shakespeare's Ocean*. New York: Continuum, 2009.

Mentz, Steven. *Shipwreck Modernity: Ecologies of Globalization, 1550–1719*. Minneapolis: University of Minnesota Press, 2015.

Merchant, Stephanie. "Deep Ethnography: Witnessing the Ghosts of SS *Thistlegorm*." In *Water Worlds: Human Geographies of the Ocean*, edited by Jon Anderson and Kimberly Peters, 119–32. New York: Routledge, 2014.

Merchant, Stephanie. "Negotiating Underwater Space: The Sensorium, the Body and the Practice of Scuba-Diving." *Tourist Studies* 11, no. 3 (2011): 215–34.

Michelet, Jules. *The Sea (La Mer)*. New York: Follett, Foster, 1864.

Miéville, China. *Kraken*. New York: Del Rey, 2010.

Milburn, Colin. *Nanovision: Engineering the Future*. Durham, NC: Duke University Press, 2008.

Montgomery, Sy. *The Soul of an Octopus: A Surprising Exploration into the Wonder of Consciousness*. New York: Atria, 2015.

Mulvey, Laura. "Visual Pleasure in Narrative Cinema." In *Film Theory and Criticism: Introductory Readings*, edited by Leo Braudy and Marshall Cohen, 833–44. New York: Oxford University Press, 1999.

Nagel, Thomas. "What Is It Like to Be a Bat?" *Philosophical Review* 83, no. 4 (1974): 435–50.

Neimanis, Astrida. *Bodies of Water: Posthuman Feminist Phenomenology*. London: Bloomsbury, 2017.

Neimanis, Astrida. "Feminist Subjectivity, Watered." *Feminist Review* 103, no. 1 (2013): 23–41.

Nixon, Rob. *Slow Violence and the Environmentalism of the Poor*. Cambridge, MA: Harvard University Press, 2013.

Nochetto, Matias. "Air vs. Nitrox." *Alert Diver*, summer 2014. http://www.alertdiver.com/AirVsNitrox.

Okorafor, Nnedi. *Lagoon*. 2014. New York: Saga, 2016.

Pálsson, Gísli. "Birth of the Aquarium: The Politics of Icelandic Fishing." In *The Politics of Fishing*, edited by Tim S. Gray, 209–27. New York: Palgrave Macmillan, 1998.

Parikka, Jussi. *A Geology of Media*. Minneapolis: University of Minnesota Press, 2015.

Parikka, Jussi, ed. *Medianatures: The Materiality of Information Technology and Electronic Waste*. Electronic book, 2011. http://www.livingbooksaboutlife.org/books/Medianatures.

Parks, Lisa, and Nicole Starosielski. *Signal Traffic: Critical Studies of Media Infrastructures*. Urbana: University of Illinois Press, 2015.

Pauwelussen, Annet. "Amphibious Anthropology: Engaging with Maritime Worlds in Indonesia." PhD diss., Wageningen University, 2017.

Peters, John Durham. *The Marvelous Clouds: Toward a Philosophy of Elemental Media*. Chicago: University of Chicago Press, 2015.

Philip, M. NourbeSe. *Zong!* Middletown, CT: Wesleyan University Press, 2011.

Pickering, Andrew. *The Mangle of Practice: Time, Agency, and Science*. Chicago: University of Chicago Press, 1995.

Plato. *The Republic*. Edited by Alan Bloom. 1968. Indianapolis, IN: Hackett, 1991.

Postman, Neil. "The Humanism of Media Ecology." *Proceedings of the Media Ecology Association* 1 (2000): 10–16.

Ricoeur, Paul. *The Rule of Metaphor*. 1975. New York: Routledge, 2003.

Roe, Charles. "ACID vs. BASE: The Shifting pH of Database Transaction Processing." *Dataversity*, March 1, 2012. http://www.dataversity.net/acid-vs-base-the-shifting-ph-of-database-transaction-processing/.

Rozwadowski, Helen. *Fathoming the Ocean: The Discovery and Exploration of the Deep Sea.* Cambridge, MA: Harvard University Press, 2005.

Rozwadowski, Helen, and David K. van Keuren, eds. *The Machine in Neptune's Garden: Essays on Technology in the Marine Environment.* Sagamore Beach, MA: Science History Publications, 2004.

Ruppert, Edward E., Richard S. Fox, and Robert D. Barnes, eds. *Invertebrate Zoology: A Functional Evolutionary Approach.* Belmont, CA: Thomson-Brooks/Cole, 2004.

Rushdie, Salman. *Haroun and the Sea of Stories.* New York: Penguin, 1991.

Rust, Stephen, Salma Monani, and Sean Cubitt. *Ecomedia: Key Issues.* New York: Routledge, 2015.

Sassi, Maria Michela. "The Sea Was Never Blue." *Aeon Magazine,* July 2017. https://aeon.co/essays/can-we-hope-to-understand-how-the-greeks-saw-their-world.

Schatzing, Frank. *The Swarm.* 2004. New York: Harper Perennial, 2007.

Schuppli, Susan. "Slick Images: The Photogenic Politics of Oil." In *Allegory of the Cave Painting,* edited by Mihnea Mirca and Vincent W. J. van Gerven Oei, 425–47. Milan: Mousse, 2015.

Serres, Michel. *Hermes: Literature, Science, Philosophy.* Baltimore: Johns Hopkins University Press, 1983.

Seshadri, Rekha, Saul A. Kravitz, Larry Smarr, Paul Gilna, and Marvin Frazier. "CAMERA: A Community Resource for Metagenomics." *PLoS Biology* 5, no. 3 (2007): 394–97.

Shakespeare, William. *The Tempest.* Edited by A. R. Braunmuller and Stephen S. Orgel. London: Pelican, 1999.

Shapiro, Michael. "Moorea's Ark." *Hana Hou!* 15, no. 4 (2012). https://hanahou.com/15.4/mooreas-ark.

Shapton, Leanne. *Swimming Studies.* New York: Riverhead, 2012.

Sharpe, Christina. *In the Wake: On Blackness and Being.* Durham, NC: Duke University Press, 2016.

Shell, Hanna Rose. *Hide and Seek: Camouflage, Photography, and the Media of Reconnaissance.* Brooklyn, NY: Zone, 2012.

Shewry, Teresa. *Hope at Sea: Possible Ecologies in Oceanic Literatures.* Minneapolis: University of Minnesota Press, 2015.

Shiga, John. "Ping and the Material Meanings of Ocean Sound." In *Sustainable Media: Critical Approaches to Media and the Environment,* edited by Nicole Starosielski and Janet Walker, 128–45. New York: Routledge, 2016.

Shiga, John. "Sonar: Empire, Media, and the Politics of Underwater Sound." *Canadian Journal of Communication* 38, no. 3 (2013): 357–77.

Simonetti, Cristián. "The Stratification of Time." *Time and Society* 24, no. 2 (2015): 139–62.

Slonczewski, Joan. *A Door into Ocean.* 1986. New York: Orb, 2000.

Sloterdjik, Peter. *Bubbles.* Translated by Wieland Hoban. Cambridge, MA: Semiotext(e), 2011.

Smith, Dorothy. "Women's Perspective as a Radical Critique of Sociology." *Sociological Inquiry* 44, no. 1 (1974): 7–13.

Smith, Jacob. *Eco-Sonic Media.* Berkeley: University of California Press, 2015.

Snyder, Joel. "What Happens by Itself in Photography?" In *Pursuits of Reason: Essays in Honor of Stanley Cavell,* edited by Ted Cohen, Paul Guyer, and Hilary Putnam, 361–73. Lubbock: Texas Tech University Press, 1993.

Sobel, Dava. *Longitude: The True Story of a Lone Genius Who Solved the Greatest Scientific Problem of His Time.* London: Walker, 1995.

Sommerer, Christa, and Laurent Mignonneau. "Art as a Living Process." Accessed May 24, 2019. http://geneticsandculture.com/genetics_culture/pages_genetics_culture/gc_w05/somm_mign.htm.

Sontag, Susan. *On Photography.* New York: Picador, 1973.

Starosielski, Nicole. "Beyond Fluidity: A Cultural History of Cinema Underwater." In *The Ecocinema Reader: Theory and Practice,* edited by Salma Monani, Stephen Rust, and Sean Cubitt, 149–68. New York: Routledge, 2012.

Starosielski, Nicole. "The Materiality of Media Heat." *International Journal of Communication* 8, no. 1 (2014): 2504–8.

Starosielski, Nicole. "Thermocultures of Geologic Media." *Cultural Politics* 12, no. 3 (2016): 293–309.

Starosielski, Nicole. *The Undersea Network.* Durham, NC: Duke University Press, 2015.

Starosielski, Nicole, and Janet Walker, eds. *Sustainable Media: Critical Approaches to Media and the Environment.* New York: Routledge, 2016.

Steinberg, Philip. *The Social Construction of the Ocean.* Cambridge: Cambridge University Press, 2001.

Steinberg, Philip, and Kimberly Peters. "Wet Ontologies, Fluid Spaces: Giving Depth to Volume through Oceanic Thinking." *Environment and Planning D: Society and Space* 33, no. 2 (2015): 247–64.

Subramaniuam, Banu. *Ghost Stories for Darwin: The Science of Variation and the Politics of Diversity.* Durham, NC: Duke University Press, 2014.

Sun, Shulei, J. Chen, W. Li, I. Altintas, A. Lin, S. Peltier, K. Stocks, E. E. Allen, M. Ellisman, J. Grethe, and J. Wooley. "Community Cyberinfrastructure for Advanced Microbial Ecology Research and Analysis: The CAMERA Resource." *Nucleic Acids Research* 39 (2011): D546–51.

Suvin, Darko. *Metamorphoses of Science Fiction.* Edited by Gerry Canavan. 1979. Bern: Peter Lang, 2016.

Szoldra, Paul. "US Spy Agency Boasts 'Nothing Is beyond Our Reach' with New Logo." *Business Insider,* December 7, 2013. http://www.businessinsider.com/nrol-39-logo-nothing-beyond-our-reach-2013-12.

Taibbi, Matt. "The Great American Bubble Machine." *Rolling Stone,* April 5, 2010.

Taylor, Jesse Oak. "Auras and Ice Cores: Atmospheric Archives and the Anthropocene." *Minnesota Review* 83 (2014): 73–82.

ten Bos, René. "Towards an Amphibious Anthropology: Water and Peter Sloterdijk."
    Environment and Planning D: Society and Space 27, no. 1 (2009): 73–86.

Thomas, Lindsey. "Forms of Duration: Preparedness, the Mars Trilogy, and the Man-
    agement of Climate Change." *American Literature* 88, no. 1 (March 2016): 159–84.

Thompson, Charis. *Making Parents: The Ontological Choreography of Reproductive Tech-
    nologies.* Cambridge, MA: MIT Press, 2005.

Tuan, Yi-Fu. *Space and Place: The Perspective of Experience.* Minneapolis: University of
    Minnesota Press, 2001.

Tuana, Nancy. "Viscous Porosity: Witnessing Hurricane Katrina." In *Material Femi-
    nisms*, edited by Stacy Alaimo and Susan Heckman, 188–213. Bloomington:
    Indiana University Press, 2008.

Uexküll, Jakob von. *A Foray into the Worlds of Animals and Humans: With a Theory of
    Meaning.* Translated by Joseph D. O'Neil. Minneapolis: University of Minnesota
    Press, 2010.

Valentine, David. "Gravity Fixes: Habituating to the Human on Mars and Island
    Three." *Hau: Journal of Ethnographic Theory* 7, no. 3 (2017): 185–209.

Vance, Jack. *The Blue World.* 1963. Walnut, CA: Spatterlight, 2016.

Vannini, Phillip, and Jonathan Taggart. "The Day We Drove on the Ocean (and Lived
    to Tell the Tale about It)." In *Water Worlds: Human Geographies of the Ocean*, edited
    by John Anderson and Kimberley Peters, 89–102. New York: Routledge, 2014.

Vesna, Victoria, ed. *Database Aesthetics: Art in the Age of Information Overflow.* Minneap-
    olis: University of Minnesota Press, 2007.

Virilio, Paul. *Speed and Politics.* 1977. Los Angeles: Semiotext(e), 2006.

Walcott, Derek. "The Sea Is History." In *Derek Walcott Collected Poems, 1948–1984*,
    364–67. New York: Farrar, Straus, and Giroux, 1986.

Walker, Janet. "Projecting Sea Level Rise: Documentary Film and Other Geolocative
    Technologies." In *A Companion to Documentary Film*, edited by Alexandra Juhasz
    and Alisa Lebow, 61–86. Hoboken, NJ: Wiley Blackwell, 2015.

Wall, Jeff. "Photography and Liquid Intelligence." In *Jeff Wall: Selected Essays and Inter-
    views*, 109–10. New York: Museum of Modern Art, 2007.

Wallen, Ruth. "The Sea as Sculptress—From Analog to Digital." *Digital Arts and Cul-
    ture* (December 2009).

Wardi, Anissa Jeanine. *Water and African American Memory: An Ecocritical Perspective.*
    Gainesville: University Press of Florida, 2011.

Watts, Peter. *Starfish.* New York: Tor, 1999.

Weinbren, Grahame. "Ocean, Database, Recut." In *Database Aesthetics*, edited by Vic-
    toria Vesna, 61–85. Minneapolis: University of Minnesota Press, 2007.

West, Ruth, Jordan P. Lewis, Todd Margolis, Jurgen P. Schulze, Joachim Goßmann,
    Daniel Tenedorio, Rajvikram Singh, and Guillermina Hall. "Algorithmic Ob-
    ject as Natural Specimen: Meta Shape Grammar Objects from ATLAS *in silico*."
    Leonardo Electronic Almanac 16, nos. 6–7 (2009): 1–5.

West, Ruth, Joachim Goßmann, Todd Margolis, Jurgen P. Schulze, J. P. Lewis, Ben Hackbarth, and Iman Mostafavi. "Sensate Abstraction: Hybrid Strategies for Multi-Dimensional Data in Expressive Virtual Reality Contexts." *Proceedings of SPIE* (2009). DOI: 10.1117/12.806928.

Wiener, Norbert. *The Human Use of Human Beings: Cybernetics and Society.* New York: Da Capo, 1954.

Wittgenstein, Ludwig. *Philosophical Investigations.* 3rd edition. Malden, MA: Wiley Blackwell, 2001.

Yaszek, Lisa. "Science, Fiction and American Public Policy." Paper presented at Society for Literature, Science and the Arts Conference, Atlanta, November 2009.

Yong, Ed. "The Lovely Tale of an Adorable Squid and Its Glowing Partner." *The Atlantic,* January 26, 2018.

Yong, Ed. "Nature's Cutest Symbiosis: The Bobtail Squid | I Contain Multitudes." YouTube, January 22, 2018. https://youtu.be/3ivMSCi-Y2Q.

Yong, Ed. "Octopuses Do Something Really Strange to Their Genes." *The Atlantic,* April 6, 2017.

Yusoff, Katherine. "Excess, Catastrophe, and Climate Change." *Environment and Planning D: Space and Society* 27, no. 6 (2009): 1010–29.

Zylinska, Joanna. "Hydromedia: From Water Literacy to the Ethics of Saturation." In *Saturation: An Elemental Politics,* edited by Melody Jue and Rafico Ruiz. Durham, NC: Duke University Press, forthcoming.

Zylinska, Joanna. *A Minimal Ethics for the Anthropocene.* Ann Arbor, MI: Open Humanities Press, 2014.

INDEX

Global Ocean Sampling (GOS) project, 130–31
Godfrey-Smith, Peter, 94
"God trick," 9
Google Earth, 122–23
Google Ocean, 116, 119–30, 138–41, 165
Google Street View, 148–49, 152–53
"Google Street View Oceans," 127, 129
GoPro cameras, 165
Great Barrier Reef, 129
Greenberg, Clement, 14
Guillory, John, 14

habitus, 12–13
Haeckel, Ernst, 117
Halberstam, Jack, xii
haloclines, 160–61
Hansen, Mark B. N., 49
Haraway, Donna, 9–10, 13, 72, 96, 127
Harding, Sandra, 10
Haroun and the Sea of Stories (Rushdie), 118
Hass, Hans, 58
Hau'ofa, Epeli, 171n70
Hawaiian bobtail squid, 108–11
Hayles, Katherine, 14, 26; database technology, 117; on inscription technology, 76, 102–3, 175n21, 180n25
Hayward, Eva, 27–28, 89, 172n75
Heise, Ursula, 121, 124
Helmreich, Stefan, 22; *Alien Ocean*, 8, 133, 173n79, 188n66, 188n69; on Darwin's diagram of evolution, 189n6; on Google Ocean, 126–27; on "life form," 189n5; "Lives We Metaphor By," 181–82n67; *Silicon Second Nature*, 135; *Sounding the Limits of Life*, 16–17
hentai (anime/manga genre), 72
Heraclitus, 64
Herschel, John, 96–97
Herzog, Werner, xii, 64
Hoffman, Donald, 38–39, 44
Holocaust, 75–76
Hookway, Branden, 40–41, 175n21
Hope at Sea: Possible Ecologies in Oceanic Literature (Shewry), 171n70
Horace, 74
Horn, Eva, 25
How Forests Think: Toward an Anthropology beyond the Human (Kohn), 27
How We Became Posthuman (Hayles), 104

How We Think (Hayles), 26
Hsu, Hsuan, 72
human-computer interface (HCI), 38–43
humanities: diving and, 163–66; ocean studies and, 16–21, 170n61; underwater museums and, 32–33
human physiology: diving and, 67–70, 174n4; sea change in, 113; spatial theory and, 78–80; in underwater museums, 144–45
Humboldt squid (*Dosidicus gigas*), 183n104
Husserl, Edmund, 11–12
Huhtamo, Erkki, 22
Hutchins, Edwin, 171n65

Icelandic ocean management, 119–22
imaginary media, 180n19
Imagining Extinction (Heise), 121, 124
immersion: interfaces and, 29–30
imperialism: vampire analogies to, 71
indigenous studies, 18–19, 168n9
information: ATLAS *in silico* project, 130–38; Flusser's theory of, 91–97
infrastructure: interfaces and, 39–40
Ingersoll, Karen, 19, 171n70
Ingold, Tim, 6, 15
inscription, 75–76; Flusser's theory of information and, 91–97; Hayles's discussion of, 76, 102–4, 180n25; sympoeisis and, 111; in underwater museums, 144–45, 150–51, 160–63
insemination, 101–2
interconnection: cephalopod body and, 72; oceans and, 171n70
"Interface" (Fuller and Cramer), 40
Interface: A Genealogy of Mediation and Control (Hookway), 40–41
The Interface Effect (Galloway), 39–40
interfaces: defined, 175n20; fathoming of, 65–67; human-computer interface (HCI), 38–43; legibility and hermeneutics of, 39; nitrogen narcosis and, 50–53; ocean as history and, 144–45; in scuba diving, 34–37, 67–70, 163–66; species-specific, 38; surface and depth and, 55–57; virtual environments and, 48–49
"The Interface Theory of Perception" (Hoffman), 38–39
interpretation: ocean as environment of, 17–21
interspecies sexuality, 72

CPSIA information can be obtained
at www.ICGtesting.com
Printed in the USA
FSHW012212180620
71298FS

9 781478 006978